Jerry M. Stubblefield

The Salvation and Nurture of the Child of God

The Salvation and Nurture of the Child of God

The Story of Emma

G. TEMP SPARKMAN

Judson Press ® Valley Forge

THE SALVATION AND NURTURE OF THE CHILD OF GOD
Copyright © 1983
Judson Press, Valley Forge, PA 19481

All rights reserved. No part of this publication may be reproduced, stored in a retrieval system, or transmitted in any form or by any means, electronic, mechanical, photocopying, recording, or otherwise, without the prior permission of the copyright owner, except for brief quotations included in a review of the book.

Unless otherwise indicated, the Scripture quotations in this publication are from the Revised Standard Version of the Bible copyrighted 1946, 1952 © 1971, 1973 by the Division of Christian Education of the National Council of the Churches of Christ in the U.S.A., and used by permission.

Other quotations of the Bible are from *The Holy Bible*, King James Version.

Library of Congress Cataloging in Publication Data
Sparkman, G. Temp.
  The salvation and nurture of the child of God.
  Bibliography: p.
  Includes indexes.
  1. Christian education—Philosophy. 2. Developmental psychology. I. Title.
BV1464.S63   1983   207   82-21349
ISBN 0-8170-0985-X

The name JUDSON PRESS is registered as a trademark in the U.S. Patent Office. Printed in the U.S.A.

To Faye,

companion in times joyful, times sad.

Contents

Preface 11

1 Foundations 19

2 Emma as Young Child—
A Child of God by Creation 43

3 Emma as Middle Child—
A Child of Promise 75

4 Emma as Adolescent—
An Affirmed Believer 109

5 Emma as Adult—
A Creative Trustee 143

Epilogue: Historical Life Cycle,
Womanhood, and Real Church 169

Notes on Chapters 173

Appendixes

    I Baptism—A Theological Question 181

    II Bushnell's Idea of
Christian Education 189

III	Coe's Theory—Salvation by Education	193
IV	Educational Theory Since 1940	197
V	The Celebrative Rites	205
VI	Image and Fall	223
VII	Tillich's Doctrine of Estrangement and Salvation	235
VIII	The Lord's Table	239
IX	Dominion, Priesthood, Trusteeship	249
X	Erikson's Wisdom	255
XI	Piaget's Discovery	257

References for Appendixes   261

Subject Index   267

Studies Index   271

The Salvation and Nurture of the Child of God

Preface

A reader deserves to know the origin of some books. This is especially true of books which set forth theories and patterns by which some critical endeavor is to be initiated and guided. This book is of that kind; therefore, at its beginning I want to sketch the lines along which this theory of nurture has come to be.

First, and naturally, I will speak of my own faith development, very much unlike that suggested for Emma. I did not grow up in a church-going family. Of the eleven in my family, only Mother was a church member. She was a Baptist, but there was not a Baptist church in the community. She was a Christian woman who prayed and read the Bible. Father had no church identity and, although well spoken of as a morally upright and deeply socially conscious man, was not known as a Christian. Some years ago, in pondering his character and style, I concluded that he would have been worthy of the name.

I don't remember how old I was when first I was sent to the Church of Christ, only a stone's throw from our house. Neither can I recall the treatment given or what was told me. It must have been friendly enough and orthodox, with a bent toward Alexander Campbell's teachings. It was not, as I remember, a significant place for me, and I did not go often.

The warm religious place for me was the home of the local mail carrier and his family, who were Baptist—the father a gospel quartet singer and the mother a strong, praying, shouting Christian. I do not recall that they ever invited me to go out to their church in the country, but I remember words like "saved," "hallelujah," "the Lord," "Jesus," and the rhythms, teachings, and sentimentalities in the gospel songs which they sang with gusto. Clearly, the mother in this home embodied something which a young child could hardly keep from being influenced and held by. Perhaps it is also instructive to record that when our family fell on hard times, I was invited to make my way down the road to this house for daily milk and a bonus of love.

When I was ten, both my father and mother were dead. Only two sisters and a brother remained at home; and the oldest of the four, though herself only in her early twenties, presided over the disposal of the home place and took her siblings off to the city where an older sister was securely employed.

The first place we lived after leaving the country was a hotel in a small village near the plant which spawned, and at the time owned, the adjoining town. The details are not significant here, but this stopping place turned out to be a beginning place for my more formal religious nurture. Some members of a local Baptist church thought it not right that a boy of my age be left to play in the hotel yard on Sunday mornings. So they asked my sisters if I might be taken to church.

Not only was I taken, but once there, I was taken in. In retrospect, I can see that this church became a substitute parent for me, and it represented all the warmth and care of a family. I was made to feel that I belonged; yet there was always an edge, or a qualification, on that belongingness. I speak of the expectation that I make a personal profession of faith and be baptized. From the time I first attended that church until, at age twelve, I went forward at the end of the worship service to make that decision public, there was pressure, sometimes gentle, sometimes frightening, but always there.

After my baptism, the same kind of nurture continued, but, of course, without the pressure to be saved. From here on it was my duty to learn the Bible and live as a Christian youth. I was active in every aspect of the church's activity—after all, the church was, as I admitted earlier, a second home, a family to me. Whenever the doors were open, I was there.

In some ways my faith journey must have seemed to most to have been one of even devotion. Yet, though devoted, it was one of inner conflict, a conflict derived from attempting to negotiate between the stern demands of my teachers and the normal lures of being an adolescent. The teachers won out, and my actions were well ahead of my internalized devotion. Thus, I did not attend the theater or go to school dances. I did not smoke, drink, or curse. If deprived of some cultural stimulation by not being at movies, and of some important socialization by not dancing, I have never felt remorse for any habits that passed me by.

In many respects I was the church's model youth, and it seemed natural that I was next in line to be a preacher boy, with all that implies in terms of life-style. That I never did become that kind of Christian I attribute to my natural interests in sports and friends and the influence of other adults in the town. Albeit, the church never wavered from its expectation that I would become a preacher, and it always seemed proud of my happy participation in its life. I am sure it was more out of lack of knowledge and experience, rather than out of insensitivity, that the church did not know how to help me negotiate a healthy Christian ethic, but rather told me what the ethic had to be, and put on considerable guilt-pressure to win my compliance.

After graduation from high school I was off to college and bigger worlds. At least two awakenings, pertinent to the theme of this book, took place in those post-schoolboy years—one in college and one in seminary.

My college experience was one of enlightenment and growth and brought with it the typical reexamination of beliefs and styles. At its end, the essential faith in which I had been nurtured was conserved, but I had come to understand more deeply the meaning of Christian freedom and had begun to set my life within its terms. I speak of it as an awakening because of its effect on my own ego strength. I came to a much healthier Christian ethic, one which I could embrace willfully rather than from fear of disapproval of significant adults. I was put in touch with cultural opportunities and with knowledge which looked toward new directions of style and thought, but the greater accomplishment was in coming to terms with being Christian without being puritan.

Still my college religious experience might be characterized as being of a zip-a-dee-doo-dah style. I was engaged by an evangelist saying that Christ in your heart puts a spring in your step and a smile on your face. Only now in middle age do I know that the spring came from my youthfulness and the smile from a happy disposition, neither very distinctively Christian. However, my faith had stirrings which went deeper than the saying and was vital enough to make me an effective Christian witness. As a student government leader and an athlete I was conscious of my responsibility to model my limited understanding of Christian living. I loved and served God and was active in the life of a congregation. At religious rallies on campus I felt strong pulls to make public commitments, and made many—all of which eventually came together to form a call to be a minister.

Another awakening came from the seminary years—it was intellectual. At least, it came through the intellectual; actually it went beyond what we sometimes consider intellectual. In those years my teachers made a critical thinker of me. They introduced me to "whys" which my adolescent devotion to religion had never heard. But, in their questioning, I sensed that they also knew about deeper answers than my entering portfolio held. In short, my teachers gave me a passion for truth. Because of their example and instruction, I could never again accept with finality what I had not personally pursued to its center, and I could never again understand truth in static terms. I did not know at the time what perilous travels such an awakening would bring.

With the seminary years behind and with a new portfolio, I set out on my ministry journey, educated and prepared for the challenges of church leadership. I met the familiar and the strange, knew success and failure. But neither my victories nor my defeats formed my central religious concern. Somewhere in these years, from seminary to middle thirty, I became engaged, no, I became overwhelmed, by the thought that God was at work in the world and that I was called to join in the enterprise as a creating participant. Here in this revelation is the turning point in my religious perspective and ministry experience. Here I found my place in creation and in the generational stream. As you read on, you will see just how paradoxically revolutionary and stabilizing an insight it turned out to be.

A second source of this theory of nurture might be called professional. What I mean to acknowledge is the influence of my career on my views of faith awakening. I have been a minister in charge of education in the congregation for most of my adult life, having served a county-seat church in Paragould, Arkansas; a military-base church in Pensacola, Florida; a university church in Bowling Green, Kentucky; and an urban church in Louisville, Kentucky. Each church, as one would already know, had its own personality, but more importantly, each made its imprint on my development as a minister. There is some of each of these congregations in this theory of how one should awaken to faith. I will not attempt the impossible, that is, to identify every strand of the theory in light of these origins, but without these real-life situations, where persons were and still are being nurtured, I should never have come to a comprehensive view of how persons come to faith.

In these congregations hundreds of persons—from infant to senior adult—came faithfully to Sunday church school and to other educational settings, and as they participated in activities for which I was responsible, they also revealed in their lives the effects, some positive, some negative, of the education that was offered. As they participated, offering both praise and criticism, I analyzed and pondered, I altered and projected. Gradually I began to generalize from all these experiences, putting them alongside my understanding of the human situation, until I had a working model for a theory of Christian nurture.

The working model was fixed when, in 1972, I left the Crescent Hill Church to take up my teaching career here at Midwestern Baptist Theological Seminary. In these ten years, freed from the rigors of the administration of education, I have had more time to move more deeply into the psychology and theology underpinning my theory. In that, the theory has been considerably enriched and made more secure. In addition, during these years of teaching I have been active in my own congregation, teaching children, youths, and adults. This experience has significantly influenced my understanding of the process of nurture.

But I must not leave the discussion of a professional source without mixing it with the contribution which my children have made to my understanding of how nurture takes place. In fact, as I look back, I must admit that as our first daughter advanced through the nursery, then the kindergarten, then the primary and junior grades, and into adolescence, so did my interest in each age intensify. Then our other children came, and made their own unique marks on my life and views.

The imaginative reader will perceive readily that in my plan for the awakening to faith there is the plaintive regret that my own children were not early placed under such a carefully formulated theory. They were left to an education that was hardly self-conscious of its goals and certainly not critical enough of its weaknesses, especially in theology. It was, after all, the eyes of my own nine-year-old daughter, as the Lord's Supper passed her by one Sunday morning, that sparked within me a dialogue which I have not, to this day, been able to end. My understanding of the awakening to faith and its attendant plan for nurture is really a hope for all children, youths, and adults; perhaps it is even an attempt to reconstruct my own religious experience in healthier terms and my own nurture along more thoughtful lines.

Before turning to that understanding and that plan, I want to confess that this theory is also of some romantic origin. In a city where I once lived, there was, and I presume still is, on my accustomed route to the church a mature hard maple, standing as if placed in its field by the Creator. Plato would have judged this tree to have been the very model of the idea of treeness. And I, well, I marveled at it in all seasons— barren in December, budded in spring, fully in leaf in July, and in autumn, aflame and dancing to October's breezes. I have, ever since, held a passion to create a tree like that one.

The purpose of this book is implicit in these confessions of origin and in the ensuing text. I want to help ministers with the challenge of ministering among a people of varying degrees of maturity. My purpose is to help ministers appreciate that persons experience salvation developmentally; that faith is a lifelong quest; that effective approaches to nurture must be formulated within the context of a worshiping congregation, be based in one's theology, and be consistent with one's psychology. While it is to ministers that this writing is made primarily, I will be pleased if some volunteer leaders in the churches, denominational curriculum makers, and students of Christian education also find it attractive. Admittedly, I also hold some hope that the wider audience of theorists in religious education, practical theology, and pastoral care will give some attention to this view.

Indulge one additional word about the organization of the book. A creative editor generously allowed me to write the theory as if it were actually unfolding in the life of a person, obviously an idea borrowed from Rousseau's *Émile* and Pestalozzi's *Leonard and Gertrude*. We agreed on the name "Emma," a representative person who moves through salvation and nurture from infancy to adulthood. This proved to be a happy decision; however, as the writing unfolded, it was apparent that the approach made some of the application sections appear arbitrarily prescriptive. On the other hand, it would have been poor style to have posed too many alternatives within the text. Therefore, I would want the reader to know that my strategies for education and nurture are suggestive and are not offered as unalterable.

This approach also raised a problem as to how to handle essential critical material which appeared to break unnecessarily into the flow of the text. This problem was resolved by including an extensive appendix. Finally, we agreed that a "foundations" chapter would add substance and clarity to the material in the Emma model. Thus, I have written in chapter 1 of foundations, such as the birth and growth of faith, a guiding theology and the like, and a summary of the theory.

1

Foundations

We are disquietingly unsure about birthings of all kinds. Though we date our age from the moment we leave our mother's womb, and though we symbolize physical birth in the cutting of the umbilical cord, there is intense disagreement over when birth occurs. We have some clear but still imprecise notions about psychological birth occurring with the earliest stroking. We lean toward establishing social birth as coming first through contact with parental figures, though some would place it later. We are even more uncertain about the birth of faith and the progress of salvation.

The Birth and Growth of Faith

Different theological families view variously the birth of faith and the coming to full faith, but generally there are two major stances. The stances are represented in the question of baptism. Two long-standing traditions and a recent emergent position shape the contemporary dialogue on baptism. The older positions are found in the churches which practice infant baptism and those which baptize believers. The third, popularized in this century, comes out of the believer's baptism family and may be termed child baptism. Unlike the first two views, child baptism has no commonly accepted, established theology but is widely practiced. Of course, in terms of practice, the history of the church will testify to all three kinds of baptism. (See Appendix I, "Baptism—A Theological Question.")

In one major stance, the baptism of the infant marks the child's entrance to faith and/or brings the child into the covenant community. In this view, faith is from the grace of God, given through the church, but not independently of human response. At one time, the next required step was for the person to confirm the faith, with the church administering a rite to symbolize that the person was taking on individual responsibility for the faith. This then opened the way for the person to receive first Communion, usually in late childhood or adolescence.

In the last decade some churches have reversed the order of confirmation and Communion, allowing children in middle childhood, as people already baptized into the covenant community, to participate in Communion prior to confirmation. In some of these churches the age of confirmation has been raised to middle adolescence. Beyond confirmation, there is no other regular ritual to symbolize a spiritual passage, although persons in these churches may and do experience religious renewal and increasing commitment to being a disciple of Jesus the Christ. The fact of the influence of the charismatic movement on adults who have grown up under the infant baptism–confirmation model demonstrates the presence of this kind of experience.

There is an altogether different stance on how one comes to faith. This view holds that entrance to the faith comes with a conscious conversion experience, followed by baptism which brings with it membership in the congregation and permission to participate in the Lord's Supper. In this approach, the faith rituals are wrapped in one package; that is, the individual takes personal responsibility for one's faith, is baptized, and then admitted to the Lord's Table. It happens all at once, and the sequence is invariant.

In this approach there is no childhood ritual and no adult one, other than the baptism of an adult convert. There is the phenomenon of rededication, which is a public act that may occur several times after one's baptism. This act signifies a religious renewal and often a new sense of commitment, but there is no rite by which to mark its occurrence. Some churches, holding to this scheme, sponsor child dedication services in which parents promise to "bring the children up in the Lord." There is no regular or common imagery associated with this service, and its proponents are careful not to leave the impression that the child is in any way changed or assured in advance of inclusion in the church or kingdom. In fact, some ministers call this service a parent dedication service.

I was introduced to the life of faith by a congregation holding to this second position, popularly called the "believer's baptism" view. Thus was I baptized as a believer at age twelve and a half. In addition to my instruction in the meaning of baptism prior to the pastor leading me into the baptismal pool, I also was told of the superiority of the mode of immersion over pouring and certainly over the sprinkling of an infant. The infant rite was not considered to be real baptism.

Since becoming an autonomous, thinking adult, I have examined the meaning of infant baptism in the writings of apologists for the practice. I have reflected on my own baptism and have studied the meaning of believer's baptism. I have read apologies for child baptism. Out of my reflection and analysis I have come to a conclusion that would not have been possible at my baptism in early adolescence. I now see that all types of baptism have historical precedent and may proceed from valid theologies, but that all positions have major weaknesses in terms of what they communicate about faith and in how they influence the practice of nurture. This is not to say that we should practice three baptisms. Neither does it mean that I have abandoned the doctrine of believer's baptism in favor of infant or child baptism. But in coming to terms with the strengths and weaknesses of baptismal forms, I have sharpened my understanding of when faith begins and, thus, how nurture ought to proceed.

One of the first surprises I met in the study of infant baptism is that it has different meanings in churches where it is practiced. Some Communions use the strong language of regeneration in the belief that salvation is effected through the vows made by godparents on behalf of the infant. In other Communions, the rite symbolizes the bringing of the infant under the covenant of faith and into the community of faith.

This is not the place to discuss the bases in Bible and history behind the practice of infant baptism. However, this is the place to affirm the clear strength of either of these meanings of infant baptism. It is this: the children, as they grow in the faith, possess a secure feeling that they belong to the church's faith, worship, and work and are not outsiders who must ask for inclusion. They view their process of faith development as steps within, not into, the faith.

Of course, it is this "secure feeling" that became one of the arguments for my forebears' rejection of infant baptism. They feared that children would become so secure that they would not face the awful fact of sin and the necessity of repentance. This weakness is especially evident in cases where the language of regeneration is used. It is much too early in the child's development for this kind of language—not too soon for grace to be at work, and therefore for salvation to have begun, but too soon for talk of repentance and renouncing sin. Repentance and declaration of faith are individual and volitional and no one can act for another in their regard. This is not to say, however, that salvation is found in isolation from the faith community or that parental influence is of little consequence.

Those who hold to infant baptism intend for the children, either in late childhood or adolescence, to take a giant step within the faith, that is, that they will confirm the faith. In its intention, confirmation does involve personal struggle and declaration, but in its practice, it has become much too automatic. According to those who advocate infant baptism, confirmation has not been faithful to its definition of personal assumption of faith, as the taking on of vows that were made in one's behalf in infant baptism. A few years ago a Swiss Presbyterian writer lamented the "lie of confirmation."[1] Others have charged that confirmation is viewed widely as a kind of graduation from church school.[2] I heard this notion one recent summer Sunday afternoon at the swimming pool. I asked a little boy, probably in fifth or sixth grade, if he had attended Sunday school that morning. His reply was that he did not have to go anymore now that he had been confirmed.

I now turn to believer's baptism and speak as an insider. The meaning of the baptism of a believer by immersion is that the person has turned from sin, has confessed Jesus Christ as Savior; and the mode symbolizes death to sin, burial, and resurrection to walk in a new life. I do not wish to discuss the doctrine but want to point out what it says about faith and what it implies about education and nurture.

First among the weaknesses of believer's baptism is that faith is seen as not beginning until one is converted. Such a view makes all other religious experience pall in significance rather than be seen as valid and highly significant regardless of the person's age. It communicates that faith cannot operate through the life of the congregation and the family. It implies that education prior to baptism is pre-Christian education and only foundational. It leaves us without a rationale for the education of our children, except to say that we are leading toward, or laying foundations for, something that is to come later.

Such a view also ignores that God's grace is at work from the moment of birth. It holds the danger of reducing faith to a rational decision, even though the meaning of conversion involves the whole person. Since conversion is a radical reorientation, it must involve more than the understanding of terms and doctrines. One has to be able to examine oneself critically. It is an emotional issue as well as a rational one. This rational danger is illustrated by a conversation at a dinner meeting of local ministers, when one reported the conversion of a six-year-old. "She knew all the answers," he said, without flinching or seeming to know what he was saying about the meaning of faith. Such an assertion would be equally inauthentic at sixteen or thirty years, for faith is richer than rational assent.

This decision also has become socially expected and mechanical. In some congregations, unless the decision has been made by the end of the sixth grade, intense pressure is applied to the child by the Sunday church school teacher and the minister. When parents bring their child to the pastor and are told that the child is not ready for the decision, they often are disappointed. I once had to tell a parent that her third-grade son did not understand the import of making such a decision or of the meaning of baptism. She became angry with me and the next Sunday sent the child down the aisle to make the decision. What I regret is that the system under which I was working had no place in it for me to tell the mother that faith was indeed at work, that what the child was feeling was real, but that the label we were putting on the experience was inappropriate. If there is a lie in confirmation, then there is also a deception here, for the person is led to believe that such a decision settles everything for all time.

Another defect in nurture under the believer's baptism view is that children essentially have no place in the wider life of the congregation until they make a public profession of faith. This is not to say that they are treated totally as aliens, but they are sent strong messages that they cannot truly belong until they make the profession of faith. This situation was driven home to me in a Sunday evening Lord's Supper celebration. The deacons were positioned around the sanctuary and the congregation clustered around them for the receiving of the elements. It was a meaningful way of symbolizing our larger corporate nature as well as our more intimate relationships in smaller groups. However, the beauty of the moment was marred in my own heart when I looked to the front of the sanctuary and saw some little children, alone, outside the circles of communion. "My soul," I asked, "what are we saying to these children?"

A story illustrates the kinds of messages we send to our children when we include or exclude them from certain activities. One minister I know would say, as he offered the Communion elements to the congregation, "This is the Lord's table. He provides what is here. If you belong to God, all of this belongs to you." One Sunday, after such a service, an older child asked his father whether he (the boy) belonged to God, whereupon the father reassured him that he did. Then the child asked, "Then why can't I take the Lord's Supper with you?"

When the doctrine of believer's baptism is combined with the doctrine of original sin, the child is put in an untenable position—a sinner by birth, but not yet old enough to choose salvation. To resolve this tension, someone or some group formulated a concept that the child is safe until old enough to be accountable for sin. Thus, the consideration of "the age of accountability" became and remains a focal point in discussions of children's faith. This "safe" notion has no basis in Scripture or in the practice of the early church, although it does acknowledge the efficacy of God's grace.

But apart from the question of grace and accountability, the "safe" doctrine bares a major weakness in our nurture of children. Imagine two fifth graders of equal religious zeal and faithfulness to the church, of equal character and intelligence. One is saved, for having made a public decision; the other is only safe, not yet accountable. The religious dynamic aside, how is the education of the two children to differ? But still more problematic is how to tell the children that they are sinners but not yet accountable.

The surpassing strength of believer's baptism is that when it follows a genuine recognition of estrangement and declaration of faith, it is a beautiful symbol (not a "mere" symbol, as some say). It does not have to represent a cataclysmic turning around in one's life, or else there would be no need for Christian nurture prior to its administration. Our children, truly reared in the faith, do not need to throw off the old life of sin and take on the new life of faith. They have, all along, been choosing faith over sin and choosing sin over faith, and will continue to do so throughout their lives. But at their baptism they are indicating that they have now faced the true meaning of sin and the effectuality of the grace and faith in which they have been nurtured. They now declare faith for themselves.

The practice of child baptism is a phenomenon in churches which have traditionally held to believer's baptism, although some parents in congregations which baptize infants have chosen to delay the baptism of their children. I now realize that my baptism in 1944, at twelve and a half, came at a time when Southern Baptists were lowering the expected age of decision from the middle teen years to the middle childhood years. When I entered seminary in 1955, the expected age for baptism in Southern Baptist churches was about ten years, hardly adult baptism, and not believer's baptism. Ten years later almost one-half of all baptisms were of children, some under six years of age. By the time I came to the seminary to teach in 1972, one-third of the total baptisms were of children, again including preschoolers.[3] The chief rationale was that the children were old enough to know right from wrong, therefore were sinners in need of salvation. Many said that it was better to "get the children early," before the "cynical" years of adolescence. That rationale is also the one I discovered when I came across the child evangelism movement.

The weakness of this theology of child baptism is that it forces us to direct our nurture toward requiring of the child a decision which is incompatible with childhood. The language and import of regeneration should be reserved for the time when a person is able to face repentance emotionally from a more mature selfhood and intellectually from a more advanced power of reason. Again, the problem is not that the reality of regeneration of God's grace has not begun. That reality operates throughout life. Neither is it a problem of when God can forgive sin. The difficulty is with leading the child to an unfitting response to such reality.

This position on child baptism does not improve on the other forms of baptism. It is fraught with the same weaknesses of believer's baptism. It is insecure about the beginning of grace and faith. It becomes socially expected, thus is potentially mechanical. It does not provide a defined place for the unbaptized child. As with infant baptism, child baptism does not take seriously the relationship between sin and conscious selfhood.

I have also met within my denomination those who have a more responsible rationale for child baptism, believing it to be essentially a symbol of the child's initiation into the Christian life. It is seen as overcoming the false promises of infant baptism and the rigidity in believer's baptism. In more positive terms, child baptism may be understood as hybrid, borrowing dynamics both from infant and believer's baptism. Whether stated negatively or positively, the argument for child baptism is couched on one hand in terms of solidarity and covenant and on the other in terms of a choice of faith.

In this form of baptism, though otherwise healthily distinguished from the abuses of child evangelism, the problem is that it calls for a profession that assumes a degree of self-understanding and acceptance not characteristic of the brightest child. Neither does it speak adequately to the documented religious experience of adolescence when sin can be more nearly understood rationally and its effects felt more personally.

Nevertheless, the beauty of child baptism is that it recognizes more responsibly than believer's baptism the current situation of the child reared in the Christian family and church. It magnifies, better than infant baptism, the simple faith of the child. Its preeminent advantage is that it comes at the right time for the church to symbolize the child's rightful place in the community of faith. In its intention, then, it is superior both to infant and believer's baptism, for it is more in the spirit of Jesus who received little children. I do not mean that Jesus was thinking either of conversion or baptism, but that in his blessing of children he meant to show their significance and place. The rationale for initiatory baptism, at least in part, promises that.

In discussing the strengths and weaknesses of nurture under infant, child, and believer's baptism, I am not suggesting that one can with integrity hold to all three. A church must have only one baptism, a person be baptized only once. My own convictions fall on the side of believer's baptism in adolescence. However, neither do I intend to argue for the rejection of infant or child baptism as valid practices. That is why when I come in the theory of nurture to the point of prescribing celebrative rites for heightened religious experience and awareness, I name more than one possible rite. To do otherwise would be arrogant and would ignore much of the history of the church and contemporary practice. This stance has brought me a greater appreciation for the theorists who, knowing the defects in the systems within which they live out their faith, still have formulated reasonable and sound theories and approaches to the nurture of the children of God.

In addition to these views on the awakening to faith, represented in churches which baptize infants or children or believers, individual religious education theorists have formulated important proposals. These fall generally within the two major views, although some theories call for significant adjustments in those views. By far the most famous is that of Horace Bushnell, of the nineteenth century, although he did not propose a lifelong developmental theory. (See Appendix II, "Bushnell's Idea of Christian Education.") From the first third of the twentieth century George Albert Coe's educational writings are the most widely discussed. (See Appendix III, "Coe's Theory—Salvation by Education.") Since Coe, there have been many important works which, though not full-blown developmental theories, have set forth guiding ideas for education and nurture. (See Appendix IV, "Educational Theory Since 1940.")

Other writers have gone further in the process of theorizing by suggesting how faith looks and how it ought to be nurtured developmentally. Some of these are based on massive original research. Some involve limited original research but are built ably on the findings of major researchers. Still others are thoughtful proposals consistent with research and with writings in the humanities and social sciences. (See Appendix IV, "Educational Theory Since 1940.")

My own perspective on salvation and nurture has elements which are parallel to those offered by others who have shared their findings and reasoned opinions with us; yet it is different in some respects. I will leave it to others to identify whatever appears borrowed and whatever appears unique. In offering this gift, I do not presume that the view holds solutions to all of the problems posed by the weaknesses of other theories. In acknowledgment of the partiality of human sight, complementarity is the best one can hope for.

The birth and growth of faith are discussed by persons in the field under varying terms. "Religious education" is the term my nurturers used for the activity by which they taught me and helped me to appropriate the faith. The Methodist church down the street called it Christian education. In the historical study of the field, one comes across other terms representing this process of faith appropriation: nurture (Bushnell), faith-awakening and socialization (Coe), Christian religious education (De Blois and Gorham), catechesis (Catholic sources), and church education (Fallaw). Other related terms are formation, conditioning, training, induction, incorporation, enculturation, and religious and faith development.

In the foregoing and following pages, some of these correlative terms are employed; however, the preference is for education and nurture. These terms are interchanged and, for emphasis, are frequently used together, sometimes with "religious," sometimes "Christian."

It is not my intention to ignore the sensitivities of those who labor for precise definition. However, if we analyze formal definitions of certain realities, we will find that, in most instances, they are inept. Definitions are for the most part synonyms. For example, the dictionary defines education as the act of educating. Educate is defined as to develop or train, to teach. Nurture is defined as the act or process of promoting development; it is also defined as education. Once the terms are identified as act or process, the definer is limited to the use of synonyms. Defining, then, is somewhat futile. Therefore, persons who wonder about my definitions will find them in the theory itself. (See Appendix IV, "Educational Theory Since 1940.")

A Guiding Theology

This is a theological view of Christian nurture; its concern is salvation. We experience our own salvation as something given, something received, something done. It is then a matter of grace, a matter of faith, and a matter of work. There is something in it with which we have nothing to do. Yet, there is something about it which is ineffectual until we willingly receive it. Salvation is something in the face of which we have to be passive and waiting, yet something which without our activity never becomes real. It comes as something initiated outside of our powers, but it applies to us only as we allow it to empower us.

This salvation takes place within the perspective of creation, which is God's continuing act. God was before all that is; God creates out of nothing. This creative activity is one coherent and purposeful process without being static or predetermined. It is dynamic without being mechanically evolutionary. All creative activity takes place within it; there is nothing outside of it. Whatever covenants there are fall within its purpose. Whatever falls and rescues there are come within its purview. Salvation is begun and completed within its boundaries with Jesus Christ as the centerpiece of that salvation and the church as the bearer.

We enter this creative process at a point in time, as persons made in the image of God. We thus are creatures and only a part of creation. But we are more, for being in God's image we also have the power to create. We cannot create out of nothing; but as we experience life, we add our own selves to its history. God expects this of us and empowers us with the ability to create. We then fulfill creation's expectation when we become a creative trustee for God in the world. It is an interlocking reality—God puts us here as stewards in a world which we did not conceive, the coming into which we had no choice. Yet inseparable with our coming and our purpose is that we also can create. As we become creative trustees, we fulfill our humanity after the fashion which God intended but which God would not effect without our participation. God initiates our being; together we work at our becoming. When first seeing this vision, the Initiator said, "It is very good."

Unfortunately, this vision has not been fully realized in human experience. Had it been, there would be no need for salvation. Existence is still good, but something is wrong. Adam is out of the garden, and

Babel's tower is down. There is a split within us, an alienation from something essential about us. We are unable to find a grounding center on which to stand and from which to make sense of experience. There is a division among us, a sense of being cut off from one another and from some higher destiny and purpose. We view the ruins of our towers of ingenuity and broken relationships and know that something noble may yet be built, something more reconciling, established. But we are unable to put our abilities consistently to purposeful and harmonizing activity or to act with persistence on our best impulses. Existence as intended is awry because in our becoming we have done something to the vision.

But God still holds faith that, in collaboration with the general vision, we can make of our particular lives and of our world something that will honor the Creator. God still believes in us and therefore is continually working to heal the inner split, to reconcile the division, to restore the unobscured and clear image in which we are made. This is no interruption but is an act continuous with God's purpose in creation. It is God's creative response to the changing nature of our existence. In collaboration with God we can put our lives back on course. That which is awry can be recentered.

The centerpiece of salvation, the impetus and model in such a recentering, is Jesus Christ, God's Son, Savior. Jesus lived, was crucified, buried, and raised from the dead. Though he came in time and out of Nazareth, he has become the meaning of God for us, has become the symbol of the way God works. He did not simply bring a saving word; he rather was a reconciling event in himself.

With Jesus Christ as the saving figure, God offers salvation. It is a given, held out by a graceful God; yet it also involves human faith and work. It is we who experience and appropriate and who witness to its reality. Salvation is of God in Christ. Along with the sin which is at work in us throughout our lives, salvation also is at work. Just as we participate in the sinful condition of humanity before we understand its import, so do we participate in salvation before we can appreciate its full meaning. If evil can work in us prior to our knowledge and responsibility, so can the holy. However, at some time in our lives we come to face the fact of our division within ourselves, among our brothers and sisters in the race, and between us and God. In facing that, we are called upon to act on that knowledge in light of the work of Jesus the Christ. If we act in faith, then we set ourselves consciously on a journey which had its beginnings long before we were aware; in short, we allow God to work in transforming our lives or in reforming us after the image.

Christian nurture is nothing less than working with this process of salvation. This is not to say that we are saved by education, for that would be contradictory to our understanding that salvation is given by God and would reduce God to the processes of nurture. It also would change faith from something active to something passive. By the same token we must also admit that God is not limited by some decision that we make, for that also would be contradictory to our understanding that salvation is given by God, and would limit God to our wishes and decisions. It would lean faith toward the mechanical and the static. God's salvation has to be understood in much larger terms than individual cognition and group processes yet must be concerned and involved with both. It must be seen in the broad scope of creation. But that brings us back to the problem. We have not been able to deal positively with the tremendous reality of a creating God, an unfolding universe, and a creative humanity.

The church is the bearer of salvation. God originates salvation, and Jesus Christ is the agent, but the church is the announcer and witness. It is depicted in strong terms: the body of Christ, a royal priesthood, the messianic community, the new Israel, and people of God. To the church has been given the very secret of the kingdom of God. God the Sovereign holds the keys. The church is the keeper of the gate, proclaiming the Good News to the world and, in God's behalf, inviting the world to come in.

But this is church in imagery. The church in the abstract does not bring persons to know God, and no one can belong to it. Let us bring it under more human terms. Actually, the church is the congregation to which we belong. It is made of people, like ourselves, being saved through grace and by faith. No one congregation is a perfect church, just as no Christian is fully the Christ. But the congregation is the people who receive and nurture salvation and is the place from which the secret of the kingdom goes out.

The church is a congregation which worships God, proclaims the gospel in concrete terms, nurtures its children, and calls its adults to maturity and mission. It is the whole congregation—in its total life of worship, of nurture, of ethic, and of mission—which brings the children of God to full stature. The church school, the Christian home, and special activities cannot be church, for they draw their life from the whole congregation especially as it is visible in corporate worship. Worship is the energizing center for nurture and missions and is the context for the preaching of the Word. Worship is irreplaceable, and where it is sterile, so will nurture and mission be defective. Where it is authentic, it puts the worshiper in touch with the holy and the transcendent. In that touch the worshiper, made in the image of God, experiences a mystical connection with the very source of the image. Further, the individual who is not involved in worshiping with the congregation will most likely not become incorporated into the nexus and faith of the community.

A moment from the eighteenth century makes the point. Jonathan Edwards required the children in his Northampton congregation to memorize and repeat the sermon outline and, of course, say the catechism in the presence of the minister. The biographer suggests that the children dutifully performed what was expected, then straightway forgot it, but that what they did not forget was that religion was a serious business.[4] That is what I mean when I say that the total context of the life of the congregation, more than any specific activity, is the true bearer of salvation and the provider of nurture.

The Theory in Summary

The ensuing discussion envisions salvation and the course of nurture in terms of four realities: Sonship–daughtership, the infant and young child years (birth to six–seven); belonging, the middle child years (seven–eight to eleven–twelve); affirmation, the adolescent years; and creative trusteeship, the adult years. Each reality has an origin, a recipient and responsible conveyer, and a pursuant nurturing task. In addition, the congregation will symbolize each reality with a rite appropriate to its theology and history.

Reality 1—Sonship–Daughtership. Children are sons and daughters of God, a status which is a gift of God. Being a child of God is not a status of salvation, for all are children of God, but not all partake of God's salvation. For that reason the church attempts to bring all under the influence of the saving Word. But in these early years its task is to convey to children that they are children of God. It will accomplish this through affective and cognitive means within the setting of a worshiping community of faith. The hope is that the children will emerge from the kindergarten age, both knowing and feeling that they are already sons and daughters of God. Later, they will learn of their estrangement from God. This positive awareness forms the basis for the other realities in the faith pilgrimage, and unless it is achieved in these years, the full dimensions of belonging, affirmation, and trusteeship cannot be experienced.

The task involves the general enrichment of the child's experience, that is, the world of oneself, parents, friends, other adults, pets, house, yard, church, and playthings. Relations with these elements, meaning their enjoyment and use, will form the curriculum. As this enrichment is accomplished, the children sense that we love and care for them. Then, as appropriate, we begin to tell them that it is the same with God and that they are children of God because they are made in the Maker's image. We do not give that kind of status by our attempts at providing an enriching environment and relationship, but we do convey it by the way we relate to the developing children.

Reality 2—Belonging. Children belong to the congregation where parents participate, a status conferred by the congregation. Our task with the elementary children is to bless them as Jesus did, to let them know that they are within the community of faith until they decide for themselves whether to embrace the church's faith. It is to tell them that they are not aliens whose belongingness waits upon conversion or confirmation or any other act of joining. It is to tell them, within the context of their emotional, intellectual, and social-moral progress, about their heritage of faith.

The hope is that just as the children emerged from the preschool years feeling and knowing that they are the children of God, so will they, during childhood, increasingly feel that they belong to the congregation's ethos and mission and are developing in belief and work. Upon a basic sense of "who-ness" (children of God) is built the sense of place, that is to say, of having a place. The children have an identity—it is children of God. The children have a place—it is as a part of the faith community. The origin is in the parental connection—not in the genes, but in the relationships. The congregation confers the belonging; the people say, "You belong here; you do not have to earn your place. We give it to you."

Reality 3—Affirmation. Adolescents affirm the faith for themselves, confirming their heritage in the church and declaring faith in Jesus Christ. In Reality 1 the task was to convey an already given sonship–daughtership; in 2, to confer and dramatize a belongingness. The task in Reality 3 is to show the necessity of and to guide the adolescent in appraising the heritage and in making a personal declaration of faith.

The task is to help the adolescents to interpret the pulls of the identity crisis and the dawning discrepancies between who the church has told them they are and what they sense about their relation to God. It is for them to see, in varying degrees, that for all of the education and nurture there is still something about this life which they cannot control. The impulse to do good is too much smothered by the impulse to do evil. The desire to be obedient is too much choked by an inclination to disobey. For all one's strength, there is much weakness. For all of the feeling about being a son or daughter of God, there still exists an obscuring of that relationship and it cannot be seen as clearly. For all of the feeling of belonging, there still exists a measure of alienation.

Reality 4—Creative Trusteeship. Adults commit themselves to being creative trustees for a creating God who is finishing creation. The task for the education of the adult is to help the adult to join fully with God in the work of creation. God is at work in both the natural and social orders and in the development of individuals. In these arenas God is supplying the essential possibilities for individual fulfillment and social completion. A measure of stewardship has been present in the growing child and adolescent, but full participation has waited upon the coming of adulthood, a time when one has put aside the play of childhood and the ego problems of adolescence to take up adult roles. Being adult

Foundations

means seeing the immensity of the issues involved in being a trustee for God, and in realizing personal responsibility for dealing with those issues. Such is the life stance of the trustee.

The trustee, out of involvement and study, develops a working theology, applying it to one's ethic and life-style. The trustee is a growing person, taking life seriously and playfully, and has a deep understanding of human origin and destiny. In all of this, the trustee is better able to deal with the unbelief, hubris, and concupiscence which compose one's alienation from God.

In addition to the theological character of this view of nurture, each of the four realities in the awakening has a critical, specific theological dimension. This is so because each reality is religious in essence and because the church needs to choose some rite by which to symbolize each reality. Such rites are by no means neutral theologically; neither is there much agreement on which rite best symbolizes each religious awakening. Even where churches agree on the appropriate rite, they hold to distinct underlying theologies. Because of this divergence in theology and practice, I have left open the question of the most appropriate rite for each reality. (See Appendix V, "The Celebrative Rites.")

Reality 1, sonship–daughtership, is based in the meaning of our created existence in the image of God and the anticipation of our participation in that good existence and in the contradicting Fall. I draw heavily from the Old Testament theologians and from some New Testament and systematic theologians for an investigation of "image of God," a basis for sonship–daughtership. The doctrine of baptism also is given attention. (See Appendix VI, "Image and Fall," and Appendix I, "Baptism—A Theological Question.") Reality 2, belonging, also has its basis in creation theology, but it is specifically to a community of faith that one comes to belong. The doctrine of baptism has to be reopened with this reality, but the theology of the Lord's Supper is also a doctrine one is to consider. (See Appendix VIII, "The Lord's Table," and Appendix I, "Baptism—A Theological Question.") Reality 3, affirmation, draws a dimension of redemption theology into a creation perspective. Because the practice of confirmation has been so mechanical and conversion has been so rationalistic, it is essential that a theology of sin and responsibility be the foundation for this adolescent reality. Tillich's doctrine of estrangement and faith best articulates the theological problem in this reality. (See Appendix VII, "Tillich's Doctrine of Estrangement and Salvation.") Reality 4, creative trusteeship, is connected theologically with our being in God's image and our role in exercising dominion over the earth. It deals with our continuing sin problem. For that, we have to return to the Old Testament scholars and to Tillich. But this trusteeship also has a base in the doctrines of church, mission, and the priesthood of the believer. Hans Küng has a helpful, perceptive statement on the doctrine of priesthood. (See Appendix IX, "Dominion, Priesthood, Trusteeship," and Appendix VI, "Image and Fall.")

The Underlying Psychology

Salvation is a religious reality. However, because it operates in the lives of persons, it has a psychological dimension. To view salvation developmentally means to move from the theological base of the substance of salvation to the question of how the reality is appropriated in the course of human development. Take some popular questions in religious education circles: When is a person ready to make a declaration of faith? Should children be baptized? When is a person responsible for sin? The substance of these questions has to be dealt with both by theology and psychology. While there is interplay between the two, theology primarily defines the meaning of the problem; psychology primarily answers the "when" of the problem.

I subscribe to the truism that we are feeling and thinking persons. It is evident to any observer that both the form and content of emotion and thought change as we move from infant to adult. As infants we whine, cry, or scream over so small a matter as a late feeding. As adults, faced by the same situation, we might be anxious or at least mildly disturbed, but would most likely express our emotion differently. By adulthood we have settled many thinking problems that confused us as children. We know that bigger does not mean older; that one can be in a city, state, and country at the same time; that meanings are found beyond concrete facts.

Two psychologists—Erik Erikson and Jean Piaget—propose sensible explanations of why and how persons progress from infant to adult emotion and thought. Their works, then, form the underlying psychology for my theory of the awakening to faith and the shape of nurture.

Erikson's psychology provides the best framework for understanding personality development and the most promising basis for making decisions about how to nurture people. In addition, his work has a certain theological character about it which undeniably connects him with the deeper questions of estrangement and reconciliation, of division and wholeness. For Reality 1, it is Erikson's insights into trust, autonomy, and initiative that are crucial to preschool education. If children do not develop basic trust, for example, how does that failure limit our ability to realize Reality 1 in the experience of the child? In Reality 2, it is Erikson's discussion of industry that is significant, especially in the relationship between the negative outcome of inferiority and the child's feeling of belonging. For Reality 3, identity is the central consideration. The question is how identity and responsibility for faith are related. While all three of Erikson's adult "ages" (intimacy, generativity, and integrity) are important, his understanding of intimacy and generativity clearly articulate the psychological foundation for the reality of trusteeship. (See Appendix X, "Erikson's Wisdom.")

The work of Piaget forms the basic cognitive insights upon which the four realities are built. How does learning that is through action and the senses determine what can and cannot be done in conveying sonship–daughtership to children? How does a basic intuitive approach to the construction of reality in the preschooler limit the kind of religious education that is possible? Why are Piaget's findings on the difference in concrete and formal thinking critical to affirmation in adolescents? These and other questions have been considered in light of Piaget's singular contribution. (See Appendix XI, "Piaget's Discovery.")

The Knowledge Problem

A recent educational television presentation on "time" ended with this word: "If you ask me what time is, I know; but if you ask me to define time, then I know that I do not know." The statement turns out to be a remarkable illustration of the problem we face with religious knowledge. That is not to say that our problem is one of definition, but that we are dealing with realities which we know but cannot prove. We are asked by others to tell them how we know some religious doctrine is true or some religious experience real. Some of us do, of course, appeal to the Bible on questions of the truth of doctrine, but anyone who has studied the history of our classical Christian doctrines has discovered that they were far from being refined in the early Christian community out of which the New Testament came. Besides, the questioner could simply ask us how we know the Bible is true. In that case and in the case of religious experience, we generally answer, in the absence of evidence, "I just know; that's all."

It would not take long for a philosopher, especially one concerned with language, to convince most of us that we know very little. Such a philosopher probes our assertions about knowing something by asking if we really know or if we only know about, or know of, or think we know, or believe that we know. Thus, do we know God or only about or of God, or only think or believe that we know God? The philosopher does not mean to play with words but is attempting to help us see that our language is too casual. However, if the philosopher in taking away our words convinces us of how little we know, then that philosopher or someone must reckon with something real that is behind what we say we know.

Philosophers who concentrate more on the substance of what we say we know and less on the language we use give us more help with our problem. We understand that some knowledge comes "after the fact"; that is, it can be supported by evidence with which others, seeing the same evidence, would agree. I know that the sun came up this morning, and anyone else who is out today also knows that. But there is a knowing which does not depend on this kind of experience or fact. Religious knowing is of this kind, for we say that we know God, and we mean more than that we know about God; also, we mean more than that we believe there is a God. All of this is involved when we say that we know God, but that knowledge is not explained by the information given or even by the experiences we have and report.

This kind of religious knowing can be spoken of as revelation. We know that Jesus is the Christ by revelation. Such revelation does not come on us directly, in disregard to our senses, our experience, our feelings, or our thinking. There is no religious knowledge that ignores these; otherwise, God would reveal great mysteries to the infant in the crib and would communicate complex doctrinal positions to people who cannot even read or write. Neither is revelation something that is added onto natural knowledge. We do not pursue knowledge to the end of our ability and then ask God to add revelation to it.

What I claim to know by revelation is intertwined with what I know naturally. Because God is over all of creation, then all knowing is, in a sense, a revelation. To be sure, some of this knowledge is mundane; some belongs to mystery. The astronaut stepping onto the moon took sophisticated knowledge, entirely available to all with competent scientific mentality. Yet he stepped into a mystery which all of mission control could not produce or even report on. What we call natural knowledge is a part of God's unveiling; the whole of creation is God's realm.

My understanding of salvation and plan for nurture assume both a positive and a negative about religious knowledge. First, I recognize that in our concupiscence we are distracted from much that God is attempting to reveal to us. In our hubris we cannot get beyond ourselves to see all that is there to be known. In our unbelief we are disconnected from the center and cannot know all that is to be known. In our dividedness we are victims of partiality and cannot even explain entirely all that we see and know. In short, our knowledge problem is that we are creatures in the image of God and given dominion over the earth but are not gods and have no kingdoms.

Yet there is a positive side. The God who is, and who does have a kingdom, makes self-revelations. This God, acting both independently of our action and in concert with us, makes it possible for us to say, out of common experiences and with common language, "I know." We understand this on the plane of human exchange. Not all who read this book will come to know the author to the same degree. Some will focus on subtle disclosures that others will overlook. But, to some degree, the reader will be able to say, "I know that man." By the same token, if you tell me that you bought my book, I would know something about you. And if you should comment favorably on some section or thought, I would know you even better. All of this may be true without our ever meeting in person.

Therefore, my theory of nurture assumes that our knowing, though partial, is trustworthy. It can be trusted in its cognitive form, though its content changes with new insights and experiences. It can be trusted in its affective result, though it varies from person to person as well as within the life span of a single individual. But religious knowing is finally trustworthy because it resonates with my belief that behind or beneath all reality there is a self-disclosing God. This does not solve the ancient problem of knowledge, but it is something, without final and absolute evidence, with which I can live and "know."

Further, to ask, "How do you know what you say you know?" is to raise the question of how we come to know or how we learn. Most of our religious knowledge is learned in the same way that anything is learned. But if revelation has any meaning, then we must acknowledge that religious learning makes a distinctive claim for itself. I can, for example, learn the basic witness of the early church to the historical Jesus, but I cannot, by learning such witness, learn or know the meaning of the event of Christ. How is it that I learn one and not the other, or that I learn both?

Just as revelation is not added onto natural knowledge and does not come directly from God without regard for one's total personality, so is religious learning not a separate or higher way of thinking. Although there is a left and right brain, we do not have two minds, one for learning religion and one for learning other matters. The mental functions in learning about God and about Einstein's theory are the same functions. Neither do we have special religious emotions. Sensations in worship and in a patriotic moment are the same sensations. As you can see then, my view of salvation and nurture has behind it certain fundamentals of learning no different from learning in any situation. But as a developmental view of salvation, my plan also has behind it the necessity of God's creative action in our salvation knowing.

Relation to Adult Conversion and Evangelism

Not everyone is going to be brought under the influence of the church in infancy or have the opportunity to awaken to faith as herein prescribed. For many persons, the Good News of grace will come during the adult years. What, then, is the effect of adult conversion on the four-realities scheme?

First, the age at which a person hears and responds to the Good News of grace does not alter the basic status of sonship–daughtership with which we are born. That status is a gift and cannot be earned or conferred by others. So anyone born into this world is a child of God, from birth to death. We are not free to accept or reject this fact, but we are, of course, free to actualize or thwart such a status. If we were free to reject sonship–daughtership, we could decide at thirty years of age that we did not want to be children of God, then, with a change of mind at forty, want the status back. Being a child of God cannot be turned off and on. It is a given status and its continued existence is not subject to our wishes. It is outside the bounds of our control, for it is in God's domain. Because it is not subject to changes due to any action of our own, then repentance, being a volitional act on our part, has no power over it.

Second, a person converted in adulthood will have to work emotionally back through the feeling of sonship–daughtership and belonging. Having not known before that one was a child of God or that one could belong to the community of faith, the adult will face these issues in retrospect and "out of time." The impetus of the conversion will probably confront the person immediately with the truth of being a child of God, for the language of conversion is heavily saturated with this theme, borrowing from Paul's belief that we are adopted as children of God. The adult will come to see that the status has been there all along, but has not been, until now, acted upon personally.

As to the reality of belonging, the adult who is converted usually joins a congregation simultaneously with the public declaration of faith. In this case, the sense of belonging, not heretofore experienced, is just beginning to be experienced. It will then have to develop alongside the feeling of being a son or daughter of God and along with the growing understanding that one is to be a creative trustee with a creative God. But this trusteeship cannot be fully realized immediately or purely on the strength of an adult conversion experience. At increasing levels, the person will come to feel the sonship–daughtership which God gives and the belonging which the church confers. A careful observation of an adult convert will demonstrate the truth of this contention.

On the matter of evangelism, it is a different but not entirely separate question from nurture. The difference and the sameness of nurture and evangelism are represented by two distinct, but overlapping, circles. Children who grow up in the church are within the overlapping region. They are being nurtured and are hearing the Good News at the same time. Children who grow up outside the church are outside the circle of nurture and therefore are not within the overlapping region of the circles. They are totally within that part of the evangelism circle which is not connected with the nurturing environment, beyond our nurturing.

The term "evangelism" cannot maintain the imperial meaning some give it to describe all that we do in the church. Neither can nurture maintain the smug meaning some give it to describe a process unrelated to evangelism. Nurture does not replace evangelism in its true sense of the telling of the Good News. The teaching of resurrection at Easter is both kerygma and didache, both witness to and instruction in a saving event. But this kerygma, this witness, does not come as completely new to the children who grow up in faith. For those outside the church, it indeed overtakes them in their course away from the God whose children they are.

2

Emma as Young Child—
A Child of God by Creation

Emma's education and nurture begin with this basic ultimate truth—she is a daughter of God by creation. And it is sheer gift. God the Maker, in creation, makes children of God of all persons who are born into this world.

This unequaled status of being a child of God is different from the earning of status through being good. Emma's behavior is not what makes her a child of God or what will insure that she continue as one. It is true, of course, that in living a morally upright life she will fulfill the Maker's grand intention for her, for no parent would want a child to be wayward. But being a child of God does not depend upon the way she lives, for she is a child by a gracious gift of the creative God who gave her life.

Emma's status, then, stands on its own. Emma, much later in her nurture, will learn of significant doctrines and will repeat confessions and creeds, but that will not add one measure to the basic givenness of her status. If she should become the most committed person on earth, while that would delight her Maker, she could not by such dedication gain any edge on others who refuse to consider or follow God's will for their lives.

Others cannot give this gift to Emma. Although her church is the earthen bearer of this good word, it is not the source. Although her parents gave her birth, they are not the source of the gift. The gift is from God and is not only to Emma but also to all children in the world.

Emma cannot refuse this gift. Just as by a process of distribution of genes she takes on the likeness of her parents and for all time is their child, so has she without choice also become a child of God. Children may be abandoned at birth or disowned in the throes of irreconcilable problems later on in life, but they remain forever the children of their parents. Although they may leave home and change their names, they cannot change their parentage.

It is the same with Emma's daughtership with God. There is, of course, no thought that God will abandon her—look at the history of the world and you will see that God could justifiably have given up a long time ago. Emma, once she becomes a willing person, might choose to abandon God, but even if she should leave "home" and change her "name," the gift will hold—she is a child of God.

There is a great mystery here. Beyond the utter wonder of her physical conception and birth, there is yet the puzzling truth that in that birth she becomes a child of God. This is not to suggest that the genes hold such power or that she was a child of God in some spiritual form and finally found a home in a fetus. The matter must be left where all mystery is left—beyond our explanation, but not beyond our appreciation. In her physical birth Emma was simultaneously made a child of God. No mind can fathom such an enigma, but we can celebrate its wonder.

But what is the mark of this mystery? In what sense is Emma a child of God? What is this mark, this sense? Clearly, it is the image of God in which all are created. ". . . God said, 'Let us make man in our image, after our likeness; and let them have dominion over the fish of the sea, and over the birds of the air, and over the cattle, and over all the earth, and over every creeping thing that creeps upon the earth'" (Genesis 1:26).

On the face of it, the Genesis text is all-inclusive. All were to be made in God's image. It was not just the Hebrews who were the children of God. Their status as people of God cannot be understood apart from the mission to which they were called. But as children of God, they had nothing that all persons did not have. All were children of God. This truth shows up in other Old Testament passages: "'For your lifeblood I will surely require a reckoning; of every beast I will require it and of man. . . . Whoever sheds the blood of man, by man shall his blood be shed; for God made man in his own image'" (Genesis 9:5-6; see also Appendix VI, "Image and Fall").

The major Old Testament theologians interpret this image as universal. They find in the texts no basis at all for a narrow view of the image of God. David Cairns, who has made an extensive study of the concept of the image of God, believes that the image applied to all persons. He suggests that this truth may have been obscured by the covenant between God and Israel but that the prophets clarified it.[1] He and others also see in this universal image the truth that all persons then are children of God. For Cairns, the parable of the prodigal son is the clear symbol that all—the wayward and the faithful—are created as children of God and so remain. Even the disobedient, the prodigal, are welcomed home; even the jealous, the older brother, are gently forgiven and reassured.

One of the problems with holding the view that Emma is in the image of God is that some assume that it is a question of salvation with no regard for sin or her freedom to choose. They argue that if you tell her that she is a child of God, made in the divine image, then you are suggesting that she is basically good and will not be held responsible for sin. However, to believe that the image belongs to Emma is not to deny that she will be held accountable for the kind of life she will live. Rather, it is to speak of who she is, not what shape her life might take.

Certainly to say that Emma is born as of God and made in God's image is not to say that she will grow up righteous and not have to face personal decisions about faith. And who can in good conscience hold that she is a child of the devil who must grow up sinful? The truth is that, as she grows, she partakes both of sin and right. Any valid system of nurture must take into account this dual development in Emma's life. It must affirm, on the one hand, her decisions for right; it must take into account, on the other hand, the fact of sin. Both of these will lead to the necessity that she declare her personal faith. But that decision is several years away for her. (See Appendix II, "Bushnell's Idea of Christian Education.")

Others will object strongly to the notion that Emma is made in the image of God because they believe that the image was lost in the fall of Adam and Eve from their original state. However, the most respected Old Testament scholars have studied the image and also Adam and

Eve's banishment from the Garden of Eden and have concluded that the image was not lost. (See Appendix VI, "Image and Fall.") Also, the most widely followed systematic theologians hold that the image was not destroyed in the Fall. (See Appendix VI, "Image and Fall.")

It seems clear that we can safely continue to call Emma the daughter of God by creation, made in God's image. She will not always reflect this image, for she will sin and hide from God, but still she is a child of God. She is brought under the influence of salvation at birth, through faithful parents. She is put in touch with the deeds and words of salvation, through the faithful church, as her parents present her to the congregation and a rite of presentation is celebrated. She grows within the community of faith. In time she will come to admit to herself that she is not adequately reflecting the image of God or living as a daughter of God. She will learn of Jesus Christ in whom the image is clear and the Sonship true. Then she will make a responsible decision.

The Nurturing Task in the Young Childhood Years

The task for Emma's church and parents is to convey to her that she is a child of God by creation. This will be done at the *feeling level* and at the *intellectual level,* within the setting of a worshiping community of faith. The hope is that Emma will emerge from the kindergarten age both feeling and knowing that she is already a daughter of God, as she was told at her presentation. Such an awareness will form the basis for her continuing odyssey of faith, and unless it is achieved during this early period of life, it will have to be discovered before she can experience the full dimensions of belonging, affirmation, and creativity.

Emma will not be told that she is either sinful or righteous, for at this tender age she is neither. In time she will become aware of both conditions and of her participation in both. Then she will see that she does not always love that which is holy; neither is she always attracted irresistibly to that which is evil. Proper nurture will predispose her to the holy, for God begins this work of grace early through religious parents and caring teachers, but she will also bow to other pressures as she grows. (See Appendix II, "Bushnell's Idea of Christian Education.")

Anyway, the "good" and the "bad" are not general concepts which

Emma as Young Child—A Child of God by Creation

Emma can understand. She does not have an ethical concept of goodness. She responds more to the ill or good effects of behavior than to any system or concept of right or wrong. Her conscience is not yet developed, though it is in the process; thus, we cannot expect her to learn right from wrong as a general principle. Take, for example, the fact that the young preschoolers must constantly be told to say thank-you after someone gives them a gift. They do not have a concept of gift and gratitude, only of receiving and liking or disliking. Thus, with no general concept out of which to behave, they simply accept the gift. Of course, they sometimes remember; but most often they are prodded, and they say, finally, "Thank you."

While Emma does not know it, she is being shaped by particular ethical values. These are, of course, the standards of her family, which, in turn, are influenced by the community values. But standards are her first contact with that part of personality known by psychologists as the superego. It is important that we not overburden her budding self-image by telling her that her innocent or deliberate actions are sins against God. While we can, and inevitably will, show our disappointment when she goes against our values, we should not put on Emma's fledgling conscience more than it can bear.

Education, at such a time of realization of good and evil, will certainly aid Emma in interpreting the urges toward the good and the bad. But this interpretation will be done against the background that she is already a child of God. Her being bad or doing bad things and her being good or doing right things do not invalidate or seal her basic daughtership.

The Feeling Level

Emma's education and nurture during the preschool and early school years will focus in both affective and cognitive growth. Affective growth refers to what some would call personality development and to what others would call emotional development. And, of course, cognitive or mental growth are other labels for intellectual development in broad terms. Let us see how growth at these two levels might bring Emma, the young child, to feel and know that she is a child of God, made in God's image.

In the case of Emma as an infant we know we have the power to shape her possibilities for future relationships by the way we feed, handle, and care for her. That is the way she will receive the world. Thus, if we want to communicate, we must do so through these available modes. In this communication to her that she is wanted, loved, desirable, and worthy, we are indeed engaging in Christian education and nurture.

In fact, at this gateway to socialization there is no explicitly religious material that we can use with Emma. She does not know the words we use; thus, we cannot teach concepts to her. Obviously, she cannot read; thus, books are of no use. This also rules out the telling of Bible stories to crib babies. It is a troublesome consideration, isn't it, to say that our traditional modes of education and nurture—words, symbols, and books—are not available to us in the religious development of the infant Emma.

That, however, is not to say that no religious education is possible. To the contrary, here in the first few months of life the very basis of all religious development is established most naturally. Yes, through these elemental physical and social needs of the infant—the need for food, comfort, physical stimulation, and others' company—we are engaged in Christian education.

The caring adult who mixes Emma's formula, changes her diapers, and strokes and talks lovingly to her is engaged as fully in religious development as the adult who sits with other adults and discusses critical biblical problems or contemporary issues. Further, when this attention to Emma's basic needs is done with quality, she will come to think of herself as of worth, that is, of enough worth that her needs are being met. She also will come to know that the adults involved in her care can be trusted to come with help, and of the right kind.

It is Erik Erikson who best establishes the wisdom that the first two years of life are the "cradle of faith." (See Appendix X, "Erikson's Wisdom.") During this brief span of months, according to Erikson, Emma will develop a basic stance toward the world and herself. That stance is that the world can be trusted to meet her needs and that, since basic needs are being met, she also is trustworthy, that is, worthy of others' care. The primary focuses of the care are the senses of taste and touch, for these are the ways she takes in the world. These are the

Emma as Young Child—A Child of God by Creation

"places" where her stimulation must be made, that is, taken, for she cannot as yet go out and get these things for herself.

Emma incorporates experience through sucking and touching and being touched. It is here that her emotional development is lodged. If this development is not fostered, because she is left without adequate care, then she will receive the negative message—"I cannot trust others to meet the needs which I cannot go out and meet for myself; thus I must not be of much worth to them." Mistrust, then, will become her basic stance toward life, and very early she will be crippled emotionally.

Erikson believes that Emma will develop according to a ground plan and that in each phase of the plan there are seeds for the next period of growth. If these seeds are carefully nurtured, they will produce, and in the next period Emma will have a better chance of developing fully. The inverse of this is also true.

Does this mean that, if Emma should come out of infancy with this negative feeling, she can never become a trusting person? No! Erikson does not offer such a disparaging and unrealistic view of personality, for it will never be too late for Emma to be loved and cared for in such a way as to establish trusting relations and feelings of worth. But the most logical time for her to develop this trust is during these first two years of life. The most beautiful and natural kind of personality development, what Erikson calls vitality, will begin rightly at this time in life so that she will move into other critical periods without the crippling deficiencies from an earlier one. That is what the ground plan calls for.

Erikson, however, has a strong word of caution about the absolute and complete nature of this early trust, and his word has a bearing on the reality of being created in the image of God. "But even under the most favorable circumstances," he writes, "this stage seems to introduce into psychic life . . . a sense of inner division and universal nostalgia for a paradise forfeited. It is against this powerful combination of a sense of having been deprived, of having been divided, and of having been abandoned—that basic trust must maintain itself throughout life."[2]

What does this caution mean for Emma? Perhaps it is this: that though even in the most trusting relationship she may have a vague, shadowy feeling of some inexplainable division, still—in spite of it—she can feel that she is a child of worth and significance. Although she is not capable of this kind of thinking, maybe what we have working here is that the Garden of Eden truly is the appropriate symbol of our inner division and separation from God and that trust must then always be against such brokenness and alienation.

In the years two to four, Emma moves into a not so pliable time when she takes on a kind of primitive willfulness and when the world is not entirely brought to her, for she can now go after it. During this time, she is not "going after" the world to the extent that she will in the early school years, but the "going after" is definitely a new behavior not characteristic of her infant years. It is true, of course, that even in infancy she actively reached for objects and persons and sought some expansion of her boundaries, but it is her new mobility as a two- to four-year-old that dramatizes this new phase of her experience.

In infancy she waited for the world to be brought and reacted to what was borne. Now she is up and walking, going after the world, and it is the adults who must react to her adventures. In such a way her needs move on to a higher plane to involve self-expression, cooperation, understanding, and forgiveness, or their opposites. For example, the child who in exploring the room comes upon and breaks an heirloom is suddenly a child in need—perhaps in need of protection from an upset parent, but most assuredly in need of some guidance, patient attention, and much love.

When such incidents in Emma's life are handled positively, she will come to sense that she is of worth, not simply through having her basic physical needs met, but because she knows she can participate, albeit in limited fashion, with trusted and trusting adults and still maintain her sense of self-worth and her trust of others. It is, then, very early established that she is liked, not simply because she is dependent; she can also take willful forays into independence and still be the desire of her parents' hearts.

The "trusted others" do not base their bringing of help upon Emma's utter helplessness, though that certainly still is a factor. No, even when the balance of dependence-independence shifts (such as when the child appears suddenly in front of company with pants hanging down, saying,

"Dirty"), the relationship holds. And Emma says, "I am still liked. I am still somebody."

Emma needs to know that though she is disobedient and therefore subject to discipline, she is nonetheless still a part of the family. The administration of discipline, punishment if you prefer, must be done in such a way as not to undercut her basic security in the face of necessary chastisement. As to how this might be done, there is no prescription to fit every single act of independence which goes far enough to deserve punishment. The crucial factor is for the attending adult to understand what is at stake in the developing personality of the child.

From this kind of treatment, Emma will in time also come to see that her being a child of God means that she is free to explore and develop and that God will be sympathetic with her, even when she makes mistakes. Thus do relationships continue to be our primary tool for Emma's religious education. While, as we shall see under the section on intellectual development, more of the normal avenues of religious education are open to her at this age than when she was an infant, the securing of the feeling that she is a daughter of God is still lodged critically in the way we meet her needs and relate to her.

Emma comes to feel that she really is somebody, and that somebody is a child of God. Admittedly, it is a transfer from human relationships, but that is all with which we have to work. Since we do not experience God directly through the senses, then we must depend upon the elemental tools of human sense and relationship to get at the reality that is God. Such a way to God is most explicit in the development of our children, for that is also the way they come to know that they have a larger family, including ancestors they will never see.

Again, it is Erikson's thought which is the foundation for what has just been said about Emma's development. The years two to four are, in Erikson's system, the battleground for the establishment of autonomy. Emma has come from infancy with that essential ingredient of basic trust, and she will work on becoming an autonomous person. Apart from the world of objects and parents, she now sets on a journey of independent personhood. Of course, this does not mean that she becomes independent, for there are many more years of dependency left for her.

But it does mean that she begins the important work of finding an autonomous self.

Such a journey is fraught with danger in Emma's mind, for it sets her over against a comfortable relationship up to this point. This dynamic is what Erikson considers to be the major theme of this age and it is focused in the anal region, whereas the mouth and the experience of being touched were the focus of her infancy period. The continuing toilet training function emerges as the specific emotional purveyor or detractor in this developing selfhood. If this crisis in her development is handled properly, the biggest early battle of her selfhood will be won. If it is dealt with negatively, then she will really doubt that she is an independent self of some worth.

There are too many stories of harsh treatment—at home, in child care centers, and in the church—to doubt that this stage is a critical one. If toilet training were not significant emotionally, then there would not be such reaction to soiled pants. If, then, we adults can get so upset during this period in the child's life, imagine the feelings of the child. Does not such a consideration then make Erikson's word more logical, namely, that much self-doubt can enter into the child's feelings during these critical years? It follows, then, that positive care will have positive results for the development of autonomy, the second touchstone for a vital personality. Emma's parents will carefully assess when she is ready for toilet training. Although by eighteen months Emma probably is ready in terms of a firm stool and developed anal muscles, her parents may safely wait a few months before training her.[3] They will tread these waters cautiously because of the danger of loosing moorings established earlier in their relationship with her.

Erikson's own words convey clearly the nature of this crisis:

> The infant must come to feel that the basic faith in existence, which is the lasting treasure saved from the rages of the oral stage, will not be jeopardized by this about-face of his, this sudden violent wish to have a choice, to appropriate demandingly, and to eliminate stubbornly. Firmness must protect him against the potential anarchy of his as yet untrained sense of discrimination, his inability to hold on and to let go with discretion. As his environment encourages him to "stand on his own feet," it must protect him against meaningless and arbitrary experiences of shame and of early doubt.[4]

Near the end of the preschool years and into kindergarten and first grade, Emma moves from the battleground of independence to a similar but in many ways very different task. If she has emerged from the previous period with a healthy sense that she is a willing self, surrounded by sympathetic adults, then she will be ready to continue, at a new and less conflict-ridden level, her lifelong movement toward independence. Whereas previously she was driven by urges to prove that she was somebody, she now acts more out of pleasure in doing so.

Emma's busy activity as a kindergarten child, while just as independent when she was two years old, is not nearly as frightful to her parents. Neither is it as threatening to her. Even her face shows the difference. Gone is the scowl of devilishment on her face after she has purposely knocked something from the table. Her actions as a kindergartner are more positive, and even her facial expression reveals that she has less conflict.

This new level of activity is, of course, also possible for Emma because of her advanced physical mobility and new verbal ability. Her repertoire of movement is made possible by some trunk development and rapid limb development.[5] She can now learn to dress herself. Her vocabulary is up to 2,600 words, and she is much more conversational.[6] These two factors, combined with her wider contact with significant adults outside her home, and her new social adeptness, accentuate her expansiveness at this age.

This period is not, however, totally free of conflict. Emma has both outer and inner conflicts. In terms of outer conflict, she often will take too much initiative and run head-on into someone else's activity. Her boundless physical energy will catapult her quickly against someone else. She may knock another child down, causing pain. She also will use words unthinkingly and thereby hurt someone else.

These outer conflicts then set in motion some inner ones. When Emma is being sensitive, she will realize that she has hurt someone else with her body or her words. As this happens, she is beginning to learn that there are limits to her initiative, that there are others who have feelings and needs like hers. But even when her activity does not affect others directly, still she will experience some inner tension about her activity. This is natural because she is trying to see to what limits her initiative can be taken.

Emma is developing conscience out of this dynamic. As she puts together or adjusts to what she feels on the inside and what she sees happening on the outside, she is shaping conscience. This is not necessarily a religious development, though one's religion certainly influences the developing conscience.

Emma is attempting to find possibilities, to find purpose. It is as if she is asking, "Now that I am somebody, what are my possibilities?" In finding the answer to the question, she has to be free to take initiative, in fact, is to be encouraged to do so. Such purposiveness cannot come from inactivity born of insecurity. Erikson says of this age that at no other time is the child "more ready to learn quickly and avidly, to become bigger in the sense of sharing obligation and performance. . . . He is eager and able to make things cooperatively, to combine with other children for the purpose of constructing and planning, and he is willing to profit from teachers and to emulate ideal prototypes."[7]

It is possible that Emma will attempt to become her own parent and thus accept limits which are far more rigid than her years would seem to be able to create or accept. This assuming of the role of her own parent causes what Erikson calls "a split between potential human glory and potential total destruction."[8] When Emma overly parents herself, she deprives herself of the natural activity of childhood so essential if she is going to develop a vital personality. On the other hand, when she gives in completely to her childish impulses, she does not learn realistic limits, which also are so essential if she is to develop a healthy emotion. If she gives in to either extreme, she will lose herself; but if she is helped to maneuver these strong pulls, she will develop vitally, as she should.

The physical locus for this crisis is the genitals. The child has much curiosity and fantasy about sexuality. Such curiosity is natural and should not be shamed. The fantasy also is natural and is far beyond the child's ability to realize. Because the genitals symbolize the taking or not taking of initiative, boys and girls often experience this developmental period differently. In Emma's case, she may hear that boys are to be aggressive while she is to be sensitive and coy, realizing her initiative goals in a less ostentatious way. Under current cultural changes in male and female styles and roles which challenge these traditional stereotypes, Emma has a better chance at developing a healthy sense of initiative. However, even then Emma will tend to identify more strongly with her mother and, even in a society which is being liberated, will learn that girls do or do not do certain things. She will be told that the differences in her body and that of a boy do not determine social initiative. Actually, it is more critical that her guardians understand this, for they are the ones who generally perpetuate the notion that the male is the initiator and the female the receptor.

During these years Emma will either build purpose on top of trust and autonomy or will stop her forward movement of vitality and become a listless, passive child. The latter would cripple her entrance to later critical periods of development. For Erikson, this stage "results not only in the oppressive establishment of a moral sense restricting the horizon of the permissible; it also sets the direction toward the possible and the tangible which permits the dreams of early childhood to be attached to the goals of an active adult life."[9]

But what is the religious concern for Emma in this initiative struggle? It is this: that she learn at the feeling level that this drive to discover her possibilities is part and parcel of being a child of God, created in the Maker's image. Indeed, the very image itself calls this kind of initiative-taking into being. Further, she needs to be shown that the most far-reaching and radical initiative on her part does not change one whit her being a daughter of God. The one who made her is a freedom giver; therefore, she need not fear a loss of status when she goes it on her own.

In summary of the feeling level, what can be said? We have utilized Erik Erikson's scheme of development to show that the touchstones of Emma's personality in the preschool years are trust, autonomy, and purpose. This development is not synonymous with religious development, but the dynamics behind them form the basis for helping Emma feel that she is a child of God.

If she finds basic trust—of others and her own trustworthiness—she will have found the dynamic by which to trust God, and in coming to such a sense of worth she will transfer that feeling to her worth in God's sight.

If she comes to a healthy autonomy, she will see that she is an independent self and that her selfhood is properly labeled "daughter of God."

If she comes to a sense of purpose, it will be because she has learned to take initiative while still being considerate of others. In terms of religious formation she will come to feel that this taking of initiative is the will of an initiating God, and even when she exercises too much freedom, she will feel that her basic status as a child of God is not threatened. Much later, of course, she will learn that though her status is secure, her relationship to God is not always as it should be.

The Intellectual Level

In the last section we discussed what we needed to do at the feeling level to help Emma understand that she is a child of God. To lead her to feel that she is a child of God is the task. Now we turn to a second facet of that task, which is to help her to identify, as well as feel, that she is a child of God. Actually the two are very closely intertwined and thus cannot be separated completely; serving is, after all, a way of knowing.

Emma, as an infant, learns through movement and the senses. She learns by responding through actions to sights, sounds, etc., in her immediate environment. Whatever is not present is of no concern, for her learning is in connection with objects that are immediate. When a rattle is placed in her open hand, she grasps it in a reflex action. When the rattle is removed, she ceases to be concerned with it. Soon Emma will show a concern for an object even though it is not in sight. Before she leaves the infancy period, she will search for objects almost endlessly.

What has happened is evident. Emma has formed in her mind some kind of mental picture of the toy so that when the toy is shown, then removed, the picture remains, and she attempts to find the toy. This is quite an advancement over the first time she was shown something but lost interest as soon as the object was removed from her sight.

Another interesting indication of the level of Emma's learning at this infant age is when she begins to recognize and respond positively or negatively to certain situations. She may react with pleasure toward a glass of milk but with displeasure at some crushed banana. Just the sound of things when either of these is being prepared educes a response from her.

Jean Piaget's study of infant learning is among the most extensive and widely quoted. (See Appendix XI, "Piaget's Discovery.") He believes that what Emma is doing is learning that there is a world separate from her body and that she is adapting to that world. From birth she is learning; she is adapting within the environment and in this process is both influencing her environment and being influenced by it. She is taking in what is around her in the environment and is also altering it according to her own unique development; she is finding and making reality.

In her first two years Emma's two main intellectual accomplishments are the discovery of a world of permanent objects and the beginning of the awareness of symbols. In the first development (the permanent object) she is learning that objects exist apart from her, thus are in a space not attached to her body, and that she does not cause everything that happens. All of this is necessary if she is to relate to the world as it actually is, and it is the kind of early intelligence so necessary to that higher intelligence which she eventually will gain. Thus Emma will be placed in a setting where she can explore her own little world and by that activity build a foundation for a later exploration of a wider, larger, more complex world.

Emma's awareness of the permanence of objects can be tested by showing her a ball then hiding it behind your back. In her first seven months she will lose interest in the now hidden ball, although she may cry immediately after the ball is hidden. When she is around eleven months old, Emma's understanding of objects is markedly increased. Now she will find the ball even though she did not see the exact place where it was hidden. Instead of losing interest in the ball, she will search for it even though it means moving other objects to get to it. Emma is doing more than playing games. She is building a universe of reality. Piaget believes that "the formation of the scheme of the permanent object is closely related to the whole spatio-temporal and causal organization of the practical universe."[10]

In the second development (the beginning of the symbolic function) Emma takes another giant step in her building of a world in which to live and a foundation for more complex intelligence. Whereas her pursuit of a hidden object is in a sense a mere continuation of an action she was already engaged in, Emma, in her second year, becomes able to evoke objects and situations long after her actual contact with them. She will demonstrate this new ability in several ways. First, she will imitate someone's behavior long after it has passed. For example, when an infant is brought to Emma's house, she watches carefully, noting the baby's actions. Hours later, she may lie on the floor, kick and scream, in imitation of the infant. This means that she is beginning to represent things in her mind.

Another sign of the symbolic function is in Emma's mode of play. She may take a book and, pushing it along the floor, make the hum of a car motor. She is using the book and her voice as a symbol for a car. This kind of symbolic play increases and reaches its climax in the elementary years. It will be significant for Emma's cognitive and emotional growth.

Other signs of the symbolic function are drawing and the mental image. The two are closely related and appear after the second year of life. In drawing, Emma is trying to reproduce what she sees in the environment. It is assumed that there is a parallel image in the mind, although this is difficult to prove. However, it seems clear that her ability to represent things in the mind is gradually becoming an image in the mind. Later, she will be able to do more than attempt to reproduce what she has seen; she will become creative in her use of mental image. Thus Emma is no longer tied to the actual objects of her sensory-motor world, for in her mind she has images that represent that world. This does not mean that she is an abstract thinker, a development that waits on her becoming an adolescent.

A final sign of the symbolic function is seen when Emma recalls an activity or a scene by the use of words. Just as she imitates the crying of the baby who had been at her house earlier, so may she later evoke the baby's having been there by saying "baby." Although there is no evident reminder of the baby in Emma's presence, it is assumed that by uttering "baby" she is recalling the baby's having been there.

Emma, in performing through the graphic image and language, is, of course, no longer an infant. She has gradually, but dramatically,

Emma as Young Child—A Child of God by Creation

advanced beyond an intelligence that is tied to the senses and to motor movement to one that is moving her closer to a more ordered, stable way of thinking—what Piaget terms "operational thought." (See Appendix XI, "Piaget's Discovery.")

Emma's thought, during the years roughly two to seven, has many limitations. For example, when she is shown two balls of clay of equal size and is asked whether they are the same size, or whether one has more clay in it than the other, she will know that they are the same and therefore she will answer correctly. However, when one of the clay balls is reshaped into a sausage form, as she watches, she will say that one or the other has more clay in it, is bigger. This is because she cannot understand that, if the sausage is restored to the form of a ball, she has the same object with which she began. Emma's thinking is limited to reasoning from particular to particular; therefore, she cannot yet deduce or generalize. She cannot get outside herself to see the viewpoint of others, for she is egocentric. This explains why she will not engage in long conversations or debate. These limits begin to break down as she moves into the school years, but they remain as elements in her thought even then.

What do these ways of learning mean to Emma's education and nurture in the church? It is obvious that they mean she is limited in the learning of religious material. She is not ready to take in even the simplest content. This should not be surprising, for neither can she learn grammar and mathematics.

It is appropriate for Emma's mother to tell her stories of a religious nature or to show her pictures with religious content. But in doing this, she must not press the instruction or expect too much from it. Probably this kind of activity aids her emotional growth more than her cognitive growth, for it is the fact that her mother is with her that is important. No doubt, the quality of that togetherness is the greatest teacher, whereas the content is of such little consequence as to be negligible.

All of this also means that children learn that adults give certain meaning to actions which can be copied by the children. The five-year-old comes to recognize that mother and father are quiet as they enter the sanctuary for the Sunday morning worship service. The child also assumes a reverent stance when entering. (Unfortunately, that reverence soon gives way, for many reasons which will be considered later.)

During these years, two to seven, in the church school the level of content should keep pace but not get ahead of Emma's intellectual development. She now has mental symbols for many of our important words—church, sanctuary, pastor, the act of prayer, Bible, etc. She may also have symbols of her own making for God, preaching, fellowship, etc. And, of course, her mental representation for Jesus is probably shaped by pictures which we have shown her. She naturally will think of God in physical terms also but will create her own symbol unless she has been exposed to Michelangelo's great concretizations of God.

However, in these preschool and early primary years Emma's thought is still mostly intuitive and spontaneous; therefore, we cannot take religious material which is essentially conceptual and simplify it for her mentality. That just will not do. She cannot understand the great themes of religion—creation, fall, redemption, vocation—for to understand these logically or systematically, she must have advanced in her ability to conceptualize far beyond the "mental symbols" phase of growth. In fact, even the children in the next period of growth will not be able to handle these themes in their full meaning.

This does not mean that Emma cannot hear any of these themes. Fortunately human cultural development protects us from such an illusion, for what "enlightened and liberated" young parents wish to hold from their children is nearly always told to the children by their grandparents. Anyway, we have learned that the removal of all myth and symbol leaves us with little to talk about. We have to speak symbolically and in images if we are to talk at all about the unseen realities which are so integral to religion. However, these realities are beyond Emma's formal cognitive ability in the preschool and early primary ages. They are not beyond her if the teaching of them is compatible with her spontaneity.

In summary of the intellectual level, what can be said? We have utilized the research and interpretations of Jean Piaget to show that Emma begins life without any distinction between her body and the world of objects and people around her. Gradually she learns to differentiate and by the end of her second year is liberated from such limitations. Emma, in a few months, builds a real world of objects and people, a world with which she interacts meaningfully and increasingly.

Beginning at two and continuing, Emma gains the ability to symbolize. This development is seen as she imitates others, and in play, art, and language. Although she still has many limitations in intellectual ability, she has, in five or six years, made great strides in moving from the self-centered infant to the interacting kindergartner. Within this development and on it, Emma's religious development depends. The very seeds of the understanding of sin and faith, of commitment and dialogue are in these preschool intellectual gains.

We are to remember that Emma's intellectual and emotional growth are connected. As she learns that there is a world of objects apart from her body, she is also feeling something about herself. This connection between cognitive and emotional growth will continue, for Emma is at once both a thinking and a feeling person, and healthy religion is built on both the intellectual and the emotional. Further, this connection between the intellectual and the emotional means that Emma approaches religious reality emotionally before she understands it in the mind. However, her emotional understanding can be seriously damaged by cognitive instruction that attempts to force on her intellect more than it can manage.

How to Convey the Gift

Let us recall what our task is: It is to convey to Emma that she is a child of God, made in the divine image. We do not confer this on her, for it is a status given to her. We make known this gift, at the levels of feeling and intellect. But the persistent question comes: How?

Emma's general enrichment of experience is what we will work on in these preschool years. Her world of self, parents, friends, other adults, pets, house and yard, church, and playthings will be the elements of the curriculum. We will help her to use and enjoy these elements in her world. We are, of course, concerned that she will come to understand the meaning of these relations, but that meaning will come through helping her manipulate and be pleased with the world around her.

In working with Emma at places where she is "experiencing," we will remember that we want her to feel something and to know something. Thus we will deal with her experiences with correct information and at the same time in conjunction with healthy attitudes. For example, in the home we can utilize Emma's dog to teach her much about life. The dog has to be cared for. He is there for enjoyment, but there is also much work that is unpleasant. He has to be trained, and someone has to clean up his messes. He gets sick, and he might die. In all of these situations we can help Emma by allowing her to be appropriately involved, by giving pertinent information, and by dealing with healthy feelings which she has.

Such a view of curriculum makes partners of all who work with Emma—parents, church school teachers, other adults in the community, preschool and kindergarten teachers, for this general enrichment comes about in the setting of her natural situations and relations. When this is done effectively, she will grow as she should and have no debilitating dimensions in her life as she moves to more advanced stages of growth.

There is, however, some suspicion by devout church workers that all of this really is not Christian education, but merely preschool humanism. Such a suspicion is understandable until one realizes that this does not mean that Emma is never told "religious" things. The point is that the religious does not become a separate element of curriculum but is part of the woof and warp of her natural experience. As she explores an orange, the teaching adult will be concerned not only with color, texture, taste, size, shape, origin, use, etc., but will also use this exploration as an opportunity to tell her that God has given her good things.

Teaching About Trinity

Emma will hear her nurturers talking about and to God, Jesus, and the Holy Spirit. But she does not have the mind for understanding the doctrine of the Trinity. She experiences God's mercy and love, and the reality of God's presence is around her, but she holds lofty and vague notions about God. She might be heard to say: "'He's a man up in the sky. He chucks down all the water and it rains.'"[11] As formal content, then, the Trinity is beyond Emma's ability to assimilate.

A part of the problem is that Emma cannot see God. In the Garden story Adam and God talk with one another, and it is written that Enoch walked with God. Jesus said that no one had ever seen God, clearly indicating that whoever had seen him (Jesus) had seen God. Still, God is not in a form which human eyes can perceive, and Jesus is not present in Emma's company.

Therefore, Emma talks about God in similar manner to adults who search for images and analogies to express their understanding of this profound mystery. Young children's conceptualizations of God are amazingly similar to the visions in the Revelation. Ernest Harms believed that "the real God experience is a fairy-tale imagination glorifying the highest fantasies which the child at this age can catch with his little mind."[12] While labeling them fairy-tale experiences, Harms supposed that children demonstrated "a kind of awe for the high and exalted" in drawings of God, a characteristic not present in common fairy tales.[13]

Emma's teachers will encourage her to talk about or express artistically how she views God. They will not attempt to make her ideas conform to theirs any more than would they criticize Michelangelo's paintings. When Emma inquires about what God looks like and where God lives, they will answer according to their own perceptions. In the end, the questions are unanswerable. Perhaps, then, our inadequate answers—such as that God lives in heaven, although that implies that God is far away—are the best we can do, at least, for now.

Emma's teachers know that she cannot receive formal teaching about God. Therefore, they will talk of God in those experiences in her life where the God-reality operates, as in touching flowers and thanking God for them. How could she or what good would it be for her to know and feel that she is a child of God if the realness of God were not shown by the adults who teach and care for her?

Ronald Goldman in discussing this problem as it relates to early primary children wrote:

> Many of these ideas [the greatness of God, who is the Creator and Giver of all things, and Jesus, the strong kindly Son of God] may confuse the children intellectually, but they provide a framework of meaning and cosmic security which they need at this stage. It is important that these assumptions should be felt emotionally rather than known intellectually.[14]

As to how to teach Emma about Jesus, we have a different matter. Jesus can be talked about more in historical terms since one dimension of his being is that he lived on earth in a certain period of time. Although we have no authentic pictures, we have an idea of what he looked like in terms of the Jewish race which gave him his birth. This would seem to mean that we talk about Jesus in similar terms to any other figure out of the past. But, of course, Jesus is more, and that presents us with a difficult problem.

Emma hears us pray to Jesus as we pray to God. She is told that Jesus is her best friend although she has never met him. She sees her other best friends often. She hears stories about Jesus when he was an adult, but she remembers mostly that he was a tiny baby. This must be confusing to her tender mind, but we have few alternatives, given our moment in the historical development of the Christian story.

One approach is to tell Emma more about Jesus' work on earth and as an adult than about his time-transcending, symbolic character. She has plenty of time, in later development, to hear and perceive the full import of the work of Jesus Christ. Of course, this approach would be for home and church school, since there is no way to exclude the symbolic form in the context of worship and still maintain the meaning of the Christ's life. When Emma worships with her parents, she will hear this complete meaning and may ask questions about it. Her questions should be responded to positively, but they need not be dwelt on or be the content of her direct instruction at this early age.

We often assume that in answering a child's question we must tell everything, as in the following story. A child asked his mother, "Where did I come from?" The mother thought this was the ultimate question about sexuality, and she responded with as much of the "full story" as she could bear to tell. To all this the boy responded, "Oh, I was just wondering. A new boy just moved in down the street, and he came from Chicago."

In teaching Emma, we should not make too much of Jesus as a baby. What other great person do we honor on birthdays by getting out the baby pictures? When we talk about Jesus, it should be in terms of his adulthood, for it was as an adult that he did the great work which has changed life on earth and given us a perspective on the eternal which is so redeeming. Besides, we don't have enough of a complete story on him from birth into adulthood to follow his development. The one

Emma as Young Child—A Child of God by Creation

incident we have after his circumcision is as an older child in the temple, separated from his traveling parents. He comes off here as a precocious child challenging the great thinkers, but Emma is likely to think of him as disobeying his parents and may wish to emulate the act. We can, of course, imagine Jesus' childhood and create interesting stories. But at best this entire matter—the life of Jesus—should be part of Emma's direct education when she is in the older elementary ages, when her intellectual ability is more conceptual, logical, and systematic.

The Place of the Bible

Emma should know that there is a book called the Bible and that it has stories in it about Jesus and others. Beyond that, however, we are faced with problems. First, the stories themselves are written in adult language and idiom. If the stories of the Bible were put in a storybook volume and submitted to a librarian, the librarian would classify them in the adult, not the children's, section. This does not mean that there is nothing in the Bible for Emma, but it does recognize that the language and concepts are beyond her abilities.

The beautiful and important stories of the Bible need to be rewritten for Emma. They then become Bible-experience stories to which she can relate, rather than straight textual accounts of what is reported in the Scripture. In addition to this, at her level, the themes of the Bible—love, cooperation, etc.—can be written about at her level, and their source identified as the Bible. These then become real-life stories based upon words and happenings in the Bible, and she can appreciate them.

Second, where Bible verses are utilized in Emma's education, some translation in contemporary speech should be used. If she is going to remember specific verses, at least the construct should be contemporary. Actually, though, as with other concepts, she has plenty of time to "hide the Scriptures in her heart," for in the middle and late childhood years she will be quite adept at memorizing and do that by natural use rather than forced rote learning.

Ronald Goldman asked children questions about the kind of book the Bible is and received revealing replies. "A six year old said it [the Bible] was special 'because you have to take it to the church. It's got a blue top on it and you take it to church.' When asked why it was called the Holy Bible, [the child] replied, 'It's got holy in it.' *'How do you mean?'* 'People get stones and chuck it at the book.' "[15] This kind of response indicates the nature of our problem. If the school child is viewing the Bible in such physical terms, how is the young child viewing it?

The Experience of Worship

Worship is to be a vital part of Emma's church experience. It should be spontaneous and immediate, happening in the setting of her experience. When she sees and touches a golden autumn leaf, Emma can be told that God made the beautiful leaves. With help she then can learn to pray, that is, to thank God for beautiful things. This kind of worship does not need to be forced, but unless it is deliberate, these experiences will pass without worship happening.

As a kindergartner, Emma will return to the worship service where at birth her parents presented her to the congregation and consecrated her to God. She will stay through the minister's story time, leaving prior to the sermon. The time with the minister is very significant to the children and becomes a way of making the minister seem more human. Upon leaving the service, she will go to a free-play or activity-oriented situation. Under no circumstances will Emma be placed in a simulated worship service supposedly aimed at her level of understanding. This activity becomes something other than worship and does not always even qualify as positively educational. By third grade, Emma will remain for the entire worship service.

Christmas and Easter

Special days in the church year present a challenge to Emma's parents and teachers. Christmas and Easter are the two greatest celebrations of the year. They are most difficult to deal with in instructional settings. In light of what has been said of Emma's intellectual ability as a young child, it is evident that some of the elements of these two special events need not be dealt with at all, namely, the spiritual manifestations.

Such an assertion, of course, does not leave much to teach Emma about Easter. She certainly does not need to be told the awful details of the crucifixion, and she simply cannot imagine resurrection or appreciate transcendence. She does not know anyone who was once dead, and she is too material minded to perceive the transcendent in her own existence. Sometimes church teachers and parents, because they are at a loss to interpret the resurrection, resort to the bunny and the eggs, giving passing attention to the symbolism of "life." It goes without saying that the symbolism in this case may obscure the meaning, for the children are caught up in the decorating and finding of the eggs.

It is best, then, that Emma's Easter teaching concentrate on brief answers to questions she might have from exposure to the event through a worship service or a television program. Again, it is not the cognitive that is important here, though our answers should be straightforward. What is important is to reassure her that what is being talked about is real to us as her parents and teachers.

Teaching Emma about Christmas is somewhat easier, though still difficult. It is still best to stay more with the fact and imaginations about Mary, Joseph, and the trip to Bethlehem than with the spiritual happenings that accompanied the birth of Jesus. These real-life happenings, even when they are enlarged by some imagination, can be more easily related to Emma's mentality and emotion. She cannot take in the spiritual side of the event intellectually or handle it very well emotionally. This dimension simply does not mean anything to her; thus, it need not be a part of the direct teaching in the home and church school.

She will hear the full story in the Advent worship services and perhaps even in Advent services in the home. Where parts of the story raise questions in her mind, the questions will be answered as simply as possible.

Here is a sample of what Emma might hear at Christmas, a story the writer created to use with the preschoolers and young children of seminary students.

A Christmas Story for Children

One day not too many years ago a happy thing happened at your house. It was before you were born. At some time during the day or night your mother told your father that she was ready to go to the hospital. For about nine months she had been carrying a baby in her womb. That baby was you, and your mother knew that it was time for you to be born. So, your father and mother got into the car and drove to the hospital.

At the hospital there was a special room for your mother. There she got ready for your birth. Doctors and nurses cared for her. They checked every few minutes to see if it was the exact time for you to be born. Your father may have been in the same room to help. Or he may have been asked to wait in a room for fathers.

During this time you were kicking and moving. You were getting ready to be born. And then, it happened. You were born. And your mother and father were very happy. They gave you a name and you still have that name today. You were put in a nursery where it was nice and warm. Many nurses took care of you. You also got to lie in bed with your mother. Your father carried you from the hospital. You went home and began to grow. You are still growing. And you are getting ready for another Christmas.

Christmas is the day that Jesus was born. His birth was like yours in some ways. But it was also very different. His mother, whose name was Mary, carried Jesus in her womb, just like your mother did you. One day her husband, whose name was Joseph, told her that they had to make a trip to Bethlehem. Mary and Joseph knew that it was almost time for their baby to be born, but they had to go to Bethlehem. So they started on the trip.

When they got to Bethlehem, the motel was full of people. The nice manager saw that Mary was about to give birth to a baby. He told Mary and Joseph that they could stay in the stable with the animals. They thanked the motel manager and went to the stable. Soon the child was born. Mary and Joseph named him Jesus. When he got older, someone added Christ to his name.

Mary and Joseph were very happy about the baby, just as your parents were when you were born. Jesus stayed with his mother, and Joseph got to be with him too. Joseph finished his business in Bethlehem. Then Mary and Joseph and Jesus went home. Their house was in Nazareth.

Jesus grew up like you are doing. He was once three years old, then four, five, six. When he learned to speak, he prayed. When he learned to read, he read from the Bible. He talked with Mary and Joseph about God. They helped him be kind to others. They helped him grow.

Emma as Young Child—A Child of God by Creation

He had happy days and sad days, like you do. He played a lot and had friends. He went to church. He loved God and his parents. People loved him too.

When he grew up, he helped many people see what God was like. He taught people how to live. He was kind to people who were mistreated by others. He helped people with all kinds of problems. Because of the way he lived, some people didn't like him. His friends kept on doing what he taught them. And today we are still doing that. So, Christmas is the time when we remember that Jesus was born. We remember all the things he did while he lived. We can be kind and helpful like he was. And we can pray and go to church.

So, Merry Christmas! Jesus was born. I'm glad, aren't you?

A Question-and-Answer Method

Another way to teach Emma, in the late preschool years, is by the question-answer method. It will be constructed simply, though it should carry profound truth. It will avoid heavy theological language, though it will be doctrinal in its intention. Emma will not be asked to analyze or discuss the content but will simply repeat it along with the other children. Later on, we can interpret the litany for her. Here is the beginning of such a method.

(Minister) *Good morning!* (Children) Good morning! *Who are you?* We are the children of God. *Who made you?* God, the Creator, made us. *How are you made?* We are made in the image of God. *Where do you live?* We live in God's world. *Why are you here?* We are here to worship and learn.

Learning Environments

At first, Emma's learning environment is the crib and wherever her parents carry her. This earliest setting will include things to see and touch, and it should be safe and warm. But its primary ingredient is the nurturing person who frequents it. This person "makes" the environment by the quality of the care that is brought. While this essential ingredient continues in future environments, soon Emma is out of the crib and able to explore her house and her room at church. Although she will make learning tools of any object she sees, she will need objects designed for special use.

In the middle and late preschool years, Emma's learning environment is any place in the world where her parents take her. Her house and yard and, in some cases, a child-care center are the primary environments. But there are also the church, the car, the grocery store, and the mall. In preschool, church, and home environments Emma needs open space with tools that will match her imagination and expand her knowledge of the world which is opening before her.

The approach to teaching Emma in her preschool and early primary years will be chiefly activity-centered. Both her emotional and intellectual development require that her education come from real contact with the environment of persons and objects rather than from verbal activity alone. She is not to be told that God is the Creator apart from some experience with nature. Thus, it becomes important to take her on nature walks and to have a nature section in the church school room where she can explore and wonder.

Emma will learn to cooperate with others through personal interaction. Thus it becomes important for the kindergarten and early primary rooms to provide experience areas in which she will be confronted with cooperation or conflict. A sympathetic adult nearby will interpret to her what is happening as she and the other children engage in free play. The younger preschoolers cannot be expected really to play together; however, they will also experience conflict as they play alongside one another. Many times more than one child wants the pretty rooster wooden puzzle, and two may want it at the same time.

Emma will be taught through the arts. By the end of the preschool years her drawings and paintings are more than an attempt to reproduce what she sees in her world. She is now creating a world. Although she cannot be expected to be an advanced artist, she may be able to communicate her deepest feelings about God, church, and others through some form of art. Anyone who has ever put a brush to the canvas knows this truth. Thus, painting and music become important approaches to teaching. Ronald Goldman suggests that this kind of activity "may help them [the children] to think more creatively, and less literally and verbally about religious experience."[16]

Besides attitudes about God, relations with one another, and artistic expression, Emma will need activities that enhance muscular development. Manipulating buttons on clothing in a home living area of the church school room or using a paint brush will help her with this development. In addition, blocks offer her a chance to turn loose her imagination in creating worlds and to develop muscular control simultaneously. As a toddler she will need the cardboard blockbuster; by kindergarten age she will be ready for small, multishaped, interlocking building materials.

At home, Emma needs a special place for art activity. This will encourage her to utilize this valuable way of learning and at the same time relieve anxieties which she may have about making messes with this kind of activity. If Emma's parents are unusually free, they might even provide her a graffiti wall at home. Of course, it is possible that she will make such a wall of her own, against the wishes of unsympathetic parents.

Through play in the home or church school, Emma is reconstructing reality. Sometimes the play results from anxiety, such as when she acts out a kindergarten scene and puts in all of the emotions she has experienced during the day. At other times, it is simply doing something pleasant. But play always represents how she sees her world. For this reason she should not be unduly interrupted by adults, for with the interrupting adult comes the adult mentality, the last thing needed in a play situation. Of course, where there is conflict or misunderstanding or danger, the nearby teacher or parent ought to enter the scene and try to help.[17]

Emma's Friends

Emma's three playmates, Elizabeth, Robert, and Samuel, also are children of God. As with Emma, God has made them children of God. However, Emma is the only one who has been told that explicitly, and her religious nurture is different from theirs.

Elizabeth's church baptized her when she was an infant. The minister held her over the baptismal font and touched her forehead with water. He talked of her regeneration and baptized her into the church, thus bringing her under the covenant of faith. Her education then is built on her already being within the faith. It is expected that, at some later date, she will confirm that faith, taking it self-consciously to herself. That decision is a continuation in faith. But it also means that she is taking a significant step in her Christian development. Elizabeth has not been told that she is a daughter of God. Neither will she told that she is a sinner in need of redemption, for that happened in her baptism. However, she will pray, with her church, prayers of confession and hear that her sins are forgiven.

Robert's church did nothing at his birth to signify that he had any relationship to the church. Neither did it tell him that he is a son of God. Robert will be baptized after he makes a decision of personal faith. His nurture then is directed at bringing him to this time of personal choice. At some point, Robert will be told that he is a lost sinner in need of being saved. His church is ambiguous on when he is, in fact, lost, for it believes that everyone born into the world is a sinner. Yet because the church knows that Robert, the young child, is not responsible for that sin, it speaks of him as safe until he comes to an age when he will be accountable for his sin, probably in late childhood or early adolescence.

Samuel does not go to church because his parents are not members of any church. Samuel may receive loving nurture as an infant and have the same quality care which Emma receives. But the religious context for that nurture is missing, for God is not a reality talked about in his home. When he plays at Emma's house, he comes under the influence of Christian people, but that is not enough. Thus, Samuel receives very little religious education and nurture, and no one tells him that he is a son of God.

Transition

Emma the young child is a child of God by creation. This status is a gift of God and thus cannot be earned by Emma or given by parents or the church. However, Emma's parents presented her to the congregation when she was a tiny infant, and the church told her by a fitting rite that she is a child of God. Parents and teachers have conveyed this fact to Emma, both at the feeling and cognitive level, through careful nurture and education suited to her infant and early years. Now she is emerging from these years both feeling and knowing that she is a child of God. She is secure in this status, for it cannot be taken away from her. It is this knowledge of who she is—daughter of God—that now accompanies her as she moves into middle and older childhood and that will form the basis for later religious experience.

3

Emma as Middle Child—
a Child of Promise

Emma, through the participation of her parents in the life of the church, belongs. She receives, through the active faith of her parents, a faith and an affiliation. It is a gift of heritage, a believing heritage, and is received through the parental connection, not as a genetic transmission, but by a power of association. Such an appropriation completes the promise to faithful parents that their children also belong and, at the same time, initiates in Emma a promise of an unfolding personal faith.

Emma's belonging is, in a sense, the automatic acquisition of her birth into a believing home. Thus, she does not have to join in order to participate in suitable symbols of heritage and belonging. Yet the church deliberately confers the belonging on her. It is necessary that the church bestow this status on Emma, for it is possible for a church to treat her and other children so as to cause them to question whether they are a part of the community. Such questioning is part and parcel of the propensity in Emma and other children to desire earnestly to have a place. They, will, of course, attempt to earn it; but how much better that Emma has been told of it in both common and dramatic ways! Belonging is a matter of awareness; thus Emma has been told that she belongs.

That Emma belongs to the faith of the church does not mean that she is a fully participating member in all of the church's activities. There are instances where her participation waits on a certain maturity, as in matters of doctrine. She is not ready to consider important church decisions and to take part in voting on such issues. Surely this was the place of children in the early worshiping communities as they shared in the activities central to the church and commensurate with their nature as children.

To say that Emma belongs falls short of saying that she is saved or converted. To be sure, her appropriation of faith through believing parents is a part of her salvation, else it means nothing. But, for Emma to feel that she belongs is not the same as experiencing that self-conscious faith necessary at a later stage in her religious development. Neither does it mean that she has faced some existential question, repented, and been converted. Emma simply belongs. Nothing more needs to be made of it.

Faith is, however, integrally involved—both the faith of parents and Emma's faith. Only some highly technical view of salvation can consider Emma's faith as non-faith. Even the notion of a borrowed faith which later will be owned faith carries some misconstruance, for faith at whatever point, immature or mature, is owned. Emma's faith is not the same in intensity or depth as it will become, but it is faith. It is Emma's childhood faith. Emma has faith. Nothing more needs to be made of it.

Because Emma's salvation involves grace, faith, and work, it seems clear that grace is the dominant reality at work at this stage in her life. Through God's grace, shown in many ways but primarily through loving parents and committed teachers, Emma is within the scope of salvation. She is partaking of the fruit of faith and work long before she can give herself completely in faith and take up her adult responsibility for the faith. Belonging, then, relates more to grace than to Emma's faith. Its conferral is a sign of grace operating through the faith-community until the day when Emma will come happily and willingly from the struggle with alternative faith choices to affirm faith for herself.

As to the faith of Emma's parents, one cannot characterize it in its details or even prescribe how intense it must be in order to be acceptable for passing along to Emma. Neither can exact measures be applied to the parents' faithfulness to the church. Faith and participation are large realities which cannot be narrowly defined, but her parents have exhibited genuine devotion to God, loving relationships with others, and

Emma as Middle Child—A Child of Promise

life-styles consistent with Christian values and have been regular participants in the worship and mission of the church. Without such character and involvement, they would have had little to pass on to Emma and would have cut her off from any church to which to belong. Belongingness in the abstract is feeble. To be effectual, it must be in the concrete for one belongs *to* or *in* or *with*. If Emma's parents, though enrolled members of church, were not themselves people of faith, she would be as the children of parents who have never made any claims to any relationship to the Christ or church.

Children whose parents do not belong to the church may be granted this belonging and made part of the promise of faith through the use of sponsors. In such cases, it is the corporateness of the church which will take in the children. Such a provision, however, will have to go beyond merely having children sit with church parents in the worship service. It will have to carry with it some commitment on the part of the church parents to be involved with the children and their parents as much as is discreetly possible.

Emma, a child of believing parents, belongs to the community of faith. Unlike her daughtership in God, which is a gift of being, this reality comes through relationship; it is a status conferred by the congregation itself. It tells Emma that she is wanted, that she is a part of what is happening. It is another necessary step in her flowering faith, a step full of meaning and promise. The congregation, by a suitable rite, will symbolize this fulfilling and promising time in the life of Emma and the church.

The Nurturing Task in the Middle Childhood Years

The task for Emma's church and parents is to demonstrate to her that she belongs, that she is already within the community of faith. Emma already has this affiliation until she is old enough to decide for herself whether to embrace her heritage. She does not have to go through a struggle with sinfulness or show signs of repentance in order to belong. Neither does she have to make a commitment to Christ or confirm faith or take any other action to earn her place in the church.

Emma will come, in adolescence, to face the fact of her estrangement and will possess the ability to make youthful commitments. In middle childhood, however, her concerns are different. She is eager to be an active member in what is happening around her, events and activities which parallel her emotional and cognitive abilities. Repentance, in the rich meaning of that term in religion, is far beyond her. Binding commitment, in the long-term dimension of that term in religion, is not characteristic of her capricious years. This does not mean that she has no loyalties, but it does mean that conventional religious expectations of conversion and life commitment wait on a certain maturity which will surely be hers in a few brief years.

Just as Emma emerged from the preschool years feeling and knowing that she was a child of God, so will she, during the school ages, increasingly feel that she belongs to the church's ethos and mission and is developing in her own belief and sense of responsibility. She will sense that she belongs to what the church believes and practices, long before she can conceptualize those beliefs or shape those practices. To the basic sense of "who-ness" (child of God) is added the sense of place, that is, of having a place. Emma has an identity—it is child of God. Emma has a place—it is as member of the faith community.

Emma's education, then, will be done in the context of belonging, rather than being directed toward convincing her of her alienation and then urging her to join. This positive education which assumes a rightful affiliation will be done both at *feeling* and *intellectual* levels. It will be both experiential and deliberate. It will be done in relational ways, through direct instruction, through involvement in the church's worship, and within a social-moral context.

The Feeling Level

Emma has successfully developed a confidence in the reliability of persons who care for her. She has learned that she can participate willingly in the normal activities of life and, even when her independence takes her beyond the patience of others, is still accepted. She has come to a sense of purpose, finding herself with the power to act with determination. Now, to these gains Emma adds the fulfillment of producing. She makes ideas and material things and in play recreates situations.

Although she has been in ordered preschool settings, Emma is now in the more structured environment of the elementary school. This new situation coincides with her capacity to work, to produce, and to learn. She is attracted to that which challenges her to act and to settings which both prescribe certain behaviors and leave freedom of choice. When her teachers require too much order, she responds out of her past gains of initiative and autonomy. When her teachers give her endless freedom, she seeks the sympathetic help of adults or searches out some familiar routine.

Emma, in these middle years, is relatively free of surges associated with sexuality. She continues to develop physically and to be curious about sexuality, but there is no crisis to match that of toilet training in the anal period. However, Emma is subject to conduct problems and to depression and other emotional disorders. She experiences anxieties and fears about major matters such as death and minor ones such as diving lessons.[1]

Although in a period of steady growth in mind, body, and social relationships, Emma's drive to produce, to fix, to solve, to complete, and to master has within it the possibility of satisfaction and the risk of failure. As she succeeds and is recognized, she moves deeper into finding herself, or her place, and will come in the adolescent years to connect these good feelings with her major identity crisis. For now, her acceptance for who she is and for the products of her inventive years is, in fact, her identity. That crisis is not yet the internal one that it will soon be.

As in the later preschool years when Emma's search for purpose led her often into more than she was prepared for and resulted in ill feelings about herself, so in these middle years she faces the frightening prospects of attempting and failing. Parents and teachers are, of course, to reassure her when she stumbles, but they must at the same time help her to find realistic limits. While every parent at one time or another overstates both praise and criticism, in the main, as parent and child work realistically with accomplishment and failure, a lasting bond is being established.

Unfortunately, the opposite also is true. The psychologist who most clearly articulates this crisis which Emma faces is Erikson. "The danger at this stage," he writes, "is the development of a sense of *inadequacy and inferiority.''*[2] The most damaging comment that any adult can make to a child of this age is the unanswerable and stunning, "Can't you do anything right?" The question is, of course, meant to hurt, and no answer is really expected. It does hurt, to be sure, and its answer is made on the tender soul of the middle child who wants so intensely to do well.

As to the sense of belonging in Emma, it comes about this way. Entwined within Emma's energetic activity of making is the wish to be as the adults around her. Emma, as with children of every age, occupies herself with that which represents for her a part in the world of adults—parent, teacher, and figures in the larger social scene. In an earlier generation she may have imitated the life of the pioneer edging westward. As with those children whose belonging involved participation in the common pursuits of the family, so does Emma find a sense of place by being included in the functions of her many societies. Erikson understands it this way: "The *fundamentals of technology* are developed, as the child becomes ready to handle the utensils, the tools, and the weapons used by the big people."[3]

What is the significance of these developments in Emma's religious pilgrimage? First, her anxieties and fears become the occasion for parents and teachers to relate to and nurture Emma. These adults will help Emma distinguish between fears based in reality and those imagined. Of course, the two are not separable in terms of their dynamics, for even an imagined fear has real dynamics. But in the long process of love and relationship, of guidance and counsel, Emma's caring adults will lead her trustingly into constructive activities that will cause some anxieties to subside and fears to dissipate. After all, earlier in her young life when her inwardness was primitive, she dealt with her fears more by activity than by anxiety.

However, there is more to dealing with fear and anxiety than mere giving of guidance and support. Genuine religion deals with such problems partly through prayer. Emma's share in the worshiping congregation's prayers of confession, praises, and intercession, and her own private prayer will be of comfort and aid to her. In this kind of involvement Emma is relating healthily to the strong emotional content in the act of prayer.

Emma as Middle Child—A Child of Promise

Emma's parents and teachers will avoid connecting these fears with some kind of religious conviction of sin. Those who do attempt such ties misuse these emotions in the child and misinterpret the dynamics of estrangement and sin. Such approaches also ignore the child's capabilities in moral reasoning. Kohlberg places the middle child in either a stage where moral decisions are made on the basis of meeting one's own needs primarily or on the basis of conformity to what the child considers acceptable and normal behavior. A child's limits of reason and emotions are to be sensitively nurtured, not manipulated.

Second, the church, especially the worshiping congregation, is one of the societies which are meaningful to Emma. Thus, as she observes that society and her parents and others whom she respects actively participating in it, so does she zealously yearn to be included. Of all the moments in her burgeoning religious experience, this one carries lasting significance for her emotional attachment to the community of faith—its faith and practice. Because emotions are seldom really formed or changed by mere words, Emma will find her place most securely and joyfully if she is, in fact, included.

One of Horace Bushnell's pivotal biblical texts supporting his theory of nurture was Jeremiah 7:18:

> The children gather wood, and the fathers kindle the fire, and the women knead the dough, to make cakes to the queen of heaven, and to pour out drink offerings unto other gods, that they may provoke me to anger.

He was not interested in interpreting the text in terms of its intention, but seized on the text's almost hidden element that the offering "is the joint product of the whole family. The worship is family worship; the god of one is the god of all; the spirit of one, the spirit of all."[4] "Acting thus together," Bushnell wrote of the family, "they take a common character, accept the same delusions, practice the same sins, and ought, I believe, to be sanctified by a common grace."[5]

In summary of the feeling level, we have borrowed Erikson's explanation of the main dynamic at work in Emma's personality growth. He holds that all children in the school years face the crisis of industry in which they realize competence or, in failing, assume an attitude of inferiority toward themselves. It is not a religious trait, instinct, or development, but it does have implications for religious experience and nurture. As for Emma, she will be brought under the umbrella of the prayer life of the congregation, and her need to belong will be satisfied through her being allowed to participate in meaningful ways in the life of the congregation. In a few years she will understand this as a foundation for an important faith decision which she will make for herself.

The Intellectual Level

Emma's thinking ability takes a noticeable turn in middle childhood. She leaves behind a stage dominated by intuition and moves into a more complex, ordered way of thinking. She does not forsake intuition, now or ever, for it will always remain a way of getting at truths with which logic has nothing to do. But she is no longer limited to intuition. Rather, she seeks facts endlessly, to be used in the pursuit of the solution to some problem. She manipulates these data in constructing and testing hypotheses on how the world is put together and functions. This new logical ability is a step toward a higher form which Emma will exhibit in adolescence.

Essentially Emma now operates on her environment. This "operation," according to Piaget, "is an internalized action which becomes reversible and is coordinated with other operations into an integrated operational grouping."[6] This means that Emma's actions are not isolated and irrelevant to each other. For example, the numbers 1, 2, 3, etc., belong to each other and can be grouped different ways, as in addition and multiplication, to produce results. Neither must her actions go in one direction, but they are now reversible. For example, Emma knows a tree on the right side of the road going north is on the left side going south, and if Hernandes is larger than Arthur, then Arthur is smaller than Hernandes. Some problems which would have challenged Emma a few years ago she now solves. For example, she will now order sticks systematically by size, whereas at one time, she gathered them by random activity. Also, she knows that although there are eighteen girls and seven boys in her class at school, there are more children than either girls or boys, as a class.

Emma as Middle Child—A Child of Promise

In addition to being able to operate on objects that do not change, as in the above examples, Emma also operates on space and time and speed. One example: She now knows that if two cars leave from the same place at the same time, but take routes of longer and shorter distances, yet arrive at their destination at the same time, then one car traveled faster than the other. Or if two children run along a track and arrive at different points when the action is stopped, it means that one ran faster than the other.

Emma's new ability is, however, workable only on objects. She cannot yet manage formal operations; that is, she cannot operate on ideas to the same degree as she can on objects. She will learn that $5 + 5 = 10$, and that $5 \times 10 = 50$, but not be able to find the value of x in an algebraic problem. The difficulty here cannot be attributed to mere limitations of mathematical skill, for Emma similarly has difficulty with propositions. For example, if we were to give her a proposition, such as "All children in this school are Mexican Americans; Jacqueline is in this school; therefore, she is Mexican American," Emma would most likely reply that not all children in her school are Mexican American. The logic of the problem escapes her because she is a victim of the concrete. In Piaget's own words:

> The same children as reach the operations just described are usually incapable of them when they cease to manipulate objects and are invited to reason with simple verbal propositions . . . . being constantly tied to action, they give it a logical structure, . . . but they by no means imply the possibility of constructing a logical discourse independently of action.[7]

Thus, Emma has attained a new level of concrete intelligence superior to earlier forms, but still far from complete. When problems involving ideas are presented to her, she makes any number of mistakes characteristic of the concrete thinker. Rather than reasoning through the situation, she will center on a word in the problem, then apply that to a whole set of ideas that have nothing to do with the problem being considered. She goes off on an irrelevant (at least, to us) tangent. Given a riddle, such as "Brothers and sisters have I none, but this man's father is my father's son," she will either make a series of intuitive guesses or give some kind of nonsensical answer, rather than reason through the riddle. A nearly nine-year-old British child said of the church, "'The disciples made it and it got bombed down, or shot down, when the Angles and Saxons came across.'"[8]

If the verbal problem relates to some religious matter, Emma might simply solve the problem through stating a conviction. If asked, in Sunday church school, why Thomas was allowed to touch the risen Jesus but Mary was not, Emma may simply dismiss it all by asserting, "We should not question the Bible." Or, if asked how Moses could have reported his own burial, she will reply, "With God all things are possible."

Emma will also demonstrate what Piaget calls syncretistic thought. She will connect thoughts as if they were whole systems because she recognizes similar words in the unrelated thoughts. Or she will simply connect thoughts on the basis of some general concept which she has in mind and then assume that she is correct without analyzing the thoughts. Her mind is replete with concepts and theories about self, others, and the social and physical environment. She utilizes these with the same intellectual vigor that she gives to social and physical activities. An example of this syncretism comes in a child's conversation with Piaget who had asked the child to match proverbs with parallel statements. One child, who understood the proverb, matched "White dust will ne'er come out of a sack of coal" with the sentence "People who waste their time neglect their business." Then the child explained that the two meant the same "because coal is black and [can't] be cleaned. Similarly, people who waste their time neglect their children, who then become black and can no longer be cleaned."[9]

The religious significance of Emma's new cognitive abilities is filled both with challenge and danger. In her more concrete, ordered mode of thinking, Emma can better understand elements in the history of the faith. The promise made in her presentation in infancy concerning being told about Abraham, Moses, the Jewish hope for the Messiah, Jesus Christ the Savior, and the church as the people of God can now be fulfilled. While this education will have an ecumenical flavor of diversity and openness, Emma needs also to know a more particular heritage of faith. Thus will she be instructed in the faith which has spawned the community of faith in which she is now participating and to which she increasingly wants to belong.

Emma is ready for a more complete understanding of the meaning of church, the Bible, God, and Jesus. Although she still has a fragmented and often dislocated time perspective, Emma can now understand the church as having a long history, similarly that the Bible as a book has been formed over hundreds of years rather than being a book written by God in a single sitting. Whereas Emma, up to now, had Jesus and God thoroughly confused, she can now place Jesus within time, as a man with a history and a life in another part of the world. Such is a prelude to understanding the incarnation, a concept yet too difficult for the concrete thinker.

Because of her concrete mind, Emma will conceive of sin exclusively in concrete terms and will not understand what is termed a "sinful condition." She understands sin as wrong acts committed or as failure to obey super-ego pressures rather than as defection from holy purpose or as an obscuring of the image of God in which she is made. Similarly, her faith declarations may be verbalisms, inasmuch as they are prior to the serious dynamics of the identity crisis and the onset of formal thought. She will deal with sin and faith concepts the same way she handled riddles and proverbs; that is, she will make connections based on key words or on some irrelevant thought, or she will simply adopt a conviction taught to her. In this light, Emma's nurturers will carefully weigh their use of phrases such as "make a profession of faith," "be converted," "be saved," "be born again," and "accept Jesus."

That syncretism which she shows, as with the refreshing intuition of early and middle childhood, is to be accepted, not condemned. In accepting Emma's misconstruances, we affirm her. But are not we also affirming that these errors of thinking may also carry profound truth? After all, our attempts to be absolutely rational and analytical have dangers of reducing truth to its several parts. Sometimes a childish connection of ideas and events will give us a missing piece of a thought puzzle. To accept, however, does not mean that we will not attempt to help Emma to back off and analyze a situation. Of course, she will, in this entire process, be making adjustments and seeing places where she has made mistakes. We can accelerate that process by joining her thought with ours. By working with her in this manner, we will help her toward a more mature mode of thinking.

In summary of the intellectual level, Emma has moved beyond major inconsistencies of thought of young childhood and has come to think more orderly about problems which earlier were beyond her comprehension. She now operates on her environment. However, she is limited to operating in the concrete and is not yet free to handle ideas and problems very skillfully. In the face of proverbs, riddles, and parabolic types of material which pose problems for her, she will employ verbalisms which, on scrutiny, break up. Her new thinking ability calls for an acceleration in religious education; however, we must not become ambitious and manipulate her beyond her cognitive ability. She is advanced in thinking ability over young childhood, and is smarter as well, but she still has a major transformation in thought ahead of her. We will work with where she is and wait for the next stage.

Social-Moral Development

Emma's social-moral development is interwoven with her emotional and cognitive growth. She is a thinking person who feels, and a feeling person who thinks. But more, she is a feeling, thinking person within a social-moral setting. How she thinks and what she thinks about, how she feels and in what she invests emotional energy are influenced by her parents, peers, school teachers, church leaders, other significant adults in her circle, and television programs.

Emma's emotional growth has already been discussed according to Erikson's understanding of the crisis of middle childhood. That crisis is, in fact, a psychosocial one. Emma attempts to achieve and enjoys success within some kind of group. Although she may be a very independent child, she ultimately will not experience full satisfaction apart from the evaluation of others. The term "inferiority," the negative result of the middle-childhood industry crisis, is itself a relative term. Thus, Emma's growth on the feeling level is also social growth.

Emma's intellectual growth has been charted according to Piaget's theory that middle children are in the concrete stage of thinking. That, too, turns out to be inseparable from the social. Emma's progress within and between stages of cognitive growth depends on interactions with objects, with other persons, and with ideas and problems that challenge her mind. This activity draws her further into the center of a stage or facilitates her passage to the next.[10]

Emma is characterized by Kohlberg as being in a stage of moral reasoning termed "instrumental purpose and exchange." He writes: "Right is serving one's own or other's needs and making fair deals in terms of concrete exchange."[11] Researchers into moral reasoning use a story about Heinz, a man faced with the dilemma of whether to steal a drug, which he could not afford to buy, in order to save his wife's life. It is quite likely that Emma would respond that it is all right to steal to save someone's life "because you may need him to do the same for you someday."[12] As one can see, Emma is thinking of herself and is making a moral judgment based on the possibility that she, too, might benefit by the action, if not immediately, then later. According to Mary Wilcox's use of the Heinz story, Emma might say yes or no, but in each case would show this egocentric kind of reasoning. Emma might say yes, "Because the druggist was cheating him, wasn't being fair, and deserved to be stolen from"; or no, "Because it's not fair to the druggist who should be able to charge what he wants because he made the drug."[13]

That Emma reasons at such a level does not mean that we accept her conclusions as valid for action. To the contrary, Emma's nurturers will tell her that they understand why she thinks such a decision is right, but that there are other factors to think about. Emma can think about those factors as long as her teachers are directing her. As she does that, she is growing toward the higher stage of moral reasoning. However, left to her own, she will exemplify the kind of judgments characteristic of where she really is with moral reasoning. These interactions with caring adults influence Emma's progress in social-moral development after the fashion of emotional and intellectual growth.

This stage in Emma's development also forbids her nurturers from giving deep theological meanings to her decisions. Sin is, it is true, in the sinning, and is concrete. But a child, who by developmental limitation cannot reason beyond herself, is innocent of the ultimate consequences of her decisions and behavior. She may, in fact, wish to join the church because she feels guilty over her self-oriented decisions. Ironically, it will be this very egocentrism which will be the basis for a true understanding of sin. This will happen when Emma is old enough to perceive her egocentrism for what it is and what it does to her relation to others and to God. But as a middle child, Emma must have her understanding of sin and her ability for moral reasoning separated.

This stage also means that the faith of the congregation is a significant social-moral setting in which Emma thinks and feels, experiences and makes decisions. This faith may be exercised through parents in the home, adults at church, or peers in the many peer settings in which Emma participates. That is another reason why the question of belonging is so critical to Emma in middle childhood.

How to Nurture Belongingness

For Emma, to belong means to be included and to appropriate her heritage. She has, of course, belonged all along and has been taking in the teaching and the spirit of the congregation. Now, at nine or ten, the feeling of belonging or not belonging is a reality of which she is conscious. As to heritage, she can now give it concrete meaning. She understands at the level of raw dimension the symbols and rituals of her faith—for example, that the Lord's Supper is a reenactment of Jesus' final meal with the disciples.[14] As to the teaching she has grown up with, by the end of the elementary years, she will be able to organize that more coherently.

We nurtured Emma the preschooler through the enrichment of her general experience. We will continue this experiential approach, especially in the early primary years, but will add to it a more deliberate instruction. For example, whereas in the kindergarten we used Bible thoughts with Emma as she participated in the learning centers in her room, we now help Emma to find Bible verses in the book itself. By the end of the elementary years we will expect her to be proficient in the use of the Bible.

David Elkind proposes that persons learn by substitution and integration, an insight in line with Piaget's discussions of accommodation-assimilation.[15] In teaching by substitution, we are expecting Emma to replace a concept with a new one. For example, if she should believe that thunder and wind are signs of God's anger against her for something she has done, we will attempt to correct her notion, not by explaining how illogical it is, but by giving her a correct explanation. In such cases, we should not expect that she will accept the new concept readily,

Emma as Middle Child—A Child of Promise

for it takes time for persons to turn concepts loose, especially those involving good or ill feelings. Further, she may not possess the ability to accommodate to what we tell her; she likely would repeat her explanation in spite of our correction.[16]

Emma's learnings will be more lasting if they are by integration, that is, if they build on what she already knows and grow out of what she is experiencing. Emma learns by substitution that "all Scripture is given by inspiration of God, and is profitable for doctrine . . . for instruction in righteousness" (2 Timothy 3:16, KJV). It is something she memorizes but does not integrate. On the other hand, in the parable of the good Samaritan, Emma sees that the Bible tells how God wants us to relate to persons in need. In this way, the Bible indeed becomes profitable for instruction, for Emma is assimilating and not merely accommodating to a substitute concept.

It so happens that learning by integration also contributes to a sense of belonging. As long as Emma is given substitute concepts which do not relate to what she knows and is experiencing, she will feel alienated from her own thinking and will experience distance from her teachers because they seem so superior in their knowledge. When she is exposed to concepts which she can integrate into her thinking, she feels an identity with the concept, an emotional identity, in fact, and feels closer to her teachers.

The two primary environments for nurturing Emma's belonging are the family and the worshiping congregation. In these settings her feelings about inclusion are at their strongest, and her incorporation into heritage is most integrative. In these places her belonging is more demonstrated than told, though it also must be articulated verbally.

Once during a rummage session a family came across some birth certificates for two of the three daughters in the home. The one whose certification of daughtership was not there became anxious, for her belongingness so tacitly assumed up to then had been threatened. The parents moved quickly with embraces and words to reassure her of her place. She seemed relieved, but the situation was not resolved completely until the certificate was found and she read the facts. On the other hand, the situation could just as easily have been one in which the certificates were in hand, but because of the quality of the relationship, the child felt excluded. Happily that was not the case, but in the end it took concrete words and evidence to enforce what in practice had long been true.

Worship: Heritage and Community

Emma will be included when the congregation gathers for worship. It is here that she must eventually find her greatest sense of belonging; here the heritage is made most visible. A part of this visibility is in the intergenerational nature of the congregation. She will not understand why the adult next to her dropped a tear as he sang, "My grace all-sufficient shall be thy supply," but she "takes in" something of that experience. Therefore, there will be no children's church for her. By third grade she will be in the entire worship service, where she belongs and where she learns belonging, where heritage and community are integral, and where she appropriates both.

The rites by which Emma's congregation celebrates religious experience and passages will be the focus of heritage and community. These, along with preaching, are central to worship. But Emma will also need to learn the hymns of the church, participate in Bible readings, and learn to pray.

Since Emma is to be a part of worship, the service will take account of her presence. There are many ways that can be done. Perhaps the most common practice is the children's sermon, but that is not enough. Emma's church will have in its treasury litanies and readings in which she can participate fully. It will have hymns which are sensitive to her thought and feeling world. It will include her and her age group as readers, as candle bearers, and choral singers. To the service she will bring banners, such as in the depiction of the Holy Week pilgrimage.

None of these features will replace the church's regular worship materials, for Emma will sing "Immortal, Invisible God Only Wise" long before she understands it. She will hear St. Francis's prayer long before she can perceive the meaning. She will hear the Psalms long before she can follow the imagery. Neither does all of this mean that all worship must conform to a childhood idiom. Some services will have more features on her cognitive and emotional level than others, just as they will at times appeal predominantly to a different age group.

Emma's education will be within a particular faith community but will be ecumenical in spirit. That is, Emma will know her denominational affiliation by the character of her church, as opposed to the character of the church her friends attend. She will feel secure, maybe even a little proud, in that identity. However, her nurturers ought never to convey to her that hers is the one and only religion. This particular identity can be nurtured in the church's ritual, for example, its way of baptizing. The ecumenical spirit can be conveyed through cooperative activities with other congregations, such as Thanksgiving union services, and through the study of religious history in which Emma will see that her church or denomination is one among many.

Elkind, in his research of religious identity in children, found that only at the ages of eleven or twelve do children understand such identity in terms of what a person believes. For example, a Jew is "a person who believes in one God and doesn't believe in the New Testament."[17] In the early elementary years, a child might suggest that a Baptist is one who puts people under water to baptize them, unlike the Presbyterian who sprinkles water on the head, obviously a definition based on what a church practices.

This probably means that sermons on "what our church believes" are wasted on Emma, whereas the presence of the central pulpit or the divided chancel, the baptismal pool or the font, and the place these have in worship are her greater teachers. It also points up how confused she could become under a rigid, sectarian education. The solution, however, is not a foundationless diversity, for that could be equally confusing to her.

Ronald Goldman found some interesting understandings of church and worship. Early primary children identify the nature of the church with its physical features and with ceremonies that take place there. From about ten to middle adolescence, children view the church in terms of spiritual functions, as represented in this response by a twelve-year-old: "'Yes, it's a holy place. . . . You get the feeling God is specially near to you in church.'"[18] Surprisingly, attention to the church as a place of fellowship does not appear until age fourteen or fifteen. This fact, however, does not invalidate our proposition that belonging is the critical reality of middle childhood. That children do not include fellowship in discussing what the church means to them does not mean that they do not feel inclusion or exclusion.

What do children like about worship? On observation, they appear to enjoy most the children's sermon, singing in choir, hymn singing, and taking the Lord's Supper. In one worship service a minister who sat next to a fourth grader (not his own child) went up from the congregation for a feature in the service and then returned to his seat, whereupon the girl said, "That was beautiful." She also held the hymnal for this minister for the hymn singing and sang with gusto. In this same congregation, as soon as the minister invites the children to the front, they jump from their pews and move with deliberate speed.

Goldman found children of all ages interested in singing, praying, and the offering. The children he interviewed did not show much liking for festivals, ceremonies, Communion, christening, and the like. However, later elementary children preferred these features more than did their younger counterparts. High interest was revealed in Bible readings, stories by the preacher, the sermon, etc., or what Goldman labels "intellectual aspects." Few children responded to questions about the effects of worship, such as the feeling of forgiveness.[19]

Family: The Natural Setting

Whereas much of Emma's nurture is in simulated settings, her family composes an unfabricated environment. Here is life in all of its realness. Here Emma and her significant others are most themselves, without airs and ceremony. Therefore, her instruction will proceed from experience and her nurture from normal activities and rituals. In the course of family living she finds a realistic standard for testing what she sees and hears in other settings. She also gradually takes on a base from which to move securely or insecurely into the wider world.

Mealtime at Emma's house most dramatically symbolizes inclusion. It also is a time for sharing family experiences. As the food nourishes her body, so does the relationship fill her life with meaning. While this time is indeed religious in the truest sense, it need not always be deliberately religious in the particular sense. That is, not every meal must include prayer and Bible reading or discussion of some religious topic. However, all of these will at times be practiced in connection with the meal.

Family travels put a family in close quarters for extended periods of time. This naturally intensifies the relationships. Such intensification holds the possibility of increased joy as well as frustration. Family quarrels are likely to result. However momentarily disruptive, these also are essential to Emma's coming to terms with herself and those around her. Without intent to eliminate all conflict, Emma's parents will plan travel activities which will involve her in expanding her knowledge and strengthening her ability to manage her emotions.

Emma's parents will be most deliberate in their religious practice and instruction in connection with major events in the Christian year. The church will help her parents with these celebrations by preparing materials for use during Advent, including readings, hymns, prayers, and instructions concerning candle color and use. It is also likely that religious discussion will intensify during the celebration of these Holy Days. Thus the church will also give Emma's parents help in understanding more completely the meaning of the events in the Christian year and of how to talk about them within the family setting. Making parents into teachers of religion, other than as exemplars and conversationalists, is not an easy task. Time is the major problem. Because of the limitations, ministers will need to focus parent education on the most critical issues.

Emma's parents will utilize the television for Emma's entertainment and education. As carefully as they prepare and control what food she eats, so will they schedule and monitor what programs she views on television. Just as she would not be allowed to eat all day, so will she not be placed in the company of television fare all day. Much of the programming is unsuitable for her, and prolonged exposure holds the danger of being emotionally disturbing. Because of its flat image, television is deceivingly innocent. Take for example, the daytime soap opera. What if a traveling drama group were to come into the home to act out these melodramatic episodes? How many middle children would be allowed to watch the performance?

The Church School

Emma's church school curriculum, in the primary years, will continue to begin with experience and avoid systematic studies. It will call for assimilation and integration more than for substitution. She can learn through units on family living but is not ready for a study of the history and sociology of the family. She might need a unit on growing things but is not prepared for a study of creation—its genesis and purpose. She will understand a unit on getting along with others but cannot comprehend a study of communication barriers.

Around grade five, Emma's church will provide her with a curriculum to take her through adolescence. While any curriculum unit must touch experience, either in coming directly from her life activity or being quickly felt by her to be related to her experience, it is in this later elementary period that Emma is ready for more order and system in her church school studies. The teaching outright of substitute concepts is still premature, for she does not have the cognitive structures with which to handle them. The life of Jesus, especially through his ministry and his teachings which have immediate concrete value, is appropriate material for the front end of such a curriculum design. The miracles, some of the parables, and the more abstract teachings will have to wait for a later place in the curriculum. (See the discussion of youth curriculum in the next chapter.)

Emma will be in open learning environments with materials for making learning relevant and enjoyable. She will, for the most part, cluster with children near her own age, but she will also need intergenerational educational experiences. At ten, she and a seven-year-old would have some difficulty discussing a unit on the life of Jesus, but they could extend one another's learning in a unit on getting along with others. In addition, she can move upwards in such mixed classes, as, for example, in a unit on when to follow and when to resist peers. She can participate with any age when the unit is built on one's experience, as in an exploration of what it means to love others or to be a part of our church.

The curriculum the church provides throughout the middle childhood years for Emma will be connected with the whole church. One church school teacher took his children's class to the sanctuary where they created "pencil rubbings" from the carved symbols on the pew ends. Another class baked bread for the congregation's celebration of Communion. Another created Advent banners for use in the worship service.

Emma as Middle Child—A Child of Promise

Just after Easter, a group interested in creative writing prepared newspapers recounting the events in and around Jerusalem.

Emma is more than a receiving person. She also can give. This will be evident as she shares with others and creates out of her own mind. But in addition, she is capable of ministering to others. She can participate in singing groups that sing for the elderly who cannot get out at Christmas. She can perform chores or run errands for persons in her neighborhood. In fact, she may, in her openness to life, be the best minister available for another child who is terminally ill.

The Minister

Emma's minister will know her and her family and will touch and call her by name. In the natural course of his pastoral office he or, as the case may be, she will more than likely visit in Emma's home. He will engage her in conversation about some important or common event in her week. While he may not want to go as far as Jonathan Edwards who required the children to produce an outline of his sermon, the minister may also ask Emma about something she has studied in church school or about some celebration in the worship service. He will visit her church school class. Because of his role and visibility, he can materially affect Emma's sense of belonging and can influence her religious development.

The Public School

Most of Emma's Christian nurture will take place in church and home. The wider community, and especially the school, is, however, an additional environment where her nurture can be enhanced or thwarted. While the religion of the public school is most generally an expression of a civil religion where God and country are closely identified, it may also in certain locales be much like what is taught in the dominant churches or synagogues in the region. Where constitutional limitations are taken seriously, the school clearly is to be neutral as regards religious practice and instruction. However, as is well known, this does not prevent discussing religion as a part of normal studies in school.

Some school systems also are open to released-time arrangements whereby children may participate in church-sponsored religious studies.

In addition, children themselves discuss religious matters, often instructing their peers with such words as, "It's a sin to cheat," or "My Sunday school teacher told me not to listen to jokes like that." These informal peer encounters, church-sponsored studies, and religious-related school studies have primary value when they feed back into the dominant settings of home and church. "Is everybody but the members of the Church of Christ going to hell?" one earnest third grader inquired. "What does it mean that Thomas Jefferson was a deist? Is that different from being a Christian?"

Teaching About Trinity

Emma will hear people pray to Almighty God, to the Merciful and Divine Creator; she will hear of God in the Psalms as a "Great and Terrible God," will hear of God in the hymns of worship as holy, immortal, invisible, merciful, loving, exalted. She will hear people pray to Jesus as well, and even to the Holy Spirit. She will hear adults talk about following God or Jesus. She will hear them say that they live by the Spirit; at other times, that they look to Jesus for guidance.

While all of this is potentially confusing, it is not terribly upsetting. Emma has her own built-in protector, namely, her point in development, which prevents her from even attempting to assimilate how a person might pray once to God, then to Jesus, then to the Holy Spirit. Because of this, she will take in as much as she can, then will respond, sometimes simply repeating as a verbalism what she has heard, at other times uttering a unique, spontaneous word. The verbalism response is seen in the six-year-old child who prayed, "Thy deliberately faith I full, faith against almighty worship God, and faith all unto you, faith against thy holy prayer."[20] The more assimilative response is in a description of God by an eleven-year-old: "He'd have little children sitting on his knee. He'd be a kind man with a beard like Jesus did, and clothes like Jesus."[21]

David Elkind distinguishes between spontaneous and acquired religion, holding that the spontaneous responses reveal the children's real concepts. He cites research which proves that children's unrestrained thinking moves in sequence from the concrete to the abstract. On the other hand, the acquired responses show no particular difference between younger and older children because children, at any age, can memorize and repeat.[22] James Fowler proposes a similar distinction by separating form and content, then demonstrating their interplay. A conversation, for example, is a change in content but not a change in form; it may, of course, precipitate formal changes. It is possible for children, or any person, to take on and repeat content but not really be experiencing any change in form or mode of thinking-feeling.[23] This requires teachers to do more listening than telling, more responding than suggesting, and that they provide more activities for experiencing than structured settings for instructing.

One might ask how Emma will move beyond her present understandings if all her teachers do is respond to her ideas. There is unrealism in such a supposition. We simply do not have that much control over what Emma will be told by others; nor do we know that much about her precise point on a developmental scale. The only way to find out where she is is to talk with her. The possibility, then, is open for teachers to expand her knowledge. Sensitive teachers will be able to recognize when their attempts at expansion are moving beyond Emma's capacities.

This gentle tugging is illustrated in a conversation which James Fowler had with Millie, a fourth grader, in which she volunteered that "God is with you all the time." Fowler asked her in what way, and she responded: "In a way God's inside you but in a way God isn't. He's inside you because you believe—if you believe in him then he's inside you, but he's also all around." At this point Fowler tested whether he could stretch Millie's thinking by asking how God could be all around. She replied delightfully: "Well, that's a good question. Um, well he's—he lives on top of the world, so in a way he's all around." Fowler, evidently perceiving that she was not ready to deal with pervasiveness, wisely moved on to another matter.[24]

Emma's teachers will therefore resist the temptation to teach the Trinity as a doctrine. It has been tried before, and children have memorized that it consists of God the Father, God the Son, and God the Holy Spirit, three in one. Teachers have used clever analogies, such as the fact that water may appear in the form of ice, liquid, or steam. Better, but still inadequate, they have appealed to relationships, showing how one's father is, in addition to being a father, also a son and a brother. The chances are that the children remember the analogies and the imagery but still do not understand the doctrine of the Trinity. They can accommodate to the formula but cannot thereby assimilate it into their mental apparatus. They can memorize the content, but do not have the mental structures for understanding the form. They can reproduce the formula as something acquired, but if responding spontaneously to questions about God, they will not suggest a trinitarian doctrine.

In teaching about God, Emma's teachers will begin with her own ideas about God and build carefully from that base. At this age of ten, Emma's view of God is quite concrete; she talks about God in terms of special attitudes and powerful acts. Andre Godin found boys from eight to ten focusing on God's miracles, while girls focused on beauty. Both, but especially girls, referred to God's goodness. Within a year or so, these notions gave way to the personalization of God, as in God the Father.[25] Ronald Goldman found children around ten and one-half moving away from viewing God in human terms toward a superhuman perspective. An eleven-year-old offered this description: "He's very very very old and wise."[26] Millie, a fourth grader in James Fowler's research, said of God: "I imagine that he's an old man with a white beard and white hair wearing a long robe and that the clouds are his floor and he has a throne. And he has all these people and there's angels around him."[27] Later, when children can think more abstractly, their ideas about God are more symbolic in nature.

Emma's teachers will accept her spontaneous notions about God without undue correction and her verbalisms without overreaction. For example, to the child who said God would have children sitting on his knee, the teachers will respond with some word about how God loves children, ignoring for the moment any consideration of God's anatomy. Even adults who have learned that God is spirit hold to similar literal views. Further, the Old Testament encourages these concrete images.

On the matter of verbalisms, the church will, in fact, encourage these by the use of creeds and hymns which are composed of concepts well beyond Emma's capacity to understand. However, it is one thing to make liturgical use of such but an altogether different matter to attempt to force an understanding of what in worship is appropriate and essential.

Emma as Middle Child—A Child of Promise

To the child who prayed that confusing prayer, an obvious jumble of verbalisms, the teachers will ask something like "What is 'faith against thy holy prayer'?" From such sympathetic inquiry, children are required to think, to assimilate. After one or two questions, they will begin to respond out of what they are really thinking rather than by merely repeating what they have heard. Their responses are their "doctrines," their working theology. It is this kind of education which Emma will not outgrow or feel she must throw away, for here form and content flow together, accommodation and assimilation associate dynamically.

Thanks to the dominant religious history, Michelangelo, and the language, Emma's teachers, parents, and ministers grew up thinking of God as man. The common speech has, therefore, been God, he; seldom God, she. However, Emma's nurturing adults have discovered that these exclusively masculine references to God limit one's understanding of the nature of God. This discovery raises a dilemma in the minds of all sensitive nurturers. How can we speak of God without giving our children the same pictures of God as man which we grew up with? Perhaps the clue is in our natural references to God as shepherd, ruler, counselor, guide, friend. Similarly, we might become comfortable in referring to God in the imagery of the mother. Thus might we pray, "God our father, God our mother." It follows that we will also speak both of God, he, and God, she. Of course God is neither, but "it" is not suitable either. As uncommon as this proposed practice all sounds, it appears to be the best we can do, given our language limitations. If this should prove confusing to Emma, the simple explanation will be that God is not a man or a woman, but that using such terms is the only way we have of talking about God, that is, about her or him.

In teaching about Jesus, Emma's teachers will begin where they did with teaching about God, namely, with her current understanding of Jesus. Goldman found children around ten as understanding Jesus predominantly in terms of his miracles. Prior to this they viewed Jesus as a good man, but one different from others. Later, they will view Jesus as specially related to God and as having a special mission, although the middle child at times seemed to be approaching this belief of a special relationship.[28] The middle child also conceived of Jesus as not being perfect because he would have been like normal children in some ways. At age six, all but one of Goldman's children saw no imperfection in Jesus; by age ten it was 50 percent; by fifteen eight out of twenty.[29]

In spite of Emma's natural interest in the miracle stories, her teachers will focus on the more common elements in Jesus' life and teaching. This is not to deny the miraculous in his ministry, but the danger in emphasizing the unusual is that it will distract Emma from gaining a balanced perspective on Jesus. She can relate more to Jesus' blessing of the children than to his raising of Jairus's daughter, more to serving wine to his disciples in the enjoyment of a meal than in turning water into wine.

Emma will learn of Jesus more in episodes than by chronology, which is more akin to the way the Gospels themselves are put together. She will be encouraged to identify her feelings about events in his life, for example, how she feels about his remaining behind at the temple after his parents had gone or how he must have felt when Judas betrayed him. In this she is building a repertoire of stories about Jesus which later on she will systematize and to which she will give greater theological reflection.

Because of Emma's limited historical perspective her teachers will not attempt to teach her the significance of Jesus to history or to identify him with Old Testament promises of the Messiah, apocalyptic images of the Son of man, or Isaiah's Suffering Servant. However, they will lead her to identify with Simeon's joy when he saw Jesus and to see that Jesus was a servant, as when he washed the disciples' feet.[30]

At Christmas, Emma's teachers will avoid as much as possible a total emphasis on Jesus as a baby. It would be better to talk of things which Jesus did and said, as we do on the birthdays of other great persons. This would give her a surer footing for a later appreciation of the unique person who Jesus was. While adults can reflect on the disparity between the innocent baby in a stall and the executed Christ on a cross, children do not make such connections. When their education approaches such realities, it is at the risk of creating diffused and vague feelings which later in one's religious development are difficult to overcome.

Realistically, however, the manger emphasis at Christmas is here to stay. We have not even been able completely to keep Santa Claus out of the religious tradition; so it is certain that we will only with great difficulty shift the emphasis from the birth narratives to the life of Jesus, for Emma will hear it at worship, at home, and in the shopping mall. We do, however, have within our power, if not our will, to remove this emphasis from the church school where it invariably is overdone. Christmas celebration belongs most essentially to the liturgical life of the congregation, and that is where it should be given heed. As Emma follows the progression of the lighting of the Advent candles until on Christmas Day the Christmas candle stands alight as the center of the worship service, she is taking in what is most essential about Christmas. The Christ has come, and still comes.

At Easter, Emma will naturally hear of Jesus' trip to Jerusalem, where he was killed, and of his burial and resurrection. She must hear of these, for they are irreplaceable in the Christian religion. However, there is really not much in these events with which she can identify. She knows nothing of traveling somewhere as a fulfillment of destiny. She does not know about the fickle crowd. She cannot fathom Jesus' words about the destruction of the temple or the curse of the tree. She does not have social perspectives from which to understand how someone might weep over a city. She cannot know that Jesus' radical lifestyle made the cross inevitable. Many of the words from the cross will be beyond her, especially the now theologically rich saying, "It is finished." Therefore, these elements will be kept in the context of worship, but not be included in teaching sessions. Of course, if Emma asks about them, she will be given straightforward answers.

Emma will be able to identify with how Jesus felt when his friend betrayed him and how Peter felt when he lied about knowing and being a disciple of Jesus. She can appreciate to some extent that Jesus did not deserve to be executed. If she has attended a grave service of someone close to her, she will understand Mary's excitement in seeing an empty tomb. If she has friends across the country whom she sees only on special occasions, she will be able to share the joy of the disciples to whom Jesus appeared. These elements, then, might be included in an Easter study. But there are plenty of other texts which raise questions of relationships, fairness, surprise, and joy. Easter is best left to worship and to wonder as far as Emma is concerned, and teaching about it is best done only in response to her interest in this mysterious event.

Jesus is the Christ, God's Son, Savior. Emma must know that emotionally before she will perceive it intellectually or appropriate it volitionally. Therefore, our teaching about Jesus as Savior will be pointed more in helping Emma express her feelings about Jesus than in attempting to teach her a full Christology or in persuading her to accept Jesus. As with Christmas and Easter, Jesus' mission in its eternal materiality in God's work of salvation is to be central in worship, but not in the church school. In worship, it all is there in its fullness, and Emma can relate to it appropriately. However, in the church school, the tendency is to overwork this truth, thus to run ahead of where Emma is developmentally. With her one-dimensional mind she cannot look at the cross and affirm with Paul that it is "the power of God unto salvation."

Similarly, Emma's teachers will teach concretely about sin and faith. Both are something she does, and her teachers will help her identify behaviors which represent sin and faith. Thus, Emma sins, and she "faiths." Of course, both sin and faith are broader than the individual act. But Emma does not understand the general sense of sinfulness or righteousness.

David wronged Bathsheba and Uriah, but he considered it sin against God. Jesus taught that love for neighbor was the same as love for God. On the other hand, the New Testament also speaks of human righteousness as ineffectual for salvation but that faith without works is not faith at all. Because Emma cannot separate all of this, the task for her teachers appears to be threefold: one, encourage Emma to do right and avoid wrong, at the same time helping her deal with the difficulties of knowing what is right and what is wrong; two, avoid confusing the specific act with the ultimate meaning of estrangement and faith; three, do not call on her to make an irreversible turn from sin or to make a life-binding profession of faith.

The Bible

Emma's nurturers know the Bible as the Word of God; Emma has yet to learn that. They turn to favorite texts in times of need; Emma may have a favorite Bible story but does not yet view the Bible according to some need in her experience. They search the Bible for answers to problems; Emma asks her parents and others how to solve some difficulty. Sometimes the adults around her talk about the authority of Scripture; Emma does not know what they mean. They give it a special place in home, church school, and worship; Emma appropriates some of this reverence but not in relation to her own involvement with Bible material. Emma's minister reads a text, then talks about it; Emma follows some of what he is communicating but seldom connects what he says with the text. Her nurturers have come through experience to see the Bible as the Word of God; Emma, if the Bible is to be the Word of God to her, must also travel that route.

Emma reads the Bible, but she finds it strange in many ways, for it is written for adults more than for children her age.[31] Further, it is a theological book. This adult, theological character shows both in the stories and the direct teachings. In the New Testament especially, it shows in the composition of the writings, as witnessed by the fact that the Gospel writers use certain materials in differing contexts, for example, the millstone warning (Matthew 18:1-6; Mark 9:38-42; Luke 17:1-2).

Take any story, such as the parable of the good Samaritan in Luke's special section (10:29-37), which children hear more as a story than as a parable. With help on some of the words, Emma will be able to read this story. She will identify with the man who was injured and like the man who helped him. She can learn the lesson on the face of the story and apply it to her own experience. But the parable is set down in a context of a question about eternal life and the great commandment and contains subtleties, such as the use of naming a priest, a Levite, and a Samaritan as characters. In addition, Matthew and Mark record a similar confrontation between Jesus and a questioner but do not include the parable. Of course, Emma does not have to know all of these things, but the use of this parable does demonstrate the adult, theological character of Bible stories.

As to direct teachings, Emma finds them in a form unlike her schoolbooks, but with help she can understand some essential lessons. She can relate to some of the beatitudes in terms of their application, although the language is strange. She will understand about people crying and finding sympathy, wanting to do right, showing mercy, attempting to make peace. She will probably not grasp what it means to be poor in spirit, and even if Luke's version, "Blessed are you poor," is utilized, she will not see how being poor and possessing the kingdom of God are associated. Similarly, she will have difficulty understanding what it means to be meek, pure in heart, persecuted for righteousness' sake, and reviled but enjoying the same reward the prophets received. Her teachers then will avoid texts which require Emma merely to accept a concept and will favor Bible material which she can integrate with experience.

When the Bible is used in Emma's learning, it will proceed from her experience as a middle child. She experiences what the Golden Rule is about, but not the verses, immediately following in Matthew, on the narrow gate. She will learn from the Lord's Prayer but be perplexed by the preceding account in Luke of Jesus' rebuke of Martha. Much of the large Judean section of the Gospels from the journey to Jerusalem to the empty tomb is foreign to Emma's experience at ten, although she can profit from some lessons, such as Zacchaeus's determination, the great commandment, the widow's gift, and the giving and use of talents. When the structure of the biblical text is too foreign to her, Emma's teachers should find other examples of character, if that is their teaching purpose.

Iris Cully uncovers in Zacchaeus a rich lesson for children, suggesting that they can relate to his having to climb the tree in order to see and to his guilt for having wrongfully used money. "How wonderful that Jesus noticed Zacchaeus and promised to come to his house," Cully wrote in capturing the way children might experience this story.[32]

Emma is not prepared for a thorough critical study of the Bible. However, her teachers will take advantage of opportunities to help her compare the renderings and placement of certain passages. For example, if the lesson should be on the great commandment, Emma, at least by eleven or twelve, can compare the text in the Synoptic Gospels and Deuteronomy and Leviticus. In the same spirit, one church school teacher, in a unit on the Exodus, had pupils prepare a map showing the possible routes the Hebrews took out of Egypt. The teacher should not make too much of differences or play with children's minds and emotions, but such differences in texts or variations in historical detail become useful in giving children a realistic view of the Bible as a book which they are going to use often as they grow up.

Emma needs to learn how to be present in a text. Admittedly, as middle child she is not all that reflective, but with assistance she can meet a text where it is in relation to where she is. Dorothy Jean Furnish suggests how to do this verbally and nonverbally. First, ask the child such questions as: "What did the story say? What did you like about the story? Did it remind you of anything? Whom did you like best? Why? If you had been David, what would you have done? What did you think about the way the story ended? How else might it have ended?" To help a child live into a text nonverbally, suggest: "Paint a picture about the story. Fingerpaint how the story made you feel. Show how you think Moses felt by the way you stand or move around the room. Act out the story using puppets."[33]

Emma will understand parables concretely. Therefore, the most appropriate ones are those where a meaning, not necessarily the deepest meaning, is on the face of the text. Emma can understand Luke's parables of the prodigal son and the good Samaritan in their upfront meaning. With help she will find surface meaning in the parables of the rich fool, of the Pharisee and the publican, and the parable of the talents. If used without the interpretation, Emma will relate to the parable of the two sons. She will have great difficulty with Luke's other parables and the synoptic kingdom parables because they require a more symbolic, abstract reasoning.

None of this is to say that there is absolutely nothing in these parables with which Emma as middle child can associate; any thoughtful lesson maker can find such connections. The point is that it is better that Emma study only those parables which are readily understandable, saving the others for the time when her thinking ability will more nearly match the depth of the parables' lessons. These are among the Bible's most penetrating insights; we cannot afford to deal with them superficially. Our children, because they are familiar with the parables, may also think they already know the parables' truths.

Ronald Goldman, in research on how children think about the Bible, found that late elementary children begin to view the Bible in terms of content more than by its physical features, as "the only completely true book, the oldest book or a book from which we learn about God and Jesus."[34] They see the Bible as a collection of many books written by different authors and as literally true because "God is associated with them [stories] and the deity can do anything."[35] They betray some confusion about what happened in Bible times and what could happen today. Concerning the crossing of the Red Sea, one child said, "'It could happen once in a million years. But there are no slaves now.'"[36]

The Bible is our pivotal book. It carries the written story which was passed orally through the generations. It preserves for us the earliest witnesses to the Christ event and the genesis of the new people of God. It deserves to be taken seriously. To diminish its import to moralisms is to trivialize it. To reduce its truth to principles is to intellectualize it. To deny its historical perspectives is to nullify it. When we overuse this treasure in instructional settings, exposing it to modes of thinking which are literalistic and syncretistic, we force the children to accommodate to the story without assimilating it to their experience. They thus grow up thinking that, because they have studied a text, they thereby also understand it. Eventually, this will undercut the force of the Bible and hinder its becoming the Word of God for our children.

Emma's Childhood Friends

Elizabeth has now been welcomed to participate in the Lord's Supper with her congregation. Her fifth-grade class in the church school met for several weeks with the minister who helped the class understand the meaning of the Supper and why they were being admitted to participation. He told them that in eating the bread and drinking the wine they were remembering the death of Jesus and celebrating his resurrection. He took them through the Holy Week pilgrimage, from Palm Sunday to Easter Sunday. They learned of the Jewish Passover and of Jesus' supper with his disciples before his death. They created dramatic readings from Isaiah's Suffering Servant passages and the words of Jesus from the cross. They acted out the Emmaus appearance and prepared banners for use on Easter Sunday.

The minister told Elizabeth and the class that they were being allowed to participate for the first time because the congregation felt that they could now best understand the meaning of the celebration, as he had

Emma as Middle Child—A Child of Promise

instructed them. But, more, he told them that their participation is a sign of Christ's presence in the church and of their affiliation with the whole congregation. He spoke of the Supper as a part of their continuing growth in faith. In speaking of continuation, the minister also was planting seeds for other times of religious experience in store for Elizabeth and the class.

Robert is active in his church. He attends Sunday church school and other activities and worships regularly with his parents. He is learning much about God's holiness as he watches his parents and others bow their heads in prayer. He, himself, has learned to pray. He has learned some hymns which speak of God and many gospel songs which sound like personal testimonies put to music. He understands some of what the minister preaches, but beyond the words he is seeing something about the importance of faith and church. He is feeling closer identity with who Jesus Christ is and regularly hears appeals from the minister for people to accept Christ as Savior.

Robert is curious about the Lord's Supper and would like to drink the juice and have some of the bread. He wonders why he cannot participate. Of course, he knows that he will be able to take the juice and bread after he has made his profession of faith and been baptized. But he hears his minister talk of remembering Christ's death and looking for Christ's return. Sometimes the minister also speaks of the communion which the church members have with each other in observing the Supper. Robert still wonders why he is not allowed to remember and anticipate and to be a part of the fellowship around the Lord's Table.

Samuel sometimes attends Emma's church when his parents take him. He also has gone to Sunday church school with Robert. But his family has not joined any church and attends mostly on special days, such as Christmas and Easter and when the grandparents are visiting them. Samuel hears just enough to be confused about religion. He does not take it very seriously. He has wanted to take the Lord's Supper when it was served at both Emma's and Robert's churches. Also, he has felt some stirrings when Robert's minister has talked of accepting Jesus Christ as personal Savior and being baptized. He is curious about the baptismal pool behind the choir. But Samuel does not talk much about these church experiences, and no one has as yet told or shown him who he is—a child of God.

Transition

Emma the middle child belongs to the community of faith. That status has been communicated in many ways to her. She has been included in the life of the congregation. She has been told the stories of faith from Abraham to the present. She has been told of her own church's expression of a Christianity which is worldwide. She has been taught the life and teachings of Jesus and has felt a fledgling mystical attraction to him. She has worshiped with the whole congregation. Formally, by appropriate symbol, the congregation has conferred belonging on Emma. She belongs where her parents participate. Now she knows her place in the community of faith. She is a daughter of God but also is a child of belonging and promise. This deep and satisfying sense of belonging takes her into the sphere of adolescent religion. The promise is hers, too, but it is her parents and congregation who hold this hope as one of their own, one of God's children, passes to another season.

4

Emma as Adolescent—
An Affirmed Believer

God gave Emma daughtership; the church gave her belonging. But neither can give her faith. No one can affirm faith for her. The origin of affirmation is in her own self-will. God gives sonship and daughtership to all; the church, through believing parents, confers belonging on all its children. Affirmation is a different matter; only the individual can affirm faith for oneself. Thus, in adolescence Emma comes to the time when she must assess her daughtership and her place in the church. She must examine her relationship to God through the Christ and her relationship to the church, and declare herself.

Emma's affirmation is voluntary. It is her own personal response, her own yes to something or someone. It is her favorable response to all that has been done for her and said to her. Regardless of how God yearns for Emma to respond positively or how much the church encourages Emma to take up the faith task for herself, only Emma can affirm it all. No one involuntarily becomes a contributing part of a community of faith or a believer in Jesus Christ.

Emma's affirmation is, however, strongly influenced by others. A free and independent decision does not mean one is devoid of influence from the outside. From early childhood, Emma's will has been developing, and she has become more independent as she has gained ego strength and mastered life's requirements at each appropriate age. The decisions she made about which toys to play with, which clothes to wear, which friends to be with, which games to play, how to spend her allowance, how to arrange her bedroom, which gift to buy for Mother's

Day, which card for Father's birthday, and about other growing matters have shown an increasing independence. But these decisions have been made within contexts of family, church, and community. While voluntary, Emma's affirmation is still social; it reveals much of the character of the loving influence of sympathetic adults who have brought her up in faith.

This influence on Emma may be termed "incorporation," or "socialization." Emma's nurturers have had in mind an education with a certain end and deliberate, but varied, means. There is no way to explain where Emma is in her religious development apart from this conscious approach to her nurture. That is why she is affirming Christian faith and not faith of some other genre. Still, that process stops short of making Emma's decision for her. Emma has been socialized in a deliberate direction and by carefully chosen methods, but she has not been brainwashed or been told to conform beyond her own will to choose and act. Effective education leads to but cannot, because it chooses not to, guarantee that Emma will make her affirmation of faith. It is that way because her nurturers understand the basic nature of faith as well as the character of a healthy process of nurture.

Emma's affirmation is radical, but not cataclysmic. Complete 180-degree turnabouts are for people who are going in the wrong direction. Emma's nurture, from birth, has set her in the right direction; thus her affirmation does not come out of having rejected God and all that is holy. She has not lived a long life of sin which has shaped her for pity but has known and loved God since her earliest years. Having never completely turned her back on God, she does not have to turn toward God. Because of her upbringing she is already facing in God's direction, already bent toward God, as a tree straightened at each critical stage of growth.

Her affirmation, then, is another step, but, oh, what a radical step, for it now comes when Emma is able to face her life situation as a participant with her whole race in estrangement from the complete purposes of God. Though turned toward God, Emma still must affirm her faith. She has been an unwitting actor in the human drama, but now she begins to see her lines in a new light and is making her own

Emma as Adolescent—An Affirmed Believer

contribution to the script. Personal decisions made from that stage are radical to the core.

With such an understanding of the nature of affirmation, what is the reality being affirmed? Emma, in affirming faith, is really confirming her heritage and declaring personal faith in Jesus Christ. She has gotten in touch with the feelings surrounding her early nurture and has examined that heritage critically and has said that she wishes to continue in it. But, more, Emma has processed the meaning of her creation in God's image. She has come to see in varying degrees that for all of her incorporating nurture there is still something about her life which she cannot control. The impulse to do good is countered by the impulse to do evil. The desire to be obedient has an opposing inclination to disobey. For all her strength, there is much weakness. For all her feeling about being a daughter of God, there exists an obscuring of that relationship and it cannot be seen so clearly. For all of her feeling of belonging, there exists a measure of alienation. Regardless of the beauty and integrity of heritage, Emma comes to a time when she senses that more is wrong in her existence than history, doctrine, worship, or community ethos and ethic can solve. She concludes that to realize her full daughtership as a child of God, she must declare herself concerning Jesus Christ. From these dynamics, she declares personal faith in who Jesus was and is and in what he did and does.[1]

Emma's decision is not simply a matter of individual salvation; it also involves some sense of mission. Along with her declaration of faith, Emma joins in a limited way in the mission of the church. It is not the intense commitment to mission which she will experience in adulthood when she will be less distracted by the problems of growing up, but it is a participation. There is much that Emma can do, both in personal ministry to peers and in corporate mission to community needs. Some promise to be this kind of Christian is involved in her confirmation of heritage and the declaration of faith.

Although Emma has been being regenerated all along, she now personally takes on the life from above as a conscious choice. Though she has been within the context of salvation all along, she now personally chooses to live within that context. Though she has made many faith decisions as she has grown in the faith, and will make many more, she now understands the import of those decisions—that is, that they lean her whole existence toward God in whose image she is made. She now sees all of these early and yet-to-come dynamics of faith in relation to her destiny as a daughter of God. The church will symbolize this new development by a fitting rite, before the worshiping congregation.

The Nurturing Task in the Adolescent Years

In the preschool years the nurturing task focused on conveying to Emma, both in word and feeling, that she was a daughter of God. Emma emerged from these years both knowing and sensing this status. In the school years the nurturing task turned to giving Emma a sense of belonging to the community of faith. She came out of these years confident that she had a rightful place in the church. Now, in adolescence, the nurturing task is to bring Emma to appraise and confirm her heritage and to declare and live by faith in Jesus Christ. This task will be defined in light of her search for identity, her social position, her new intellectual ability, and her religious development.

Emma is an adolescent! The very word means to grow up. It is marked by puberty at its beginning and by entrance to adulthood at its end. In our culture it is a period of life between childhood and adulthood and partakes of both, as Rousseau said of Émile, "He is neither a child nor a man. . . ."[2] It is for some, but not for all, a time of intense upheaval.[3] For all, and for Emma, adolescence is a time of facing new dynamics and challenges. It is a time when she will encounter and resolve numerous conflicts. There will be concern over bodily changes, relationships with parents and significant adults, acceptance among peers, questioning of prevailing values, doubting or at least analyzing religious beliefs—altogether a list too long to enumerate.

Emma's entrance to the common adolescent identity crisis is not wholly one of feeling. Although fraught with emotion, the identity crisis for Emma is affective, social, and cognitive.

A New Social Position

Psychologists Kurt Lewin, Erik Erikson, and Jean Piaget hold that Emma the adolescent is qualitatively different from Emma the child and that the social milieu is a primary factor. Lewin best characterizes this

Emma as Adolescent—An Affirmed Believer

difference as one of social position.[4] Emma's behavior is best explained by the fact that she is in a different region from that of her childhood and not yet accepted in the adult world. She is a marginal person. In this marginal field Emma overlaps both with childhood and adulthood. This immediately widens the field. Consider the expansion of Emma's geography, especially once she has "wheels."

This widened region, overlapping as it is with her childhood and the yet-to-come adulthood, is then unfamiliar. Emma is placed in situations that are new to her. Obviously she has strong feelings about all of this, often wanting to withdraw, often wishing for the right words to speak or even the right way to sit, and wishing she knew what to do with her hands. She will also be in positions that are almost entirely contrary to what she has been taught and has known to be right. The intensity of her emotional struggle, so markedly advanced in its consequences over new situations in childhood, is an adolescent phenomenon.

There is another feature of this new social position. Besides being social and affective, it also is cognitive. Emma is right off faced with a cognitively different field. She has heard much of the language before and has her own repertoire, but she now is forced to call on deeper thought resources. Her perception of her position can no longer be managed by the simpler modes of childhood thought.

This new situation, composed as it is of the social, the emotional, and the cognitive, explains Emma's moments of uncertainty, her sudden shifts in behavior, her exasperating changes in mood, her sometime abandonment of calm for an unreasonable turbulence. Emma's behavior, however, should be as understandable and expected as that of an explorer in a new world in space.

In Erikson's view, Emma is in a period called a moratorium, provided by her society in order to give her opportunity to find an identity continuous with what she has been becoming and with what she envisions for the future.[5] To a sense of trust in those who cared for her in infancy, Emma added a personal willfulness to act. To self-will Emma added the pursuit of reality with purpose. She then began to put that purpose to useful production, demonstrating her ability to create, to make, and to make well. Now, to all of these dynamics, Emma adds identity, essentially a sense of continuity. She now longs to see in herself the person she has been becoming and wants to continue to become. She wants to see her history as lining up with whatever she can perceive of her hoped-for future. She wants to find in the present an identity, a fidelity to what she has been and what she might yet become.

In this quest Emma is going to draw on the gains from the conflicts faced and, with the help of loving adults, resolved in earlier years. Of course, these gains are positive, but they have come out of facing the negative aspects of growth as well. Emma's trust is stronger because she also appreciates the terror of not trusting. Her will is more intact because she knows how she can alienate and be alienated from others in her desire to be autonomous. Her sense of purpose is more creative because she understands the good or ill which she can do. Her competence is surer because she has faced what it means to feel inferior. The positive gains from these growing years have put Emma in a stronger position to face the identity crisis.

Without such gains in the development of vitality, Emma would enter adolescence as a cripple. Thus, each conflict would recall her disability, as physical contests betray one's physical handicaps. However, even in the best of health, these adolescent conflicts will test Emma's ego strength. In the face of such conflicts she might choose a negative identity. That is, she might view her facelessness and simply assume a face, select a face from others or from a crowd or cult or from an ideology. Such is the critical importance of the positive accomplishments of Emma's experience in the preschool and elementary years.

Emma's quest then is both psychological and social. She is not acting simply as an isolated individual attempting to manage inner conflicts brought on by puberty and neuroses held over from earlier experiences. Rather, she is actively in pursuit of identity and is engaging in the contest within a social context. She reacts psychologically to the context and acts on the context individually. By the same token, the social context receives her individual activity and acts on her. It is a mutual activity. By it, Emma establishes a sense of identity, a fidelity, and thus avoids entering adulthood with a confused understanding of self.

Piaget also understands Emma as entering a new social region.[6] She now feels more adult than child and is drawn toward adulthood by the adoption of a life plan. In such a plan Emma will order her values and ideals, will set tentative long-range goals. This is no mere intellectual exercise, but it is an intensely emotional, social experience in which Emma is raising herself above the child she was. She is realizing, in part, the adult she thinks herself to be. She attaches stronger feelings to her ideals and values than she once did. As a child she gave only passing feeling to injustice, perhaps momentarily concluding that some adult had been unfair, as, for example, in Little League play. But as an adolescent Emma invests emotional energy in matters held dear. Note the persistent theme of perceived injustice in the way adolescents are treated in the social setting of the high school.

Lewin may be right that Emma is a marginal person, but Piaget is also correct that she considers herself equal with adults and, thus, in a position to criticize on equal terms. She will then also hold to systems which promise to solve the world's problems and will put those solutions out for public consumption, though not yet for public criticism; criticism will come soon, however. Because Emma is a social being, relating to significant adults but grouping mostly with peers, she will receive encouragement and criticism from both groups. Her social relations will draw her into new and challenging situations as well as provide a necessary challenge to her seemingly unabated confidence in her theories.

However, the social setting is not the primary determiner of Emma's behavior. The heart of the matter is that Emma is in a different position now because she has attained new structures of thought. Once her intelligence came through the senses and was expressed at the actional level. To this she added the simple representation in the mind of what she was seeing in the external world. She then was characterized by a capriciousness because she was deceived by what her eyes beheld. Once she was bound in her thinking by what was concrete. Now in adolescence, she can operate formally on her environment.

With this advanced way of thinking, Emma is now freed from the present moment to imagine the future. This is more than the simple imaginative beauty seen in children; it is a serious projection of what the "not yet" might look like and be. It involves enumerating the possible even though the facts do not point in that direction. Only by imagining what is possible can Emma formulate her vision for the future. Otherwise, her future would simply be dictated by the limitation of what she knows in the present.

Emma now can think about her own thought. At first she will not do this consistently, because of her infatuation with what she has formulated. Considering herself equal with adults and thinking that she has the theory for making sense of life, she is reluctant to admit her system is flawed. Because she formed it, she invests it with a certain infallibility. However, as she interacts with others, she will become critical of her own thinking. She will come to stand back and look in on her own mind and will learn what is effectual and what is defective.

Emma now makes combinations of thought. She connects thoughts logically which in childhood she might have joined intuitively. But now her connections are not guesses, although they may actually represent leaps beyond what is apparent to others. She is more able to deduce conclusions from general laws and, at the same time, to induce from individual experiences to form broad generalizations. To the question "If Sue is larger than Jane and Jane is larger than Mary, is Sue larger than Mary?", Emma, as a child, would have answered that she would have to see them side by side. Now she can solve the problem at the verbal level, knowing that if A is larger than B, and B is larger than C, then A is larger than both B and C. If she sees in her class that all the children who have blond hair also have blue eyes and all who have black hair have brown eyes, she will be able, without looking, to tell you the color of a child's eyes when you tell her the color of the child's hair. Back in the concrete state, she would have had to look at the evidence.

The Identity Crisis and Faith

Lewin, Erikson, and Piaget agree that Emma the adolescent is in a new social position. All agree that Emma is experiencing real psychological dimensions as she negotiates this position. Lewin contributes the most illuminating depiction of the overall nature of this new position. Piaget, more explicitly than the others, takes into account and describes her cognitive gains, still in relation to, but by no means determined by, the social setting. But it is Erikson who contributes the most complete characterization of the particulars of what Emma is experiencing.[7] Using his discussion of the dimensions of the identity crisis, but also drawing from Lewin and Piaget, let us examine more closely what Emma's search for identity looks like.

In addition, let us thoughtfully pursue the relationship between identity development and religious identity and growth.[8] Emma, in emerging from adolescence with a vital sense of continuity and fidelity, is not thereby Christian. To be more fully human is, of course, in its broadest terms to be religious. The old prophet laid down a vision for a humanity which would do justice, love mercy, and walk humbly with God. This is fundamentally religious but does not define what we mean by affirming one's faith. Emma's psychological-social health is not one with an affirmation of faith. Psychological-social adjustment is not salvation. Finding her place in her new social region is not the same as finding her place in the Body of Christ. Attaining formal operational thought does not guarantee that Emma will find ultimate truth.

On the other hand, can we not be equally certain that Emma's faith will have more than a passing effect in her general development? The opposite notion is unthinkable. When she confirms her heritage and affirms faith in Jesus Christ, she is doing something that will make a difference in how she negotiates the winding paths of adolescence. Faith's work is to make her whole.

Now, let us move on to the particulars of the identity crisis and religious identity. First, Emma is coming to a perspective on time, that is, that it has duration and is made up of cause and effect. Time does not in and of itself negotiate or solve problems. Emma is coming to terms with the fact that her actions have some relationship to external causes and that they in turn have their own effects. She connects solutions and accomplishments with her actions rather than with some magical phenomenon. She separates the dreamy wish from the earned accomplishment. Associated with this development is that her sense of history is not as flat as it was in childhood; both her backward and forward views are deeper. She has a better understanding of the ordering of events. With this understanding comes a better grasp of how time works and of its relative position with all time. This accomplishment is the difference between the digital clock which simply registers the moment and the common hour clock which shows the moment in the context of the hour. Emma's critical-thinking powers contribute to this accomplishment because she can reflect on her own thought and can transcend the actual to suppose what might someday come to pass.

At the simplest level of application, this new time perspective facilitates Emma's retrospective journey into her heritage. She begins to perceive that the faith she has known was lived out in the lives of real people who, rather than drifting through life, made deliberate decisions about faith, about right and wrong. She connects the faith of her nurturers with the fact that she had a Christian place in which to grow. She sees that her heritage is the effect of such actions. It will be many years before she will find her own role as the guarantor of that heritage for another generation, but it is now that she can confirm such a heritage.

At a deeper plane, Emma's sense of time makes it possible for her to begin to conceptualize eternity and transcendence. As a child, Emma heard the words "eternal," "everlasting," "forever"—"His steadfast love endures forever"; "who believes has everlasting life"; "And I give you eternal life." The obscurity of these words slowly ascends like an early morning fog, and the horizon broadens. Her own time is a part of what was and is to come. The promise which faith makes of eternal life is partially apprehended then as continuous with God's purpose, unfettered by the boundaries of her individual life or the confines of history. Whereas in childhood Emma was perplexed by how one could live in Kansas City and Missouri at the same time, she finds herself a part of both time and eternity.

Emma's newly acquired historical consciousness also enlightens her appreciation of grace. As an innocent child she acted out cause and effect with but a primitive awareness; as an adolescent she perceives it fully. Yet the word of the church to her is that for all of its love and concern for her, it cannot give her God's grace. The church tells her that for all of her love for God, she cannot earn God's grace. How, then, does this reconcile with the law of cause and effect? The answer is that it lifts the law to a higher plane so that Emma now better understands her transcending quality and God's eternity, and she celebrates that the Great Giver offers grace and mercy independently of her personal action.

Can Emma the young adolescent, up to fifteen years, visualize and verbalize such perspectives? No, not fully, but her sight is becoming clearer, and the old promises about God's faithfulness enduring through all generations are beginning to make sense. In later adolescence and young adulthood Emma will ponder more penetratingly the meaning of transcendence and grace. It is then that she will best understand her "mortality taking on immortality."

Second, Emma is attempting to find a self which when mirrored by others turns out to be the same. Her self-conscious behavior in familiar as well as unfamiliar situations demonstrates this concern with self. Emma's criticism of herself is heightened and ranges from a pimple on her face to her personality. She wants to know how others view how she views herself. This concern is partly due to her new social position, her change in group belongingness, her movement out of childhood. That she is in between, though not in a static manner, draws attention to herself. For Emma, the expectations of childhood were clear, but as a marginal person she is not sure what to expect either of the present or the anticipated adulthood, for the terrain is different. If she were clearer about the present and the future, she would not experience such uncertainty.

This concern may also be explained in part as Emma's penchant for turning her reflective power on herself. Now that she is able to do second-order thinking, it is inevitable that she should focus that ability on self. In all of this exchange—her critical view of herself, others' responses to her—Emma overcomes the temptation to become apathetic about her life. Thus, instead of doubting that she has a place, she realizes an important certainty about herself.

Emma's nurturers have laid the best foundation for this sense of self-certainty. They have shown her that she is a child of God and have given her a warm place in the community of faith. Her heritage tells her who she is; to paraphrase what Tevye said in *Fiddler on the Roof*, "Tradition gives us balance." Although the dynamics of adolescence will hold up this reality for questioning, there is no unchallenged certitude that, in order for Emma to become her true self, she will have to break with such a rearing. To the contrary, it is just this kind of nurture that should, above all else, reassure her of who she is and aid her in finding the particular shape of her daughtership.

However, the unity Emma seeks in her search for identity seems elusive to her. As Emma looks for a unifying reality in her new social position and ego struggle, she finds it in what the church has been telling her. The task of the church is to interpret this elusiveness as estrangement, as a sign of an ancient, universal division that obscures her daughtership and works against the singularity of the image of God in which she is made. It is the source of whatever hubris, concupiscence, and unbelief she possesses. (See Appendix VII, "Tillich's Doctrine of Estrangement and Salvation.")

This is not the first time Emma's nurturers have told her about estrangement, alienation, and sin, for this reality has been present and interpreted in many settings in the church and home. However, she is now able to grasp more fully the meaning of sin and to make some personal decision about sinfulness and the meaning of Jesus Christ. It is not the first time she has heard about Jesus Christ, for she has heard about him as Savior in the hymns, prayers, and preaching of the church. And while Emma has followed the teachings of Jesus as best she could and has trusted him at appropriate levels, she now can better understand the import of the redemptive work of the Christ.

Emma clearly is capable of this kind of thinking and is ready emotionally to face questions of selfhood. However, she does not yet have a fully developed "I" or a comprehensive world view from which to do this kind of thinking or manage this kind of emotion. She is not yet entirely sure that she has a center of awareness which she can trust to help her put her experiences in their proper places.[9] This does not mean that she cannot make an independent decision. What it does mean is that this independent decision is made within the expectations and conventions of the nurturing context. Again, the context is not forcing conformity on Emma; neither is she merely conforming. Her decision is not automatic to the situation. No, it is a free choice.

Emma does not have to break with her heritage in order to find the religious dimension of self-certainty. But she does have to process the church's teachings for herself. As a young adolescent she is connecting that process with what she has known and experienced. We, of course,

Emma as Adolescent—An Affirmed Believer

want it that way, for why else would we have placed Emma in a carefully prepared context of nurture? Yet we also want it the other way. That is, we want to make sure that as she processes faith within the very context which we have hoped would bring her to a commitment, she truly makes her own choice.

Third, Emma is questioning if she wants to take on the roles to which her family and culture have committed her. But she views these with ambivalence. The adult world is pluralistic, and Emma is confused. She is deciding if she is going to be middle class, chaste, temperate, religious. She cannot accomplish this task in the abstract. Therefore, she will experiment with various roles, sometimes in the extreme. The extremes betray her position in the overlapping region. They also indicate her lack of a fully developed, conscious "I," and a not yet complete sense of intimacy either with herself or others. These extremes may also demonstrate her adolescent certainty about the theories and systems which she constructs with her new reasoning ability. Of course, experimentation in one case may teach her what to expect should she entertain testing other roles. A test of her sexuality limits, for example, may teach her something about what role she will assume in other domains. That is to say, we are not to expect that Emma will go to extremes in the testing of every role which is modeled by her family, church, and a diverse society.

The right kind of education will help Emma with the expected testing of roles. Because Emma has not been brought up under a rigid system of education, she will not rebel completely or choose a negative identity which could complicate her personality growth for years to come. Because she has not been taught with a heavy-handed authoritarian approach, Emma will not make a premature decision out of fear of disappointing her elders or for the sake of pleasing them. On the other hand, because Emma's nurture has not been thoroughly permissive, she will not bear the bitter fruit of desperate experimentation born of rootlessness. Emma might visit another very different church or participate actively in a religious group at school, both of which represent alternatives to her normal religion. Should she perchance do more than experiment with these and actually adopt them, that would represent a conversion. There is no way, short of severe and persistent brainwashing, to protect her from such a possible choice. The expectation is that none of these is in store for Emma. But if she is to confirm the heritage, trust and declare faith in Jesus Christ genuinely, she is going to have to test roles.[10]

Fourth, Emma is concerned with what useful purpose to put her ability. She can no longer talk, as she did as a child, of some ill-defined modeling of persons in her society. The wish in childhood to grow up to be an astronaut does not carry the same emotional load as to plan in adolescence for becoming a space explorer. Emma moves, in early adolescence, from global vocational ideas to differentiated career ideals and plans. By late adolescence her skill in reflecting on her experience makes it possible for her to appraise her gifts and at the same time facilitates her attempts to construct a life plan.

Of course, this same competence in thinking about the future carries its own peril, for Emma can imagine more futures than she can ever devote her energies to. Her marginal position in society also adds to her insecurity and causes her to question whether she will, in fact, find a role that will both fit her interests and give her a fitting place in the adult milieu. She will at times even doubt that she will find a fulfilling vocation. This doubting often shows in her temporary inability to get on with some school task, though she certainly has the necessary intelligence for doing the work. As she, with the patient guidance of parents, other adults, and friends, persists, she will weave a fabric of occupational confidence.

The church can be of help to Emma in this quest for a life program. The task is to bend her toward a career that promises fulfillment and not simply toward a job that will assure her a living. In this guidance, which should come more from theology than culture, Emma's nurturers will avoid encouraging her toward traditionally expected roles for women. They will also resist the middle-class temptation to encourage her toward the careers which society has designated as the appropriate and successful ones. Positively, the church will hold up life programs which are part of God's activity in the world and which are worthy of Emma's ability and investment of energy. A career in the ministry fits this positive direction, and the church will help Emma to be sensitive to God's call to career ministry. But she will not be taught that she has

Emma as Adolescent—An Affirmed Believer

to become a minister to fulfill a life program. Other life programs align with God's work in the world and are compatible with her own gifts and person.

Fifth, Emma is establishing a sexual identity. Though she has been prepared by wise parents to explore and celebrate her body, she will experience some concern over what is happening to her body as puberty sets in. In terms of changes in life space, Emma's genital maturation is to her as a new region uncharted. Her body, once prone, then creeping, toddling, and finally walking, once awkward and then coordinated, now takes a new turn. This turn, to say the least, requires Emma to reintegrate her body into her total picture of herself. Urges only mildly incipient in childhood now intensify, putting increased strain on Emma's ego as she attempts to balance the inner drives with the prohibitions.

Even though Emma may adjust to these changes without inordinate upheaval and fear, she still is faced with finding a female identity. Actually, she is, in her drives and interests, both male and female, as society defines these. She will, however, likely be uncertain about feelings she has for other girls, and not yet ready to manage feelings about boys. Though possessing both male and female characteristics, her main task is to understand herself essentially as female. Once this is accomplished, she will be able to appreciate her bisexuality and relate healthily to both male and female. Without a firm sense of femaleness she will be confused about her sexuality and not be able to find that true intimacy necessary to productive relationships with others.[11]

Emma's sexuality is as natural a concern in her Christian upbringing as these other dynamics. Of all the dynamics, however, this one is the most sensitive in the minds of Emma's parents and teachers and certainly is the most precarious in her own mind. Neither society nor the church has always known what to do with adolescent sexuality, either theologically or practically. Some still hold that the sin in the garden was sexual intercourse, that the sin of the flesh is one's sexuality, and that to deny the flesh means to abstain from sexual activity.

Emma has not been taught that sexuality is tied theologically with the sins of the flesh, or that the sin of Adam and Eve was sexual intercourse. Therefore, her struggle for sexual identity will not be complicated by religious puritanism. Her religious rearing will, however, have an effect. She will utilize the religious values of personal dignity, self-esteem, the worth of others, and social considerations in finding the proper use of sexuality. Emma has been taught to appreciate her body, to explore it unashamedly, to affirm it naturally, and care for it religiously.[12] Although that body has just undergone profound and potentially puzzling changes, Emma will continue to be told the facts, honestly and unhesitatingly. Of course, she is now in a quasi-youth culture in which there is strong pressure to act sexually in real-life situations.[13] This means that her instruction must include guidance in values as well as facts of anatomy.

Emma's parents have also helped her with conflicts she has faced in relation to the sex roles her parents have demonstrated. She remembers that they combined roles, sharing equally in caring for her as she grew, making decisions together. She now perceives how they manifested mutual authority and respect. She has not suffered the identity confusion which characterizes some adolescents who have grown up in a family where traditional male and female roles have changed radically in the last two decades.

In this setting and with this kind of care, Emma will discover her femininity, its beauty and its purpose. Her faith will help her celebrate the former and manage the latter, but not without some degree of testing as she faces the pressures common to her age.[14]

Sixth, Emma is struggling with when to follow and when to resist authority. She knows that her social position is not that of an adult; yet in her cognitive competence she feels equal, if not superior, to adults. In her idealism she assumes the role of the critic, calling for standards which she herself cannot produce in terms of moral behavior. She really does not wish to live without any authority, but neither does she hold parental, official, or peer authority in complete awe. She is impatient with adults who are capricious in their use of authority. Also, she will be disturbed by the uses to which peers put their authority. The world of school is especially critical here because in it she is persistently reminded of her marginal position, while also being told by her teachers that she is an adult. At the same time her peers may give her a position in which she may choose their "authority" when she makes choices.

As a young adolescent, Emma is not creating her own authority, although at times her experimentation may make it seem so. She is still too conforming for that. When she selects peer standards in a given situation over school standards, it appears that she is shaping her own authority. When she favors a teacher's instruction over a parent's value, it appears that she is formulating her own mind. Actually, Emma is, in such situations, mostly choosing authorities which are external to herself. She is applying her critical powers to such situations but is still too much identified with the social setting to make her own way in complete autonomy. In later adolescence and young adulthood she will view these social settings more as systems within which to behave or to resist, but she does not yet possess defined principles by which to judge these systems. She judges them, to be sure, but not systematically from a set of principles.

Emma's education can complicate or enhance her position in reference to authority. Her nurturers will not appeal to authority without validating it in religious experience. For example, such teachings as the Ten Commandments will be utilized in terms of the principles of justice, respect, and order which they represent and of the effects those have in the lives of real people. Emma will not be told that she has to do something because some authority said she must. To the contrary, she will be taught to follow leaders because they deserve to be followed, not because of their position. While she will need help with such discrimination, it is a necessary part of her adolescent education. To approach Emma in this way does not mean that she will grow without any sense of having to submit to authority. Everyone is under some authority. It does mean that she will develop a healthy sense of authority.

The task is to provide Emma with a setting in which she can feel secure in her social position, yet exercise her competence and move toward the realization of her life plan. This calls for a society which is neither recklessly permissive nor suppressingly narrow. Then will Emma learn when to follow and when to exercise authority on her own.

Seventh, Emma holds to certain ideologies firmly while experimenting with substitutes for other ideologies. She may be fiercely loyal to her school, church, and country. On the other hand, she may experiment with religion by attending another church or entertain some specific disenchantment with her country. In a way she is like the deft debater who can assume with ease the pro or con of any argument and with power persuade the judges. She may even, in real life, experiment with some radical cause, especially in late adolescence when she is more exposed to competing philosophies and loyalties. Emma is nearing the time in her development when she will fix on a system which will prove to be a useful tool for taking her into and through adulthood.

Some of this ideology testing can be attributed to Emma's position in the middle zone between child and adult. Much of it, however, derives from her intellectual maturity. What she once accepted as true because it was told her as truth, she now can test and question. She now can compare ideologies in their particulars as well as in their overall thrusts and general effects. She sees through and can pinpoint with precision the weaknesses of family, school, church, and society. Though still attached emotionally to familiar belief systems, she applies her logic to them. When she does formulate a belief, she holds to it as if it were true because she herself holds it.

In this kind of activity, Emma is really engaging more in ratifying beliefs than in analyzing them from a well-developed world view. In this activity she is showing a marked advance over childhood when her values and beliefs were predominantly verbalisms. But it falls short of a later development when she will be able to disassociate herself more completely from the belief system in which she has been nurtured. So Emma, while critical of the ideological setting, does not yet move outside her conventional setting.

Emma's parents and teachers have already set the pace for challenge and free inquiry. Her nurturers have modeled a devotion to, yet a certain independence of, the prevailing ideology. In observing, she has gradually understood that ideologies differ because they are formulated by persons, not delivered mystically. They are established by power or consensus, regardless of appeals made to ancient authorities. Emma will, at her own level of understanding, participate in criticizing beliefs and systems. Eventually, she may even attempt to change them. If she has been told that the rule and ideologies are from the Spirit of God, then she will also have been taught that she has access to that same Spirit, thus may be equally guided to submit or resist, accept or reject.[15]

Teaching for Affirmation

The phrase "teaching for affirmation" includes both what is done prior to and after Emma has made the affirmation of faith. Our concern, then, is with Emma's education and nurture during the entire span of middle school or junior high school, senior high school, and post–high school or college. During this period Emma will examine her heritage critically and learn the meaning of estrangement and faith. She will therefore need a curriculum made up both of material and experience content. It follows that Emma's learning environments will be varied and open.

Heritage, Estrangement, and Faith

Charles Stewart noted that if the church-going adolescent simply belongs to the church as to any other social group, it may "block him from real grappling with the issues of his life and from experiencing the world as it actually exists."[16] By leading Emma through a review of her heritage of faith and an examination of estrangement and faith, we are putting her in touch emotionally and intellectually with a history which she has lived but to which she has not given much reflection. We hope thereby to avoid the aborting of her religious awakening.

In helping Emma appraise her heritage, Emma's minister will first remind her of the rites she has participated in as she has grown from infancy to adolescence. This remembering will be done at a time when the church is celebrating the infant rite of presentation and the childhood rite of belonging, so that Emma will have them fresh in her mind. To complement this actual participation in the context of worship, Emma's minister will give her copies of whatever statements or documents the church has prepared for these rites. The minister will involve Emma in reflection on and analysis of these texts.

As an example, consider this excerpt from a "covenant of presentation" prepared for presentation of the infant to the congregation and consecration to God. The minister asks, "What can we affirm about Emma?" The congregation replies, "That she is made in the image of God and is a child of God by creation." (See Appendix V, "The Celebrative Rites.") The minister can then ask Emma questions, such as "Do you remember when you first realized that you were made in the image of God? How has that realization unfolded in recent years?

Do you experience any particular feeling when you think of yourself as made in God's image? In what sense do you suppose you are made in God's image? Do you think that your life reflects the image of God? How so or how not? Do you recall the first time someone told you that you were a child of God? Was that confusing to you at the time? Do you like being told that you are a child of God? What about now? Do you think you live as a child of God should? How so or how not? Does anyone you know live like a child of God? What would the world be like if most people lived that way? What questions do you have about the 'image of God' and 'child of God'?"

The same kind of exercise would be done for the childhood rite of belonging. However, in this case Emma has the advantage of having been a conscious participant, and now as an adolescent she may remember how she felt either in her baptism or in participating in the Lord's Supper for the first time. The chances are good that Emma will remember the emotional content of such celebrations, perhaps even some of the persons who made overtures toward her at that time. Of course, she should know some of the words and phrases used in these services because she repeats them regularly as the worshiping congregation celebrates the birth and belongingness of other children coming along.

Both the infant and childhood rites will raise theological questions in Emma's mind and lead naturally into an exploration of the church's doctrine. Emma will be interested in the image of God, children of God, baptism, the Lord's Supper, the church, and the Trinity. The task for the minister is to keep the focus on the doctrines with which Emma herself is in touch. There is time and a place in the continuing curriculum for a more intense study of particular Christian doctrines.

Somewhere in this process of heritage review, Emma will face the incongruity between the ideal of being a daughter of God, made in God's image, of belonging to the congregation and being vital to it, and her actual experience of not feeling as if she reflects God's image, of not acting like a child of God, of not being very committed to the congregation which has given her belongingness. If the dynamic is not present, Emma's minister will have to avoid the temptation of forcing its emergence. Of course, there is also the danger that the minister will

Emma as Adolescent—An Affirmed Believer

not even attempt to explore these dynamics. As with other occasions of education, Emma's minister should suggest and probe, but not implant and manipulate. Where there is a trusting relationship between Emma and her minister, simple questions will reveal her depth of feeling and understanding. "Do you consider yourself as being in the image of God?" is as good a beginning question as any.

As Emma faces the paradox, she will be ready to look into the meaning of estrangement and faith. She will be confronted honestly with the puzzling nature of sin as both sin in the concrete and sinfulness as a generalized condition, and of faith as essentially action but also as life-style. Her minister will avoid confusing sin and sinfulness with mores and morals, and faith with being good and taking a middle-of-the-road position on every issue, or with knowing and agreeing to doctrinal statements. Once Emma is ready to face the real dynamics of sin and faith, she will be ready for understanding the mission of Jesus Christ. With the Nativity stories behind, as well as the childhood view of Jesus simply as a special person who did good and helped many people, Emma can begin to understand Jesus' role in the whole process of salvation, that is, as the centerpiece. Emma will come to see Jesus as the Christ, God's Son, Savior. As that formula suggests, the fish and the ichthus may be an appropriate symbol by which to initiate with her the meaning of the Christ. It holds the special mystery of humanity and divinity, of incarnation and transcendence.

We might ask by what mode Emma can be expected to respond to our questions and provide her own questions and insights. James Fowler holds that she will respond predominantly from a conventional mentality until she confronts contradictions in values and authorities, diverging opinions and perspectives on religion and faith, and other disruptive dynamics which lead to a transition toward a style of faith which may be termed individuative-reflective.[17] As to her responses to the meanings of symbols, Emma, once past the early formal stage, is able to find meanings in the symbols by which we incorporated her into the church. Later in her development she will be able to exchange symbols and meanings, to ascribe new meanings to old symbols.[18] This ability will help her better understand the variety of doctrines the church holds, for example, seeing that baptism may symbolize covenant for some Christians and repentance for others. For now, however, our primary concern is with aiding Emma in focusing on the meanings of Jesus, baptism, Supper, church, estrangement, and reconciliation, while heeding Fowler's warning that "the expectations and evaluations of others can be so compellingly internalized (and sacralized) that later autonomy of judgment and action can be jeopardized."[19]

Curriculum Content: Material and Experience

Emma will have a curriculum to take her from about grade five into early or through college. Such a curriculum will be built around realities consistent with Emma's increasingly sophisticated cognitive ability, emotional management, and symbolic functioning. As examples, Emma will move from a consideration of the simple facts of the life and ministry of Jesus to a grappling with the problems of comparative religions. She will advance from relating to Jesus as a special person in history to one who at the deepest emotional level centers her life. She will change from a recipient of the church's symbolic rites to one who can give her own meanings to church celebrations. By middle adolescence she will be capable of examining the full range of religious history, Christian doctrine, and Christian experience.

The content of this curriculum will include both material and experience content. There are times when Emma needs objective material as the focal point of the learning event. At other times, she needs to share what she is experiencing, a sharing which, when joined by the experiences of the group, becomes the focal point of the learning event. Take for example, the meaning of baptism and Lord's Supper. There are aspects of the meaning of these celebrations which Emma would not learn from a group sharing experience, for there are doctrinal and historical "givens" in baptism and the Supper which individual experience may not consider. One cannot experience how different modes of baptism came to be practiced. On the other hand, a study of these as doctrine cannot elicit their full meaning, for the given meaning needs the enrichment of the experienced meaning. The theology of the Supper as belonging and anticipation cannot, for example, express the dynamics of acceptance and hope. Out of this kind of dialogue both material and experience content will become more responsible and relevant.

Ronald Goldman found that adolescents bring four major intellectual problems to religious study: The problems of literalism and authoritarianism, of two worlds, of Old Testament teaching, of biblical relevance.[20] First, they hold on to literal and authoritarian teachings from childhood and the concrete stage of thinking, as in holding the Bible to be true because it is old. Second, they have conveniently separated the thought world into two parts: the one at church where it is taught that God created man and the one not at church, as for example, in science class and school where the teaching says humans evolved from lower forms. Third, they are confused about various teachings in the Bible, especially in relation to the Old Testament and, thus, need to be helped to find a unity in Scripture based on the full revelation in Jesus Christ. Fourth, they view much of the Bible as containing events of long ago which cannot happen today, such as the belief that God spoke from a bush to Moses but does not do that kind of thing today. A predominantly material content will aggravate these problems, whereas an experience content will form the basis for a realistic resolution of them.

The weight of the curriculum, therefore, is to be on experience content. Consequently, the teaching approach will begin with and emphasize Emma's experience throughout the learning event. If the doctrine of the church is the topic, the teacher will begin by asking Emma how she experiences church. From this base, and the contribution of others in the group, the teacher can help Emma develop a theology of the church. At some point in the unit, of course, material content, such as from Ephesians, will have to be introduced into the discussion, if the doctrine is to be complete. This dialectic between experience and material, beginning where possible with experience itself, will help Emma develop a more realistic belief system and make Bible and history more relevant to her.

Emma will meet the curriculum in different settings: the worship service, the church school, the family, the youth group, and the youth choir. She will make contact with some aspects of curriculum in school environments, particularly in para-church groups and in studies in history and humanities. Association with the ministers of the church is another essential setting where Emma and the curriculum will come together.

Worship: The Central Setting

The worship and fellowship of the congregation is the focal point of Emma's nurture, for here the congregation makes its life visible. Emma will be included as a full participant in this worship and fellowship. She may sing in the choir, read the Scripture, lead a prayer, usher persons to their pews, or carry and light candles. She might be invited to create worship materials, such as banners, hymn texts, and contemporary readings. But even if she does none of these, she will be in the congregation, singing, praying, reading, and listening. She will be taking in and appraising her heritage, strengthening her understandings of Jesus Christ, and making important decisions.

The worship of the church will include Emma during significant passages in her life. Baptism and first Communion are, of course, the pivotal celebrations, but there are other occasions meriting attention, such as entrance to middle or junior high school, obtaining of a driver's license, graduation from high school, and the like. Special recognitions and gifts are fitting, for they confirm the unfolding of life and create bonds of mutual support and trust. Some examples are a certificate for baptism, a cup for first Communion, a book on growing up for entrance to middle or junior high school, a subscription to a favorite magazine on getting one's driver's license, a book on faith at high school graduation.

Emma will not be isolated in a youth worship service supposedly structured around the idiom of her generation. Nothing is as detrimental and counterproductive, for it legitimizes a subculture mentality which will in the end retard Emma's movement through adolescence into adulthood.

Wherever the church is worshiping, Emma will be present and participating. Anything else cuts her off from the richness of that heritage and takes from her the raw material by which to assess whatever heritage she might possess. It takes her out of the fellowship of the congregation that has watched her grow, thereby depriving the adults of a sense of accomplishment and satisfaction and signifying to her that she canno

Emma as Adolescent—An Affirmed Believer

any longer receive from these adults. It implies that Jesus would have to wear designer jeans in order to speak to her contemporary situation, an implication which, to be sure, may have its counterpart in adult worship but which, in any case, distorts gospel and church.

In one church, while the congregation celebrated the Lord's Supper, the youths were in another part of the church in their own service. In another church, on the day of their baptism and first Communion, four youths passed the bread and cup to the congregation for the celebration of the Supper. They "learned" what books, sermons, and youth services could never teach.

But will Emma want to be in worship? There is, of course, no way to assure that she will. The pressures and pulls of other ideologies and communities are strong. But that she desire to be present in worship clearly is our hope and goal. If we have been faithful in our task and if Emma has been participating all along, there is reason to believe that she will continue. If our nurture has been faithful to her development and needs and has taken seriously her adolescent passages, there is good reason to believe that she will want to remain a part of it all.

The task, however, is broader than including Emma in worship. The worshiping church must model for Emma what affirmed faith looks like. Then, and only then, can the church truly call her to heritage and declaration. If the church tells her that Jesus is Lord, but she sees in the life lived by the church that power and influence rule, the teaching will be for naught. If the church tells her that they are the people of God in the world, but she sees them as people of the world in the church, the teaching will be anemic. If the church tells her that all are God's children, but she sees that some are treated more like sons and daughters than others, she will perceive the modeled message. With the church modeling genuine faith, it can call Emma to personal responsibility for declaring herself in relation to her heritage and to Jesus Christ.

The Church School: Structure and Comprehensiveness

In the structured settings of the church school, Emma needs a curriculum which will be organized around the major life concerns and faith experiences of the span of years from about ten to twenty. A mere listing of Emma's passages and developmental journey in those years will demonstrate the viability of such a curriculum. Once these concerns and experiences are identified and plotted over the entire span, the curriculum makers will formulate appropriate learning events and then find appropriate supporting or study materials.

Here are some examples. One, if the conflict between science and religion is plotted at ninth grade, then the learning event would be something like "a study of the creation accounts in light of scientific findings and contemporary attitudes and opinions." Such a study might proceed from the experience of the learners to a study of the creation texts and even expand into a study of the nature of the Bible. Or, the study might begin with material content and then be applied to current problems. Two, take the matter of one's declaration of faith. If this is plotted at about fifteen or sixteen years, then the learning event would be "an exploration of the heritage of faith and of the meaning of sin and faith." Three, take the pluralism of religious beliefs. If plotted at grade twelve or early college, this learning event would be "a study of world religions, their origins and truth claims." Or this study could be turned into a witnessing event, defined as "understanding and witnessing to persons of other religions."

This is difficult work, but it can be done. One church used the now aging Cooperative Curriculum Project areas and themes.[21] It spread them out over the youth years, then found from diverse sources the materials needed for group discussion. In some cases, persons in that congregation created the discussion materials. Some examples from this curriculum work are as follows: The curriculum area "Life and its setting: The meaning and experience of existence" with the theme "Man's relation to the natural order" was plotted as the first study of the fall session of the church school. Because this is material content, a book, *My Place in God's Creation,* was utilized. The curriculum area "Vocation: The meaning and experience of discipleship" with the theme "Discipline in the Christian life" was scheduled for a pre-Easter study. This theme could be either material or experience content, but it lent itself more to experience; therefore, no book was selected for this unit. The leaders employed group building and sharing techniques to involve the youth in talking about their faith and in exploring meditation, prayer, and Bible reading.

There is a need for curriculum which can be used in crisis situations which cannot be anticipated. As a youth group gathered one Sunday morning, it learned of the death of one of its members the night before. The youths and their teachers were equally stunned. Some of the teachers were able to help the youth group deal with the initial shock and confusion. With foresight on the part of leaders, and training on the part of teachers, all the teachers can be prepared to shape curriculum out of an immediate crisis. Such a curriculum can be built on drug raids, natural disasters, international crises, and the like.

In most cases, however, the curriculum is formulated and packaged at a publishing house, and the church simply buys into the system, taking what is in the books without regard for an intentional educational experience over the span of the youth years. Even then we can take this given curriculum and improve it by augmenting sections which publishing houses make skimpy or in which they are reluctant to deal with critical issues. We can delete units which are irrelevant to the age group or which reinforce unhealthy, superficial religion. This adding to and taking away can itself become instructive as the learners see the material in the book and hear us offering a different interpretation or deleting the material altogether. This makes for dialogue.

One church found that the denominational materials included units on the declaration of faith too early in the developmental process. That church substituted other material for that one unit. In another instance the church was using a book from another denominational publisher which contained a section on the sacraments, a term not in the vocabulary of that church. The teachers made advantage of the discrepancy by dealing with sacrament and ordinance.

Some religious education writers, teachers, and ministers, in looking at the church school, especially for youth, wonder if it is worth the effort. As long as youth continue to attend and we know that we are dealing responsibly with life needs, the answer is yes. The church school complements and stimulates what goes on in worship, in the family, and other settings where life and faith are discussed.

The Family: Natural and Intergenerational

In the home we have raw experiences from which to build curriculum. Emma will come home from school one day and tell about someone who copied a paper and made an A when she worked all weekend on her paper and made a B. She will come in late some night soon after she has learned to drive and will show signs of stress from being placed in new settings where her moral standards were challenged. Here, curriculum is being made on the spot and no fabrication is required.

Because of their pervasive influence, the mass media amount to an environment all their own. However, it is in the setting of the family where Emma comes under the media mystique. The printed media are replete with news accounts and commentary which reveal values and attitudes and show existence in its full humanness, both the positive and the negative, the noble and the demonic. Television, however, holds the greater potential for power over Emma and for family dialogue. She and her family will view programs peddling life-styles which are radically different from the ones modeled by Emma's parents.

Television, however, also has a quite positive contribution to make to family religious education. Apart from its inability to model any healthy religious family life, television offers Emma and her family informative and artistic programming. History's tragedies, such as the Holocaust, become existential in the configuration on the monitor. Its absurdities, such as slavery, are arrestingly real in serial documentaries. History-changing events, such as the development of the atomic bomb, are professionally reviewed. These raise ultimate, moral questions. This is not to suggest that Emma will want to discuss at length every such program. But she will ask questions as the script unfolds, and so will her parents.

The family setting has the advantage of being intergenerational. In such situations the perspectives are sometimes shockingly disparate. Suppose that at a mealtime Emma should propose that the family install a swimming pool in the backyard. She doubtlessly has in mind a whole set of images: friends dropping in, poolside parties, and, of course, private sunning. Her little brother sees himself and his close friend having fun there, with no one else around, including Emma and her friends. Mother and Father may have different images from each other,

Emma as Adolescent—An Affirmed Believer

but it is certain that one of them will see dirty water that has to be cleaned often, repair bills, refreshment tabs, and wet carpets, along with, one hopes, some images similar to those of the children. And what if there is a grandparent present? Well, Emma's suggestion could ignite a rigorous discussion of values, rights, relationships, and regulations, a discussion which would include perspectives from several generations.[22]

The Youth Group: Groupness and Mission

Emma will be an active part of the youth group, a phenomenon without which her youth experience in the church will be lacking. She will look to this group for social-emotional support and for an outlet for her study of and commitment to mission.

Emma's youth group will give social-emotional support which will minister to her, and as a participant she will be ministering similarly to others. This kind of mutuality will bind the group to one another and hold together the other aspects of youth ministry. A healthy group will provide Emma with a laboratory for testing relationships, for sharing feelings and developing trust, for raising questions which she might not ask in the church school or even in the family. Here she also will find stimulation and motivation for being faithful in worship, the church school, and other activities of the congregation.

Because it is essential and is based so intensely in social relations, the youth group holds the potential of becoming so subculture-oriented that it interferes with the church's broader goals for its youth. In its weakness, it is like the youth group which the entire community talked about because of its annual trips to all parts of the country. These trips became the focal point of the program and most of the group's energy and the youth budget were spent on them. One had the uneasy feeling that should the annual trips be canceled, the youth ministry would collapse.

In church school, Emma will study about missions; in worship, she will hear the mission call; in the wider life of the congregation, she will see the mission task. In the youth group she will become a missionary herself. The youth group not only is a laboratory for social relations, but it also is a natural group for doing missions. The unique power of involvement in mission action will draw Emma away from herself, yet cause her to ponder her own life and faith. If Emma's youth group takes food to a needy family, she will feel deep empathy for the receiving family while at the same time wonder how she would feel if she were in a deprived condition. Perhaps she will even begin to ask questions about faith and poverty. A youth group thus involved will be less turned on itself and at the same time be more secure in its existence.

Youth group mission action projects may range from the simple to the complex. It takes very little planning or training to field a youth team to rake leaves or provide other yard and house services for the elderly or the ill. On the other hand, consider the youth group which organized a hot line for talking with troubled young people. The participants had to be trained in telephone technique, in listening, in reassuring, and in knowing how to refer people to professional help.

The Youth Choir: Music and Integration

The youth choir serves a multipurpose in Emma's nurture. Its foremost function is to expose her to the church's musical heritage, but she will also learn much about voice, reading, music theory, and choral singing. The choir leader will select the literature for Emma's choir with the same goal of comprehensiveness as curriculum planners do for the church school. Emma's voice development, what she is capable and not capable of, what will enhance and not injure her voice, will be a major consideration. For example, Handel's *Messiah* is unsurpassed in the church's heritage, but the voice of the young adolescent is not adequate for performing it.[23] This developmental consideration will not, however, justify the use of inferior music.

Because of the theological nature of the church's hymnody, Emma will, in choral activity, integrate many of the themes and doctrines which she studies in other curriculum settings. In this instance music fulfills its role as a holistic, poetic art form. A look at the hymns of the church will validate the unique contribution which music makes to Emma's theological formation. Along this line, the youth musical can be turned into an effective tool in teaching sound theology and in reenacting the epochs of religious history. As the performance of musicals is under preparation, a teacher should be a part of the choral team for the purpose of giving background and clarification to the text.

Emma as Adolescent—An Affirmed Believer

The youth choir fulfills a social role for youth and may be used as a mission action tool. Some churches utilize their youth choirs to sing in shopping malls, retirement homes, and the like, a mission-witness involvement which will appeal to some youth who otherwise would not be attracted to more direct ministries.[24] This kind of activity builds the fellowship of the youth group.

Southern Baptists have inaugurated a Sunday evening program for youth which joins fellowship, music, and study. The youth meet for choir, a supper, and then hold discussions around the overall topic of discipleship. This kind of activity has the potential for becoming the energizer of the youth group, leading to more meaningful participation by the youth in worship and the church school. It may also stimulate religious dialogue in the family, the youth group at large, and the school.[25]

Other Settings: Diversity and Dissonance

Emma will find herself discussing religious questions in settings other than church and family. Being an active member of her church, she might be attracted to a religious group at school. Because these groups generally emanate from religious centers outside the denominations, Emma will find herself in touch with divergent theologies and subjected to additional appeals for her time commitment. The hope is that Emma will put this activity in perspective and not allow it to become "church" for her. If it should become a substitute for the wider religious character of her congregation, the chances are that she might be thwarted in her movement toward adult religion and participation.

Emma will confront difficult questions in some of the school curriculum offerings. Here is the legitimate place for "religion" in the public schools. Take history, for example: How does one study colonial history without studying religious history? How does one examine religious history without raising theological questions? How does one raise theological questions without centering on one's own faith? A competent teacher can manage such a situation without violating constitutional safeguards or denominational forms of religion. At a deeper level, all history and literature should stir religious dialogue, but the public school is not to be expected to encourage such stirrings.

At an awards program at the end of a school year, a physics teacher, in presenting the science awards, said, "Regardless of what you hear about who is most important to the future of this country, it is the scientist who is the hope for our country." Emma and her parents should be able to turn that conjecture into fruitful religious conversation. At that same event, there was conspicuously more applause for the monetary awards carrying the greater money value. Such spontaneous response holds deep implications for valuing, a fit subject for Emma and her nurturers.

Emma's Ministers: Continuity and Guidance

While not a curriculum setting in the strict sense, Emma's contact with the ministers in her church is a vital ingredient in her religious development. Emma sees them as the baptizers and the celebrants of the Lord's Supper. She sees them as worship leaders, preachers, and congregational leaders. She sees them acknowledge and celebrate passages in the life of the congregation. All of this gives Emma a sense of continuity in her religious journey.

In addition, ministers offer counsel during times of heritage appraisal and are available for support during critical times in young people's lives. They are teachers as well. With all these roles in Emma's clear view, the ministers will frequent the youth activities. They will know Emma's family and call her by name.

Emma's Adolescent Friends

Elizabeth, at sixteen, affirmed the vows given in her behalf when she was baptized as an infant. This affirmation came at the end of a confirmation class in which she was instructed in the faith of her congregation. She was told the meaning of her baptism and studied the actual words used in that baptism. She was reminded of her first Communion and why she was allowed to participate. Doctrines which she received only in story form as a child, she now has studied in a more formal way. She examined more seriously than ever before the meaning of sin and faith. She was told that only she could confess her faith in Jesus Christ and become a more loyal participant in the life of the congregation.

By an appropriate rite, Elizabeth, on her own, made personal vows of faith in Jesus Christ. The congregation made additional pledges and celebrated Elizabeth's public confession.

Robert, at sixteen, has also made a public confession of his faith in Jesus Christ. He did this on a Sunday morning, coming forward to greet the minister during the invitational hymn following the sermon. Robert and the minister had already talked about this decision, but the minister, before the congregation, asked Robert about his experience. In answering, Robert told the congregation that he was confessing his sin and professing faith in Jesus. The congregation approved of Robert's decision and received him for baptism.

At a later service, Robert was baptized, symbolizing death to sin and rising to a new life. Baptism also made him a full member of the church which, among other things, means that he now participates in the Lord's Supper with the congregation. He also attended a new members' class after his baptism. Robert is, for the first time, called a Christian. He will remember this time as his conversion, his salvation experience, before which he was lost, but after which he was saved.

Samuel still visits Sunday church school and sometimes goes on youth trips with Robert. He attended Robert's baptism. Robert's minister has talked to Samuel about making his profession and being saved. But Samuel seems both uninterested and uncertain about it all. He and Emma sometimes talk in a casual way at school. Emma and Elizabeth also attended Robert's baptism, and once, after that, Samuel, who had seen Emma at the baptism, asked her if she understood what was going on. Emma told Samuel that she did understand because many of the same things were said at her public confession. Samuel did not respond and neither he nor Emma pursued the matter. Samuel is sixteen; some have tried to persuade him to become a Christian. Still no one has told or shown him that he is a child of God.

Transition

Emma is an affirmed believer. In that affirmation she has made more complete the words uttered when she was presented to the congregation as an infant and has received more deeply the belonging conferred on her when she was a child. She has now understood the paradox of her being a daughter of God, belonging to the community of faith, but not fully in touch with God and others. She has come to understand her estrangement from something essential about herself. With that understanding, she has received the gift of healing which Jesus Christ provides. The congregation has heard her confession and celebrated her experience. What existed only as promise is now a reality. She has much growing and learning to do, much to learn about complete commitment, much to learn about life and genuine doubt. With this self-chosen reality Emma has a vital faith to take her into the greater responsibilities which await her in adulthood. She moves toward such duty as an affirmed believer.

5

Emma as Adult—
A Creative Trustee

Emma's faith has come to full flower, and its beauty is that it conforms more perfectly to the image of God in which she is made. Emma commits herself to being a creative trustee for a creating God who is finishing creation. It is a voluntary act of will that moves Emma closer to the singularity of the image of God. It is a radical act, moving her closer to the centeredness and devotion which would characterize all existence were it truly faithful to the image of a creating God. Through her years in the church, Emma has faced the propensities toward estrangement from her Maker. She listened to the call to stewardship and has caught a vision of what God is doing in this world. She now sees her faith as meaning that she also has a stake in such work and comes to join God in that activity.

Emma takes on for herself the assignment to her forebears to have dominion over the earth and all living things. She does not assume that to have dominion means that she is to trample creation under foot or to lord it over animal and earth. She understands that creation had God's blessing and was pronounced as being good; that God gave humankind the collective responsibility for taking care of it. God meant for Adam to be the caretaker, the steward. Further, Emma puts this vocation in the context of covenant and law, of new covenant and new commandment in Jesus Christ, and of servant and priest in the early church. Emma accepts her creative trusteeship, and the church lays hands on her.[1]

The commitment to creative trusteeship builds on Emma's early nurture. She is a daughter of God by a gift of God. She belongs to the community of faith by conferment of the congregation. She is an affirmed believer by her own confirmation of heritage and declaration of faith. As an adult, she has laid aside the toys of childhood play, negotiated adolescence, and put the school years behind her. Now she completes that process, not automatically, as by the power of decisions which are predetermined and irrevocable, but by free, delightful choice. Emma's life has not been one smooth course unencumbered by the exigencies common to all human experience. She has met life head-on, though she has not always been entirely self-conscious of the conflicts and resolutions, and has emerged with a Christian self intact and stronger.

Emma has, of course, already been involved in some measure as a steward. It is not as if she affirmed faith in adolescence then waited to become an adult before she participated in God's mission in the world. No, she has in varying degrees had some share in that mission from her childhood days. But now, in middle adulthood, she is overtaken by a heightened awareness of her daughtership, a renewed appreciation of her belongingness, and a new perspective on her affirmation of faith. She is more capable mentally to think about the meaning of being in God's image. The belonging which she once only felt, she now can articulate. In reflection she can feel even that belonging more intensely. The affirmation of faith which was real when made is now viewed in more independent terms and seen more clearly for the self-chosen act which it was and is.

This renewal, this commitment to trusteeship, may have come from one or more of several religious experiences which are the fruits of normal adult experience. It may have come from marriage, the birth of the first child, the entering of a new career, the meeting of a new and engaging person or idea, the death of someone close. The renewal may have more mystical origins, as in contemplation of existence and self or in a transcending worship experience. Involved at some significant point in this experience is Emma's continuing worship of God in the community of faith to which she belongs. She has held the bread of the Lord's Supper in her hand and pondered the depth of God's concern for the world, and, in eating, she has felt God's energy. She has drunk from the cup of the new covenant and known God's blessing.

There are seven marks of the creative trustee.

Life Stance—The basic mark of Emma's trusteeship is that she is aware of being a redeemed daughter of God through Jesus Christ and a trustee for God in the completion of creation.

Origin—Emma, as a creative trustee, lives out of the humility that there is gift and mystery in existence in the image of God which she cannot measure or explain.

Mission—Emma understands that the creative trustee is on mission in the world, through the church which is the Body of Christ in that world.

Growth—Emma is actively learning, fulfilling her potential as a person, just as God works in an expanding universe and an unfolding social order.

Working Theology—Emma knows that a creative trustee is to be a theological thinker, putting in perspective the realities of life and the givens of faith.

Ethics—Emma applies her working theology to the formulation of ethical principles and working hypotheses which she takes into situations where she must make ethical decisions.

Style—Emma's creative trusteeship shows a style of living which is rooted in piety and at the same time is playful, balancing life's seriousness and the weighty reality of the devotional with the lighter delights of play.

The Nurturing and Mission Task in the Adult Years

Emma is a middle adult. Whereas in childhood and adolescence she had loving nurturers around her, as an adult she has become a nurturer and missionary. Of course, this does not mean that she herself is no longer in need of education and care. That would indicate that as an adult she is static, when, in fact, the word "adult" itself is from the same Latin root for adolescence, which is to say that the adult is also growing. Thus, Emma is both giver and beneficiary of nurture. This makes the task of adult education that of providing a continuing context in which Emma can flower as a Christian and establish a framework in which she can live out her creative trusteeship.

Generativity and the Adult Crises

As a middle adult, Emma is far removed from the uncertain social position of the adolescent. The social status she longed for earlier is hers. She is an adult in an adult world of adults, youths, and children. It is a new position for her, and it alters how she sees herself and relates to others. Her new place in the order of things is characterized by Erikson and called "generativity." Some have called these middle years the settling-down period, the deadline decade, the productive years. Erikson's term, "generativity," is superior in its wisdom.

To understand Emma as a generative person, we need to go back momentarily to the identity crisis of adolescence and the intimacy crisis of young adulthood. The adolescent period was unique in Emma's life because in it she drew from the positive residue left over from the earlier stages of development. The trust, autonomy, initiative, and industry gained from infancy and childhood enhanced Emma's identity formation. These contributed to her maturation in regard to time perspective, self-certainty, experimentation with roles, and vocational direction.

At the same time, her identity quest anticipated certain incipient dynamics which mature in adulthood. Specifically, her activity in moving toward a healthy sexual identity makes it possible for her to establish intimate relationships as a young adult. Her youthful, realistic dealings with authority aid her in resolving the generativity crisis. Her fledgling commitment to and testing of ideologies will contribute to her personality profile in old age.

The young adult intimacy crisis challenges Emma to maintain close relationships with others. Of course, she has been close to others before, but now such relationship is between two persons who, with their identities intact, are able to provide complete mutual satisfaction for each other. But this intimacy may also be toward institutions and causes. While she is not ready to form a lifelong relationship with these, she is developing toward a thorough involvement. Contracts and covenants mean more to her now than they ever could have in the experimental days of youth. If Emma fails to manage this crisis, she will fall away into tragic isolation from others, from causes, from institutions. Such a failure would leave her alone and without direction. This is the work laid out for Emma, the young adult.

With intimacy established, Emma moves into the middle adult years to work on generativity. The first focus of this stage is in the bearing and rearing of one's own children. It means that Emma has genital power and mutuality with a partner and that she and her partner give themselves to the rearing of the next generation. However, the meaning is much broader than that, for it extends to her ability to take her place in the scheme of history where generation follows generation. Just as the adult generation of her days of youth brought her to adulthood, so does she feel responsible for the coming generation. It is now her time to support the institutions, uphold the civil power, and maintain the continuity of history.

Generativity is bound up in how Emma views the movement of history and the dynamics of change. It depends on her cognitive style and ethical sensibility. It depends on her commitment to growth and her living style. It depends on a total social system which permits Emma to apply on the adult level the autonomy and initiative gained in childhood. It depends on a milieu that permits Emma a significant place in the adult work world where she can find achievement not unlike the competence she learned in middle childhood. Oppressive systems, because they limit possibilities and destroy hope, do not provide a vital sense of generativity. In closed social systems she would be able to provide continuity for the next generation, because in such systems the alternatives are fewer and less threatening. But she would not be able to realize her potential in the fullest sense.

In either case, Emma might experience stagnation instead of generativity. Under the rigid system she would have little choice and little hope. Under the dynamic system she could choose to turn her intimacy on herself, spend her ability on self-pursuits, and ignore her responsibility to others. Eventually, she would waste away, as would the institutions which waited for her care. And the coming generation would be impoverished.[2]

Eventually Emma will leave these adult ambitions behind just as she once put away the fantasies of childhood. She will enter the years of wisdom, reflecting on the years past and quietly accepting the passing of former abilities and conquests. It will be a transitional period from active pursuit to satisfactory retirement. Emma will not view it as a time of dying but as one of making serious preparation for the irrepressible waning of her physical energy and the irresistible day of death. In this crisis Emma faces the possibility of cynicism and despair. But here in middle adulthood, those years are of only passing concern to Emma.

What about Emma's intellectual level as a middle adult? Emma attained in adolescence the upper stage of reasoning described by Piaget. Although some researchers believe to have found a higher stage, more than likely what they have discovered is that some adults, with increased experience and opportunity, have more fully developed these formal reasoning powers. This would seem to be the case inasmuch as others have found many adults unable to perform consistently at the formal reasoning stage.[3] As a middle adult, Emma is bearing the fruit of years of mental stimulation. She has been encouraged to apply her full thinking power to every problem. In doing that, she has not moved to a new stage, for there probably is not one. Rather, she has simply progressed through levels of formal reasoning begun in the transition from child to youth.

We should remember that in adolescence Emma thought that her newly found intellectual conclusions were right because she had conceived them. It was called egocentrism or, by some, the ability to compartmentalize insights so that one does not see conflicts in or between them. But this eventually changed to a viewpoint from which Emma saw the conflicts involved in divergent opinions and values. At first, she felt that she had an either-or choice before her, but that gave way to an ability to perceive that there is truth in both positions. In coming to this point, Emma dialogues with both opinions or, if the case be, values. Eventually she will arrive at a new sense of equilibrium as she utilizes what she perceives as valid in differing ideas, opinions, and values.[4]

Generativity, Estrangement, and Trusteeship

Emma is, in psychology's terms, a generative adult. In theology's terms she is a creative trustee. Psychology views her as in the time of life when she will either take the torch from the older generation and run with it for the sake of the next generation or drop out of the race. Theology views her as ready to see the complete meaning of being in the image of God, that is, as a daughter of God called to be a steward in God's world. While the two are complementary, that Emma is a generative adult does not mean that she must or will be a creative trustee. However, she cannot become a trustee in the complete sense until she faces the dynamics of being a generative adult. In seeing Emma resist stagnation and become a generative adult, fulfilling the purpose for which she was made, God will repeat that pristine declaration, "It is good. It is very good."

Though a creative trustee, Emma still participates individually in an order estranged from its Maker and Keeper. She still lives with measures of unbelief, hubris, and concupiscence. Yet she is overcoming these, for she cannot be a creative trustee and be bound by these particular manifestations of sin. Just as her development as a generative adult depends on successful progress with identity and intimacy, so does her progress as a creative trustee depend on her liberation from the sin that imprisons the image of God. Emma is learning that bondage to sin and effectual stewardship for God cannot coexist, that she cannot serve two masters. In this, she is experiencing the healing of the remnants of division within herself and between her and God which the years of nurture could not completely heal. She is experiencing new being to an intensified degree. She is accepting the wonder that God accepts her in spite of her war with her essential self and estrangement from essential purpose. (See Appendix VII, "Tillich's Doctrine of Estrangement and Salvation.")

We have already noted briefly the marks of the creative trustee. Let us take another view in order to see more fully what Emma as trustee looks like. In working with the first three marks—stance, origin, and mission—Emma is coming to terms with the full meaning of unbelief, hubris, and concupiscence. Some dimensions of these marks are evident in early middle adulthood, whereas others are developed over the long span of middle adulthood.[5]

The Creative Trustee and Life Stance

The basic mark of Emma's stewardship is that she is aware of being a redeemed daughter of God through Jesus Christ and a trustee for God in the completion of the divine plan. In the years since Emma declared faith in Jesus Christ, she has furthered her understanding of his person and work. She first heard of him as the baby in a Bethlehem stall, and she held to vague notions about him as an adult who was killed but who came back to life. Later, her perception of Jesus was sufficient enough that she was able to declare faith in who he was and in what he did and does. Now she more clearly relates the Jesus of Nazareth with the Jesus of Emmaus, seeing him in his full humanity and as resurrected Lord. She experiences him as a man out of time; but because he came in the fullness of God's time, she experiences him as a man for all time. He becomes to her "the inspiring and disturbing presence"[6] who gives meaning to her everyday experience and at the same time calls her to the new and the demanding. Emma takes Jesus Christ as her model.

This stance is not individualistic. Emma as a unique individual is a person in relation to others. It is not provincial. Her place in creation is part of all places. Emma assumes Buber's I-Thou stance toward persons and reality, seeing them in their sacredness. She works toward redeeming relationships and meaningful group experience. She offers her gifts to the oncoming generation. The legacy she has received, she now passes along. In this stance Emma is truly ecumenical, for she views self, others, and reality in a universal perspective where all is God's and all are God's children. She is joining God in response to her given daughtership, knowing that she cannot earn it. She is responding to what has already been freely given and what is now more fully celebrated.

In assuming this stance toward life, Emma is taking a significant step in overcoming the sin of unbelief. Her life would be off center were it cut off from this perspective—she would not be truly related to the Christ or serious about her place in God's order. In understanding the depth of the meaning of Jesus Christ and the import of God's call to her to be a creative trustee, Emma is reestablishing a cognitive connection which was damaged in the Fall. She is strengthening her resistance to that unbelief which could cripple her effectiveness, a resistance begun long ago but now renegotiated in adulthood.

The Creative Trustee and Origin

Emma, as creative trustee, lives out of the humility that there is gift and mystery in existence which cannot be fully measured by her explanations. She knows that both the gift and the mystery are wrapped up in her being in the image of God and that this existence cannot be fathomed in all of its dimensions. As Moses before the bush, she hears what she cannot see or comprehend. In the light of this experience she takes off her shoes and learns how to listen. She senses that her life has a quality and a purpose which transcend the raw materials which she can see and touch, and she is reverenced by it. Unable to rationalize, she feels and contemplates and lives within the paradox.

Because Emma understands her origin, she knows her destiny. She accepts the fact that death is inevitable, but her perspective is that while life is moving toward death, life calls to life. Out of this kind of perspective, she is free to respond both to life's tragedies and its joys. She is no artificial flower unable to open to the sun's warmth or indifferent to nature's storms. No, she is a real person who suffers with suffering and dances with joy. With such a perspective she is overcoming the sin of hubris, knowing that she is no phoenix able to rise from the ashes by her own will and energy. She knows that she can do nothing to stay the onslaughts of the tragic and the absurd, that she is not in control. She breaks with Adam and Eve who sought to be more than their Creator intended and in the doing became less than they were meant to be. She admits that unlike Elohim, she cannot bring something out of nothing.

The Creative Trustee and Mission

Emma understands that creative trusteeship is done in the context of the world, God's order, but that the church is the Body of Christ in the world. Further, she understands that the Body of Christ is more than metaphor—she, in fact, is a part of that reality. She knows that she is to give herself to the work of the church as it is faithful in the world. In this, she is not the stoic Marxist worker who is merely the vassal of the party. Rather, Emma is the autonomous, committed disciple who in joining in the cause is at the same time fulfilling her own personal destiny. Her own full humanity is bound up in the church's own full being.

Here is Emma's battle with concupiscence. The sin is to relate to the world primarily in terms of one's own desires and pleasures, to view all reality from a selfish point of view. Deliverance from this sin is found in turning one's view outward. Emma does this; she sees that being a trustee for God puts her legitimate self-interest in the proper context. Just as in her individual sinning she contributes to the collective sin of the human race, so in her personal commitment to mission she participates in the salvation of what God has made.

Emma sees the natural order as God's domain. She knows that God provides the seed but that she must plant, cultivate, and harvest. Life's basic energy is given, but she has to work to harness, preserve, and use that energy wisely. The beauty of the earth is evident, but she can mar or enhance it by human neglect or care. Emma joins the dilemma over the wise use of resources and the preservation of the environment.

Emma wants to work with God in the social order. She sees in every liberation movement God's own spirit of freedom and in every status quo movement something of God's own propensity for order. As they come from God, the two are never in contradiction, though in their manifestation in the human drama they often appear as opposing forces. Emma joins the ambiguity, attempting to discover where the energies of God are flowing and then collaborating with the movement.

In this sense of mission, Emma redeems the dignity of work. She is able to understand that God's command for her to have dominion over and replenish the earth establishes work as integral to her purpose in being in the world. In the image of God, she is to see work as a necessary and joyful component of God's grand design. She was not made for the pursuit of endless pleasure. And work is not a curse pronounced because of the misuse of pleasure. No, it is inseparably a part of Emma's status as a daughter of God. As a trustee who understands her mission, she restores work to this rightful place in the design.

Emma now sees through the distortion of unbridled technology. She believes a part of her mission is to show that to subdue the earth does not mean to conquer and destroy it. While she would not attempt to limit the reaches of human ingenuity, she knows that the far reaches of technology have to be balanced by equally far reaches of inner strength. She joins the fight to raise moral courage above technological necessity.

Emma wants to witness of her faith to individuals who have not grown up in faith as she has. She is grateful for the fullness of humanity which she knows because she has faced the meaning of her existence and found it complete in being within the will of God. She does not boast of it as a possession which she created or earned; neither does she pride herself as more worthy than those who do not have what she has. Rather, she embodies in her life what it means to be a creative trustee for a creating God, and she tells others about her joy and duty. Further, she invites them, in God's behalf, to respond to the same Good News of salvation and purpose.

The Creative Trustee and Growth

Emma is actively learning. She is not passive to ideas or to happenings. She believes with the apostle Paul that she has not arrived at complete maturity but must "press toward the mark." This pilgrimage involves Emma in the gaining of new information and the formation and expansion of concepts. She acquires new skills and assumes changed behaviors. She alters her values and attitudes. In each of these dimensions of learning she has some stability, but she remains open to new experience and insight. She reads, listens, and dialogues with others. Her model is the creating God for whom she is a steward. God calls her to fulfill her potential as a person. It is a part of her being in God's likeness. Her inspiration is the unfolding universe out before her, the social order around her, and the creative people with whom she lives. All of these invalidate the staid and the static and call Emma to openness and growth.

The Creative Trustee and a Working Theology

Emma knows that a creative trustee is to be a theological thinker, though not a dogmatic or systematic theologian. She takes seriously and critically analyzes tradition, Scripture, and church history. She understands the stories, symbols, rituals, and meanings of the church in which she has been nurtured. She also is aware of the larger ecumenical context. Her contemporary experiences with children, career, and relationships are thought about and acted upon from a religious perspective. She is actively trying to make sense of the givens of faith and the raw materials of life.

Emma is a nondogmatic person, for it is not fixed statements of doctrine which she is forming and applying. She sees herself as living out of a dynamic theology rather than subscribing to a static system of doctrine. This does not put her on equal terms with the theologians who work out coherent systems; their work has a dimension for which she has no training. She has inherited a system as part of growing up in the church. Because she feels it is her responsibility to preserve the past, she will not abandon these doctrines capriciously. But she is not satisfied that these express fully what is real about God and persons and life. She knows reality to be more elusive than that. Hers then is the critical work where her life and her problems intersect. She must be the theological thinker, judging the past, examining the present, and projecting into the future on the basis of working theological terms. This is the functional aspect of Emma's overcoming the unbelief that cuts her off from the true life stance expected of a creative trustee.

The Creative Trustee and Ethics

Emma applies her working theology to the ethical decisions she has to make. As she has a dynamic rather than a static theology, so does she make ethical choices from an energetic stance. She does not go into such situations unarmed, waiting to see what the situation itself is like. After all, the situation also is dynamic and is, in fact, determined by the forces that produced it and by the persons who are involved with it. Any of the social issues on the current scene illustrate the point. If she did indeed enter such situations entirely unprepared without a sense of right or wrong, she would be devoured. Further, with such naivete, she would not be able to bear any witness for God in the resolution of any crisis. She would be drowned by persons with divergent aspirations and questionable methods for solving problems.

Emma takes hard-won ethical principles and working hypotheses into ethical problems. She then assesses as objectively as possible the dimensions and consequences of the problem. She weighs the validity of the dimensions and the import of the consequences. She puts her judgments alongside her ethical principles. In the dialogue, she may alter the application of a principle because it conflicts with a newly perceived higher one. Or she may have to be unyielding. In either case her ethics are enriched, for they have been tested in the real world where decisions have to be made and not simply exercised in the safe quarters of discussion. As an adolescent, though capable of making independent choices, Emma stayed faithful to the contexts in which she was living and acting. As a young adult she was better equipped to judge her life setting, but she was still working on the development of principles by which to make moral choices. Now as a middle adult she is able to see these conventions in terms of how and why they came to be. She is able to evaluate these origins. She can participate in changing the present system and in forming new systems on principles of the sacredness of life, the necessity of justice, and the right to liberty. She will lean toward moral decisions that uphold responsible agreements and that preserve what is worth preserving in church and society. However, she will show in her morality some movement toward that more completely independent moral position where the principles of life, liberty, and justice are absolutely applied.

In devoting her mental powers to the formation of a working theology and ethic, Emma is overcoming the sin of unbelief. Rather than allowing her mind to be the victim of the depravity which has set in over the human race, she gives her mind to high purpose. Rather than allowing her mind to atrophy with disuse or be distorted by misuse, she takes to heart a part of the great commandment to love God with the mind.

The Creative Trustee and Style

Emma's creative trusteeship shows a style of living that is rooted in piety and at the same time is playful. Because she knows her origin and destiny and fully appreciates the tragic and the absurd in her world, she gives herself to contemplation. She has learned that being on mission carries its price. She has experienced the absence of energy and has had to draw back from activity to get in touch with the roots, to drink from the well of meditation. She knows that ceaseless activity can turn into frenzy, magnifying her alienation from the center. With Lao-tse and the psalmist she believes in waiting, for by it she gets back in vital touch with the center—the unobscured image of God.

Emma balances the weighty reality of the devotional with the lighter delights of play. If unchecked devotion to the cause can precipitate rootlessness, absolute piety can take away the joy of one's salvation. Both overactivity and radical piety need the curing medicine of play. She is not frivolous and impetuous, but there is a playfulness, a certain unpredictability about her. Emma learns how to synthesize the playfulness of the child and the seriousness of the demands made on the adult. She is like Robert Frost whose poetic mischief keeps us from taking life too seriously. In this synthesis Emma realizes the transcendent quality of her life. This delivers her from regressing to juvenile behavior on the one hand and being confined by abject existentialism on the other.

Practicing Creative Trusteeship

Emma, as these marks of the creative trustee indicate, is a person who is both reflective and active. She will give attention to the inner life of devotion and worship but also will be involved in mission and ministry activities. She will receive care from and, in turn, give care to others, as an act of individual ministry or in cooperation with others in group activities through her congregation.

Study, Care, and Mission

Emma the creative trustee will be involved in study and caring and will be on mission, as opposed to being stagnant, isolated, and uninvolved. She will participate in these dimensions of her trusteeship in ongoing groupings where study and care are primary components, in study groupings, in mission groupings, in wound-embracing and support groupings, in geographic family groupings, and in individual activity within and beyond the congregational setting.

The Curriculum: The Seven Marks

The church's curriculum for Emma will build on the youth curriculum, for one never learns everything; new experiences raise new questions. The focus of the curriculum will be in the seven marks of the creative trustee: life stance, origin, mission, growth, a working theology, ethics, and style. In the explication of these marks, the church

Emma as Adult—A Creative Trustee

will find the goals for Emma's adult curriculum. Take, for example, life stance. If the basic mark of Emma's trusteeship is that she is aware of being a redeemed daughter of God through Jesus Christ and a trustee for God in the completion of creation, then a major goal for Emma's nurture will be this awareness and its attendant commitments.

The first three marks—life stance, origin, and mission—will require that Emma's curriculum include material and experience concerned with major themes: First, God's creative activity is the context for human existence. Second, salvation is the end in creation. Third, Jesus Christ is the centerpiece of salvation. Fourth, mission is the human participation in the salvific experience. As Emma is put in touch with these themes, she may study some fundamental theology, such as the image of God, or recount her own experience within the sphere of salvation. She may study Pauline Christology or tell how she experiences the living Christ. She will study the nature and mission of the church and will find her own role within a particular community of faith. She will witness to her faith through involvement beyond the congregation.

The next three marks—growth, a working theology, and ethics—will require that Emma's curriculum include material and experience concerned with these themes: First, as creatures within God's creation we become as we open ourselves to experience. Second, within the dialectic of study, experience, and reflection, the creative trustee develops a working theology. Third, the trustee faces situational dilemmas requiring ethical choices. As Emma meets these themes, she might study process thought, philosophy, psychology, education, and/or theology. She might ponder her own development, thus perceiving and sharing how she has become uniquely who she is. She may study particular theologies, such as Brunner's doctrine of God, or reflect on her own experiences with God and from that reflection postulate the nature of God. She may study the Ten Commandments or ethical theory or share with others how she has made decisions within actual life situations.

The last mark—style—will require that Emma's curriculum include material and experience concerned with these themes: First, the tragic and the absurd require contemplation on life's meaning and end. Second, work, routine, and the reflective life necessitate the balancing power of play. Emma may study, through novels, for example, the weight of human existence or, as in times of grief, tell others what it means to suffer helplessly in the face of the absurd. She may study about others' enjoyments and diversions or share how she keeps her work from being her life and how she keeps from routinizing existence.

Emma's ministers will provide ideas and suggest resources for individual and group learning events. One minister in a church which formulated its own adult curriculum for the church school published twice a year a study idea booklet which included brief book reviews, listing of stimulator papers, listing of local human resources, services offered by the church library, and references to curriculum tools in the minister's possession. In looking for curriculum categories or areas, curriculum makers may look along the following lines: (1) Person in context: Creation and salvation, (2) Personal issues and development, (3) The faith community, (4) Fundamental theology of the Christian faith, (5) Religious history, (6) The Bible, (7) Social issues, (8) Ethics and decision making, (9) Vocation, (10) Family living, (11) Social relations, and (12) Training for leadership.

Ongoing Groupings: Study and Care

Emma will be a member of an ongoing group for the purpose of study and care. In this group she will meet the full range of the curriculum in terms of the learning event. And in it she will receive and give care in regular as well as special times of need. Although this group will not be directed by the church to perform the outreach function, it will by its nature generate among nonmembers an interest in belonging. In some churches this kind of group becomes the primary one for reaching persons who move into a community. As Emma finds satisfying stimulation and has her needs met, she will invite others to join her group.

The study function may be met through the church's regular curriculum, but preferably through one built around the meaning and shape of creative trusteeship. Without such an intentional focus, the curriculum can turn into one seemingly endless, directionless drudgery. So-called Bible study programs which lack this kind of focus end up being superficial and irrelevant. With this direction laid down and known to the group, the group can elect its studies. Where this election is the

Emma as Adult—A Creative Trustee

case, the ministers will periodically advise a group whether it is weighting its study in a few popular areas to the exclusion of equally vital ones.

Emma's caring—both what she gives and receives—will consist of regular sharing as well as the meeting of particular crisis needs. She and her group will interact meaningfully as they meet together, learning to care for one another as they take one another seriously. Healing ministries are often given in these normal, casual exchanges. She will also be available to visit a member who needs counsel or to take food and provide other mercies in times of special need, such as in death or at the birth of a child into the home. This group becomes the church's front-line ministry team, filling needs which the minister cannot and investing time and energy which the minister does not have.

Emma's group will be organized around study and caring. It will elect a study leader who will lead the group in decisions about what to study. The group will decide if one of its members will lead a particular study or if an outside resource person is needed. In addition, the group will elect a ministry leader who will lead the group in the caring function. This person will be the hub in getting help to needy members. This person also will keep the group informed of wider ministry opportunities, such as the need for a church to maintain a clothes closet or food pantry.

Emma's group will consist of approximately twenty persons; it will be divided into permanent groups for caring purposes, and on occasion into smaller study groupings. The group will meet weekly, most probably around the church's worship service. In one church a group of single adults who enjoyed sleeping late on Sunday morning met on Sunday afternoons for these very intents of study and caring.

Study Groupings

Not all of Emma's learning needs will be met through her regular, ongoing group. She will want additional opportunities. Her church will provide studies on the basis of interest, taking from the same curriculum themes as utilized by the ongoing groups. One church offered such an approach on Sunday evenings and some weekdays, billing such topics as "The Election Year and the Moral Issues," "The Crisis in the Public

Schools," "Enriching Family Life," "The Christian Year—Faith and Drama." The schedule also included current book studies and biblical and theological studies. Further, this format will carry the task of training leaders for the church and for orienting persons for mission group assignments which they have undertaken.

The ministers will select a study committee to administer this program. The committee will survey the congregation for interest and analyze the contemporary scene, will decide which elective courses to offer, and then enlist the teachers. The study groups are temporary; they last only as long as the study lasts, generally four to six weeks, or in half-day, all-day, or overnight conferences. They carry no function other than study. If a group should raise an interest in caring or in mission action, it will be reconstituted according to the church's programs for support and mission involvement.

Mission Groupings

Emma's church is on mission; Emma as a creative trustee is a missionary. Therefore, in addition to her activity of caring for others in her ongoing group, Emma will find a mission group through which to take her church beyond itself, into a world of persons and structures not especially interested in religion or in coming to church. This going beyond may be to two kinds of persons: member potentials and ministry potentials. Emma might be a member of a visitation-outreach group which visits regularly to enlist persons into church membership, such as when a family of the same denomination moves into the neighborhood. Predominantly, however, the mission groups will go to ministry potentials, persons who will not likely come to or join the church. In such cases, self-giving ministry is the motivation. Some of these projects will be end-term mission projects, such as the sponsoring of a refugee family, and long-term projects, such as ministering to families of prisoners in a nearby penitentiary.

Depending on the nature of the mission, Emma and the group will need special training. In such cases her mission group will become a temporary study group during the weeks of preparation for mission. It is also possible that because of the nature of the mission, Emma's group will decide that it ought to worship together and share at deep levels.

Emma as Adult—A Creative Trustee

It is possible that such a group may become "church" for Emma. While this cannot on a long-term basis substitute for worship with the whole congregation, the ministers ought to be free enough to allow this to run its fulfilling course.

The ministers will select a mission committee to survey the needs and lead a congregation to decide realistically which projects it can support with financial and human resources. These then are publicized and members are urged to affiliate with a group where their gifts can best be utilized. Of course, individuals on their own may organize mission groups. One minister gives time in the regular worship service for such individuals to explain their conviction and issue a call to others to join them. Except where this requires the financial support of the congregation, these should be openly encouraged. If the group needs funds from the treasury, then it will normally enter the process at the appropriate time, working with the mission committee. It is possible, however, for a church to allot an undesignated mission fund for this kind of individual initiative as well as for unpredicted mission needs. Such flexibility will keep a church vitally on mission.

Wound-Embracing and Support Groupings

There is yet another potential setting for Emma, namely, the support group. While the ongoing group provides regular and crisis care, there are life experiences which require more intense, often professional, and sometimes long-term caring and support. For this, Emma's church will provide wound-embracing groups for persons who experience death in the family or who themselves experience divorce, loss of job, or any other grief-producing event. When death comes to the family, for example, the caring is immediate and intense, but it subsides, of necessity, soon after the funeral. Some persons would be strengthened by being in a wound-embracing group of persons who have experienced the same, but who are past the time of intense grief. Divorced people need similar support, as do those who lose jobs; and while the church is awkward in giving a total response to such crises, it can offer its ministry through the wound-embracing group. One such group meets regularly, inviting to its meetings persons who have lost children in death. Often the most effectual healing is in seeing that others have survived what at the moment seems insurmountably crushing.

Besides the wound-embracing groups, there is also the vocational support group. This group is a group of persons who are in similar vocations, such as business persons, who meet to share common problems of living out their faith in their vocation. One has to take care that these groups focus on supporting roles and do not become success-oriented groups which add despair to frustration and in the end appeal only to those with trophies to share. To the contrary, this should be the group where a member, say an architect who has just lost a job, can find help. While such groups are not qualified to be therapy groups, and ought not to be, they can often open up potential job markets for members who fall on hard times.

Geographic Family Groupings

Emma's church will provide clusters composed of families living within a small geographic area for purposes of intergenerational fellowship and ministry in times of crisis. This cluster, consisting of about ten families, will have no formal organization except for having a deacon assigned to it. The deacon will sponsor three or four social occasions for the families in the cluster and will mobilize the group in times of crisis. Otherwise, there will be no meetings of the group and no further organization. In most cases, families wish to choose their associations on bases other than geography. In some instances, this clustering might prove convenient for intergenerational education, but that should not be a stated function or one that is encouraged. Such a group may also discover prospective members in the community and invite families to the group fellowships and to the church.

Individual Study and Activity

Emma is not dependent on her church to supply all of her study and caring needs or to direct her when to care for others. Out of her own perception of areas in which she needs to grow, she will seek helpful and inspiring literature. Out of her own sensitivities to the hurts of others, she will find ways of caring for others.

Emma also will be on mission at her own initiative, not waiting for the church to organize a mission group. She might share God's mercy through hospital volunteer service or show God's concern for the social order by participating in critical public hearings. She might take on more intense assignments, such as running for election to the school board or seeking appointment to some public board. In cases where Emma expresses her missionary call primarily through public service, the congregation should commission and applaud her as surely as it recognizes persons who channel most of their service within the programs and structures of the church.

When Emma chooses to serve within the church, she might be a choir member, a teacher, a committee member, or a deacon. It is not as if one must pit public service against in-church service. Both are God's work. While Emma cannot be totally involved in both at the same time, there will be seasons when one or the other is a priority in her trusteeship for God in the world. When the devoted service is outside the congregation, it does not exempt Emma from worship and study. In fact, that service will most likely intensify her need for both. Further, Emma will most certainly support her church through regular financial contributions. She will not recognize any legalisms concerning the giving of money, for she is aware that all is God's. A creative trustee does not give God a portion; she orders her existence around God's gift and claim.

Devotion and Witness

Emma's church will call her to devotion and witness. This enrichment of her devotional experience and of her witness to the faith may occur in individualized ways or group settings. Both of these dimensions of Emma's Christian life have an ongoing character, but they require seasonal attention. A most appropriate time in the Christian year for these emphases is in the pre- and post-Easter seasons.

Pre-Easter Devotion

On Ash Wednesday Emma will begin her preparation for Holy Week and Easter. She has learned that the joy of resurrection is greater when she has made her spirit ready through devotion. At the church's service on Ash Wednesday she will commit herself either to a schedule for private devotion or to participation in a group-sharing experience. At this service the minister will serve the Lord's Supper to each member of the congregation who chooses to come to the altar. As Emma approaches the minister, she will make her pledge known, then will receive the bread and cup and a blessing from the minister.

If Emma chooses private devotion, she will select an appropriate book, such as Augustine's *Confessions,* Pascal's *Pensees,* or a periodical containing daily Bible readings, thoughts, and prayers. Another option for this private approach is the keeping of a daily journal. The season might include a pilgrimage to some religious shrine or to a place of special significance to her heritage and faith. Sometimes our deepest and most hidden emotions are stirred by returning to the place of our birth or to the church in which we were baptized.

Emma's church will sponsor group-sharing experiences. If Emma chooses to join such a group for the pre-Easter season, she will share with the members of the group what is happening in her faith development. If her needs are for therapy or intense encounter, she should find other appropriate groups; the church's sharing group is designed for sharing how one's faith and life are bound together. The seven marks of the creative trustee might become the focus of the sharing.

The sharing groups, also called devotion groups, discipline groups, or Lenten groups, will meet weekly. Their time together will include the following:

First, the reading of an appropriate Bible lesson and/or an article from a religious magazine or a selection from a devotional classic. This will be done in silence.

Second, the breaking of the silence. Someone in the group will be designated ahead of time to say, after an agreed period of silence, "I now break the silence."

Third, the sharing around the marks of the trustee. The person who breaks the silence may be the first one to share out of the reading and silence.

Fourth, the reporting on faithfulness to the group covenant. The group will have agreed to certain commitments, such as the doing of a caring deed for someone outside the family each week, the attendance at the church's worship each Sunday, and the keeping of daily meditation.

Fifth, praying together.

After-Easter Testimony and Dialogue

Emma's post-Easter experience will reflect her season of devotion and her participation in the Holy Week pilgrimage and Easter celebration. It is a time for testimony and dialogue. Emma's church will sponsor testimony services in which members of the church will be asked to tell how God is at work in their lives. Such affirmations will not be preachments or a recounting of one's conversion experience, for these often are used to evade talking about faith issues. Rather, they will be a witness to God's present activity in one's experience. This activity speaks to several marks of the creative trustee but is especially relevant to helping the trustee think theologically. That may be why it is no easy thing to do and may explain why many prefer to go back in time to their conversion.

The testimony services will run for about six weeks. The testimonies will last ten minutes each and will be accompanied by opportunities for dialogue with the speakers. If the affirmations are to be during a morning worship service, then a separate dialogue session, such as on Sunday or Wednesday evening, will be scheduled. The preferred way to manage this is to have the affirmations and the dialogue in the same service, such as on Sunday or Wednesday evening. Two persons would be invited each week to share how God is at work in their lives. Then the group would dialogue with them about their testimonies. This activity may be given special flavor by going ecumenical, periodically inviting someone from another church to be the affirmant.

Ongoing Witness: Individual and Group

As a creative trustee, Emma will be a witness to her faith in continuing ways. Emma has received God's grace and acted in faith. That has enriched her existence. She now wants to bring others within the sphere of salvation. This witness may be within the family setting, the work place, or the community setting. It will involve both the witness of the life lived by faith and the witness of telling others about God's activity in the world and Jesus Christ's work of salvation. She will do this individually, or she might participate with others in her church in an organized witness group. Such a group exists for the sole purpose of taking the gospel to persons outside the fellowship of the church.

Worship: Celebration and Renewal

Emma was first brought to worship at her infant presentation. As a kindergartner she participated in most of the worship service and as an early primary child was present for the entire service. In worship she was given the rite of belonging; it was the setting where she made her declaration of faith and was baptized. She has been in worship all these years, and if Emma is to become a creative trustee, it will be partly the fruit of her continuing participation.

The Experience of Corporate Worship

In corporate worship Emma hears the Word of God and in the hearing is energized for trusteeship. Here she celebrates God's good creation and is renewed in the joy of her salvation. Here she finds some resolution to the paradox of her daughtership in God and her separation from God. Here she acknowledges both her continuing estrangement from essential being and from God's purpose and her continuing intent to be faithful. Here she brings her scatteredness and finds health. Here she continues her sense of belonging to the community of faith. Here she keeps her place in the generational stream. No other activity qualifies as a substitute for this participation—not worship on the lake or the highest hill, not fellowship within an ongoing study and caring group, not an electronic religious service.

The Worship Event

Of course, Emma's church may not offer this kind of worship. It could be entombed in dead forms without relevance to the contemporary situation or be a prisoner of culture without relevance to the gospel. If her church is to proffer worship which is true celebration and renewal, then its worship will be characterized by at least the following: be based in God's transcendence and holy presence; offer the Lord's Supper and baptism as a sign of God's continuing grace in the eschatological community; celebrate the Supper as both memorial and Eucharist; be viewed as art, created in the context of the drama of faith represented in the Christian year; include preaching which is rooted in Holy Scripture and pertinent to the worshiper's experience, admitting to being the preacher's words but promising the possibility of becoming the Word of God; expect persons to respond to the Word and therefore issue a call to declaration of faith and to creative trusteeship; draw from the church's rich heritage of hymnody and choral music; be participative rather than spectator-oriented; be intergenerational, from early childhood on; make visible the larger life of the congregation's fellowship and mission.

The Church Choir

The church choir supplies a role in worship where the holistic function of art and the universal beauty of musical score bring to life the themes of creation and salvation, of Christian living and mission. In special choral productions the epics of faith can be reenacted in uncluttered and moving simplicity, as, for example, Bach's *St. Matthew Passion,* Mozart's *Requiem,* and Handel's *Messiah.* Whether or not Emma continues as a member of choir, it is an essential activity in her nurture and she enjoys the fruit of its ministry.

Emma's Adult Friends

Elizabeth is a religious adult. She participates regularly in the worship of the church. She is a member of the altar guild. She seems satisfied with her religious experience, although it is not something she talks about very much. Other than sharing her faith with her children and worshiping on Sunday, Elizabeth's faith is pretty much a private affair. She is active socially and in her community. She is a member of the school board but does not connect that activity with her faith. Her last public demonstration of faith was at sixteen when she affirmed her baptismal vows.

Robert is a religious adult. He is rearing a religious family and is active in the activities of his church. He teaches in the Sunday school. At home, church, and work, he talks about his faith. He talks often about wanting to be more dedicated to the Lord. Since his baptism at sixteen, he has made two rededications of faith. He is the president of his local union and witnesses to other members of the union, but he sometimes feels guilty that his union activity takes him away from church activity. He does not see his union work as a part of his religious vocation.

Samuel is a religious adult. His religion is a rightist group which is active in local and national issues. He once had a confrontation with Elizabeth when his group pressured the school board to remove certain books from the school libraries. They remembered each other from school days but had no religious greeting to exchange. He and Robert bowl in the same league. Both are known as dedicated men. Whereas the church is the center of Robert's commitment, Samuel's creed is the rightist group's constitution; his mission is the group's purpose. Robert has tried to persuade Samuel to become a Christian, but he retorts that his organization is the hope of the country. Samuel still does not know that he is a child of God.

Transition

Emma is a creative trustee for God in the world. She works with God happily and with purpose. She increasingly bears the marks of creative trusteeship. This fulfilling understanding of self and sense of mission take Emma into old age and to her time to die. In her declining, she lives on the rich harvest of a life given over to God's purpose and on the sure hope of her salvation. She knows that being creature means to die; being in the stream of salvation means to be resurrected. In her ending, she reaffirms within her inner being what was true at her beginning—she is a child of God, made in the image of God.

Epilogue

Historical Life Cycle, Womanhood, and Real Church

How quickly and smoothly Emma has moved from infancy to adulthood! She has grown to adulthood within the brief span of the writing of this manuscript and for you, the reader, in the few hours it has taken to turn these pages. But real life cycles exact more from us and are cast in historical settings. There is, of course, an unending dialectic between the two, for we are set down within forces produced by our collective existence, and to varying degrees we early on begin to exert our own influences on the collective experience. Consider, for example, how the tiniest infant, innocent to the exigencies of the birth context, reshapes the entire routine of the household so that parents can hardly visualize what life was like before the thankful intrusion of this little, eight-pound living package.

If Emma were at my age of fifty years, her parents and congregation would have consecrated her to God in 1932, against the gloom of the Great Depression, hardly, by earthly perspective, a time to speak of the gift of God and to anticipate an unfolding future of Christian nurture. With Pearl Harbor etched in their psyche and their hearts heavy over the evil loose in Germany, Emma's congregation would have conferred belonging on her. Would she have noted any reservation in the congregation's joy as it both welcomed her to the Lord's Table and added new names to the war memorial list?

Emma would have affirmed her faith in the euphoric early postwar era, sure of what she was doing, but along with her parents and church unaware of the moral significance of the atomic clouds over Hiroshima and Nagasaki. Her commitment to creative trusteeship would have come during the tumultuous mid- to late sixties, a most opportune time for a Christian to see the movement of God in the social order and to pledge oneself to serious involvement in the mission of the church. In her retirement, Emma would see the end of the century of her historical life cycle; let us not speculate on the context of those years.

In addition to adding reality to my view of Emma's nurture with this brief reflection on real history, we must speak also of Emma as woman. When women of necessity left home for the factory during World War II, womanhood took a turn. There was, of course, the postwar baby boom which required that a resident mother be on hand, but women were in the work force to stay and child-care centers were increasing in number and acceptance. But women are still given marginal status in the working world, society, and church. Women have long been allowed to assume service and teaching roles in the church. In the last few years there has been some progress in welcoming them to decision-making positions and deaconship. But the prospect that Emma could become a priest or senior pastor is not bright. Somewhere we must face the discrepancy of consecrating Emma as an infant, embracing and baptizing her into the fellowship of the church, but not allowing her to express her creative trusteeship in the fullest sense to which she feels called of God. Somewhere the rituals to which she is welcomed must be matched by a prophetic word concerning her dignity and her place.

One additional consideration is appropriate. As a part of my duty to the seminary and to students who enroll in our doctoral program in ministry, I visit ministers in their churches. Toward the end of the completion of this manuscript I attended a small church in northwestern Missouri. There were about sixty persons present, including a little girl of about four. I wondered if her name might be Emma, and if this little congregation could do for her what I have envisioned for Emma and all children of God. I pondered the young child sitting in front of me and that congregation around me (a real one, while Emma's church is fabricated, middle class, and endowed with unusual talent). Then I concluded—yes, yes, indeed this real congregation with its strengths and inadequacies has the necessary ingredient to convey to its children that they are children of God, that they belong to the community of faith, that they must affirm their faith if it is to be vital, and that they are called to be creative trustees for God in a real world. The vision holds!

Notes on Chapters

Chapter 1

[1] Walter Neidhart, "A Declaration of Faith in Swiss Presbyterian Churches," *Religious Education* (July–August, 1965), p. 297.
[2] See this view and others in a valuable symposium, *Religious Education* (September–October, 1963), pp. 411-442.
[3] The 1955 and 1966 data are from the *Quarterly Review* (Sunday School Board, SBC), July–September, 1967, and Clifford Ingle, *Children and Conversion* (Nashville: Broadman Press, 1970); the 1972 data are from the same periodical, July–September, 1973.
[4] Ola Elizabeth Winslow, *Jonathan Edwards, 1703–1758* (New York: Collier Books, 1961), p. 144.

Chapter 2

[1] David Cairns, *The Image of God in Man* (London: SCM Press Ltd., 1973), p. 28.
[2] Erik Erikson, *Childhood and Society* (New York: W. W. Norton & Company, Inc., 1963), p. 250.
[3] Paul H. Mussen, John J. Conger, Jerome Kagan, *Essentials of Child Development and Personality* (New York: Harper & Row, Publishers, Inc., 1980), pp. 159-160.
[4] Erikson, *op. cit.*, p. 252.
[5] Mussen *et al., op. cit.*, p. 171.
[6] John F. Travers, *The Growing Child* (Palo Alto, Calif.: Scott Foresman and Co., 1982), p. 278.
[7] Erikson, *op. cit.*, p. 258.
[8] *Ibid.*, p. 256.

[9] *Ibid.*, p. 258.
[10] Jean Piaget and Bärbel Inhelder, *The Psychology of the Child* (New York: Basic Books, Inc., 1969), p. 15.
[11] Ronald Goldman, *Religious Thinking from Childhood to Adolescence* (New York: The Seabury Press, 1964), p. 89. Used by permission.
[12] Ernest Harms, "The Development of Religious Experience in Children," *American Journal of Sociology*, vol. 50 (1944), p. 115. The report on his research, which led to his conclusion, is on pages 112-122 of this periodical.
[13] *Ibid.*, p. 115.
[14] Ronald Goldman, *Readiness for Religion* (New York: The Seabury Press, Inc., 1968), p. 93.
[15] Goldman, *Religious Thinking*, p. 70.
[16] Goldman, *Readiness*, p. 94.
[17] See Erik Erikson, *Toys and Reasons* (New York: W. W. Norton & Company, Inc., 1977).

Chapter 3

[1] The sophisticated understandings of anxiety and fear are discussed by Britton K. Ruebush in *Child Psychology*, published by the National Society for the Study of Education, pp. 461-466. Of more immediate help is the discussion of this problem, including defense mechanisms employed by children, in *Essentials of Child Development and Personality* by Paul Henry Mussen et al., (New York: Harper & Row, Publishers, Inc., 1980), pp. 284-292, and in John F. Travers, *The Growing Child*, (Palo Alto, Calif.: Scott Foresman and Co., 1982), pp. 472ff.
[2] Erik H. Erikson, *Identity and the Life Cycle* (New York: W. W. Norton & Company, Inc., 1980), p. 91.
[3] Erik H. Erikson, *Childhood and Society* (New York: W. W. Norton & Company, Inc., 1963), p. 259.
[4] Horace Bushnell, *Christian Nurture* (New Haven, Conn.: Yale University Press, 1967), p. 74.
[5] *Ibid.*
[6] Jean Piaget, *Six Psychological Studies* (New York: Random House, Inc., 1967), p. 78.
[7] Jean Piaget, *The Psychology of Intelligence* (Totowa, N.J.: Littlefield, Adams and Co., 1976), p. 146.
[8] Ronald Goldman, *Religious Thinking from Childhood to Adolescence* (New York: The Seabury Press, 1964), p. 200. Used by permission.
[9] Bärbel Inhelder and Jean Piaget, *Judgment and Reasoning in the Child* (London: Routledge and Kegan Paul, Ltd., 1969), p. 232. Also, see Piaget's *The Language and Thought of the Child*, trans. Marjorie Gabain (New York: World Publishing, 1962), chapter 4, where he discusses syncretistic thought in some detail.

[10] Piaget discusses reciprocity of socialization and its effect on attaining equilibrium within a stage as well as facilitating transit to a higher stage in several works. See "Social Life and General Coordinations of Actions," in *Biology and Knowledge* (Chicago: The University of Chicago Press, 1971), pp. 359ff., and "Social and Affective Interactions," in *The Psychology of the Child* (New York: Basic Books, Inc., 1969), pp. 114ff., and pp. 243 and 337ff. in *The Growth of Logical Thinking from Childhood to Adolescence*, coauthored with Bärbel Inhelder (New York: Basic Books, Inc., 1958).

[11] Lawrence Kohlberg, *Essays on Moral Development*, vol. 1, *The Philosophy of Moral Development* (San Francisco: Harper & Row, Publishers, Inc., 1981), p. 409.

[12] *Ibid.*, p. 148.

[13] Mary M. Wilcox, *Developmental Journey* (Nashville: Abingdon Press, 1979), pp. 70-71.

[14] *Ibid.*, p. 240.

[15] David Elkind, *Children and Adolescents* (New York: Oxford University Press, 1981), pp. 59ff.

[16] This does not mean that we should not challenge children with content that is ahead of their performance. That would retard their progress. Learning comes as persons accommodate to the new, then assimilate it to their own mental possessions. This accommodation is set up when teachers introduce a cognitive dissonance to the pupils' minds. If the pupils cannot even attend to the dissonances, then we know that they are not ready for the new learning and we back off lest we force them to substitute what they really can only learn by integration. If the pupils can indeed accommodate to the new, then we proceed to help them assimilate it to their present structures, that is, to integrate it with what they already know.

[17] David Elkind, *The Child and Society* (New York: Oxford University Press, 1979), p. 265.

[18] Goldman, *op. cit.*, p. 201.

[19] *Ibid.*, pp. 194ff. We need some research on the worship experience among children who are regular participants in worship services.

[20] *Ibid.*, p. 1.

[21] *Ibid.*, p. 89.

[22] Elkind, *The Child and Society*, pp. 255-256.

[23] James Fowler, *Stages of Faith* (New York: Harper & Row, Publishers, Inc., 1981), chapter 23.

[24] *Ibid.*, p. 139.

[25] Reported by Andre Godin in *Research on Religious Development*, ed. Merton Strommen (New York: Hawthorn Books, Inc., 1971), p. 114.

[26] Goldman, *op. cit.*, p. 90.

[27] Fowler, *op. cit.*, p. 138.

[28] Goldman, *op. cit.*, pp. 157ff.

[29] *Ibid.*, pp. 162-163.

[30] See Godin, chapter 4, in Strommen, *op. cit.*

[31] The Revised Standard Version is the best one for middle children. It has the advantage of contemporary language yet does not attempt to change the structure of the texts by articulating them in contemporary idioms. Children, then, should not be permitted to grow up with the *Good News Bible* or *The Living Bible* as their only Bible.

[32] Iris V. Cully, *Christian Child Development* (San Francisco: Harper & Row, Publishers, Inc., 1979), p. 152.

[33] Dorothy Jean Furnish, *Exploring the Bible with Children* (Nashville: Abingdon Press, 1975), pp. 106-107. (Also see her later work, *Living the Bible with Children*.)

[34] Goldman, *op. cit.*, p. 70.

[35] *Ibid.*, pp. 74-80.

[36] *Ibid.*, pp. 82-83.

Chapter 4

[1] If it sounds contradictory to turn suddenly from the progress of childhood faith to talk of disobedience, evil, and alienation, it is an inherent part of our human situation. As much as we might propose or wish, life is not smoothly evolutionary. The tragic and the absurd are ever present. The split in our being will not heal completely. No scheme of education can assure a pilgrimage unmarked by crises; no view of human nature can ignore the individual and collective estrangement of humankind from God.

[2] "Excerpt from *Émile*" by Rousseau, reprinted in Carol J. Guardo, *The Adolescent as Individual: Issues and Insights* (New York: Harper & Row, Publishers, Inc., 1975), p. 9.

[3] See Albert Bandura's chapter in Guardo, *op. cit.*, for a discussion of this popular notion that adolescence is of necessity a time of intense upheaval.

[4] See Kurt Lewin's chapter in Guardo, *op. cit.*

[5] For a discussion of moratorium, see Erik Erikson, *Identity: Youth and Crisis* (New York: W. W. Norton & Company, Inc., 1968), especially chapter 6.

[6] Piaget's critics have suggested that he, in his zeal for logico-mathematical structures, has ignored the affective side of human development. While it is true that he did not research personality as such, he has written of the significance of affect in cognitive development. See *The Growth of Logical Thinking from Childhood to Adolescence* (New York: Basic Books, Inc., 1958), chapter 18; *The Psychology of the Child* (New York: Basic Books, Inc., 1969), where the affect is discussed in each major section.

[7] This more detailed investigation of the identity crisis is found in Erik Erikson, *Identity: Youth and Crisis,* chapter 6. Henry Maier discusses these in *Three Theories of Child Development*, chapter 2, and in Guardo, *The Adolescent as Individual,* section 6.

[8] Thomas Droege, *Self-Realization and Faith* (Chicago: Lutheran Education Association, 1978), chapters 3 and 4.

Notes on Chapters   177

⁹See *Identity: Youth and Crisis,* chapter 5, for Erikson's discussion of the conscious I as "the verbal assurance according to which I feel that I am the center of awareness in a universe of experience in which I have a coherent identity, and that I am in possession of my wits and able to say what I see and think" (p. 220).

¹⁰Adolescents often will use speech to run the gamut of these crises, talking through extreme alternatives without any intention of acting on their words. They also use peer groups to act out these conflicts, often acting more extremely than they wanted to, thus, one hopes, turning back with a healthier sense of identity. In the extreme, some will engage in bizarre group behavior which has no precedent in their past behavior and no promise for the future—orgies, for example. The forays into experimentation need not be viewed by adults with alarm, but these severe, isolated group behaviors indicate a generation without roots and without anticipation of any future. In short, such persons are without identity. Clearly, that is not the vision we have for our children.

¹¹John S. Dacey, *Adolescents Today* (Glenview, Ill.: Scott, Foresman and Company, 1982), discusses the movement of persons through three stages of sexual feelings: autosexuality, homosexuality, and heterosexuality. He reports on research which postulates that about one-third of all adolescents have engaged in sexual play with someone of the same sex at least once. However, "It appears that in most cases such behavior results from curiosity rather than latent homosexuality of the adult variety" (p. 241).

Sexuality is integrally connected with dynamics in adolescent development. One's physiology, commitments, and culture are also involved. Mussen *et al.,* in *Essentials of Child Development and Personality,* report on research which indicates that, in the case of physiology, boys show signs of sexual excitation more frequently, whereas for girls the arousal is more diffuse. Further, even where sexual arousal in girls is high, girls are more likely than boys to put that in relation to "needs such as self-esteem, reassurance, affection, and love" (p. 355). It is now a myth, however, that men have a greater capacity for sexual gratification. In terms of commitment, "politically conservative and religiously oriented youth are more conservative in sexual attitudes" than their peers (p. 357). Cultural differences do not need to be documented here.

¹²The youths of the 1940s did not explore their bodies to the same degree as those of the 1970s, according to Mussen *et al., op.cit.,* pp. 356-357, who report that both boys and girls masturbate earlier than did their parents' generation. However, John S. Dacey, *op. cit.,* suggests that "there appears to have been no marked changes in masturbation during the past 30 years for either sex." Nearly all boys have masturbated by the end of teens; 80 percent of girls, by age 14 and over 90 percent by age 18 (p. 249).

¹³For an instructive discussion of the subject of a youth culture, see *Youth: Transition to Adulthood,* the report of the Panel of Youth of the President's Science Advisory Committee, 1974, pp. 112-125.

¹⁴Are today's adolescents more active sexually? Dacey reports that both sexes engage in petting activities earlier than 30 years ago; that premarital coitus

increased in frequency in males so that the 18-year-old in the 1970s was as experienced as the 19-year-old of the 40s, and females equaled males in terms of experience reported. In the 1970s premarital intercourse increased among adolescents from 27 percent in 1971 to 35 percent in 1976 (pp. 249-250).

Mussen *et al., op. cit.,* reported increased sexual activity especially among girls who are educated and of a higher economic status. In the general population, 3% of the girls at 16 in 1940 had sexual intercourse. In 1970 the percentage jumped to 30%. Among boys the increase was from 39% to 44% (p. 356). Contrary to popular opinion, there was not an accompanying promiscuity (p. 358). Papalia and Olds report on studies in 1974 which found that 1 in 3 single white women had experienced sexual intercourse by age 17. This study found that premarital sexual intercourse doubled among women in late teens and mid-twenties from 1953 to 1974 (p. 285). If an anonymous Yale University physician is correct, then the pressures for losing one's virginity are strong; he suggests that sex has become an ideology which holds that it is one's duty to have it and that if you don't, then you are maladjusted (Papalia, p. 286). Diane Papalia and Sally Olds, *Human Development* (New York: McGraw-Hill Book Co., 1978).

[15] It is the research of Fowler which will not permit us to hold that the young adolescent is capable of standing completely outside oneself and one's system. For Fowler, adolescent faith is more synthesizing and conventional than reflective and individuative. Though adolescents have the ability to think their own thoughts and to turn this ability on themselves in adolescence, Fowler did not find adolescents that independent of the conventions of their life setting. What can we make of all this? It appears to me that while Fowler holds with Piaget that a new ability for reflection and second-order thinking emerges in adolescence and is utilized extensively, in the end the adolescent engages in this critical activity still within the system. Of course, we do not want our youth at this stage in their religious development to feel that they have to break with their heritage in order to affirm it.

[16] Charles W. Stewart, *Adolescent Religion* (Nashville: Abingdon Press, 1967), p. 168.

[17] James Fowler, *Stages of Faith* (New York: Harper & Row, Publishers, Inc., 1981), p. 173.

[18] *Ibid.,* pp. 244-245.

[19] *Ibid.,* p. 173.

[20] Ronald Goldman, *Religious Thinking from Childhood to Adolescence* (London: Routledge and Kegan Paul, Ltd., 1964), pp. 242-244.

[21] The Cooperative Curriculum Project produced two documents: *The Church's Educational Ministry: A Curriculum Plan,* Bethany Press, and *Tools of Curriculum Development,* Warner Press.

[22] See Margaret Sawin, *Family Enrichment with Family Clusters* (Valley Forge: Judson Press, 1979), and Lela Hendrix, *Extended Family: Combining Ages in Church Experience* (Nashville: Broadman Press, 1979).

Notes on Chapters

²³Paul F. Roe, *Choral Music Education* (Englewood Cliffs, N.J.: Prentice Hall, Inc., 1970), p. 191.

²⁴See Dan Boling's chapter, "Involving Youth in Mission and Witnessing," in *Knowing and Helping Youth,* ed. G. Temp Sparkman (Nashville: Broadman Press, 1977), p. 150.

²⁵For information on Disciple Life, write the Sunday School Board, 127 Ninth Avenue North, Nashville, TN 37203.

Chapter 5

¹After working with several terms for Reality 4, I finally settled on "creative trustee." All along I have been attracted to the word "creativity," although Erikson warned that neither it nor the word "productivity" adequately represented what he meant by "generativity" (*Identity and the Life Cycle* [New York: W. W. Norton & Co., Inc., 1980], p. 103). Then after seeing what one writer on psychology and religion did with the term, I decided there would be no way to redeem it as a separate term for Reality 4 in my theory. I forthwith abandoned the term as a separate word, but kept it as the first in a compound term to signify our participation with God who continues to create in the world order. (See Appendix IX, "Dominion, Priesthood, Trusteeship.")

²For a deft and stimulating treatment of generativity, see Don S. Browning, *Generative Man: Psychoanalytic Perspectives* (Philadelphia: The Westminster Press, 1973).

³Papalia and Olds report on research which found evidence that not all adults operate at a 100% formal operational level. In one test among women, college students did best, with 67% passing. Only 54% of the middle adults passed the test (*Human Development* [New York: McGraw-Hill Book Co., 1978], p. 373).

⁴For discussions of compartmentalization, dichotomizing, and dialectic, see Mary M. Wilcox, *Developmental Journey* (Nashville: Abingdon Press, 1979) and James W. Fowler, *Stages of Faith* (New York: Harper & Row, Publishers, Inc., 1981).

⁵I have some difficult problems with these marks of the creative trustee. First, I have to ask if a person must be able to have an awareness of creative trusteeship in order to demonstrate it in real life. Some of the marks require a higher degree of awareness and an articulate ability than others. However, some awareness is necessary in all or else the trustee would be a passive servant simply taking orders or a faithful worker doing one's duty. Second, I wonder if my Reality 4 is nothing more than a Christian baptism of what it means to be fully human. Apart from the explicit Christian references, devout religious people of other faiths doubtlessly qualify as creative trustees. When I attempt to convince myself otherwise and worship at the altar of narrow Christianity, the first person I meet in turning from the altar is Abraham Heschel. I accept this as a lifelong struggle. Third, I become uneasy about some of these marks in relation to Fowler's work. I have intended to characterize the adult from

around 35 to 65. Some of the marks of the adult trustee correlate with Fowler's young adult stage which he calls stage 4, "Individuative-Reflective Faith." Some more nearly parallel his middle adult stage 5, "Conjunctive Faith." There are some elements of "Universalizing Faith," stage 6. However, in Fowler's sample only 14.6% of the respondents ages 31-40 represented stage 5 "faithing"; 12.5% from ages 41-50; 23.5% from 51-60; 16.1% from 61 years plus. Most adults 31-40 years were at stage 4, the typical stage for persons 21-30. An equal number of adults from 51-60 were at stage 3 or stages 4 and 4-5. No one under 61 was a universalizer; 1.6 over 60 were in stage 6 (James Fowler, *Stages of Faith* [New York: Harper & Row, Publishers, Inc., 1981], p. 318).

[6]This is taken from *Jesus: Inspiring and Disturbing Presence* by M. De Jonge, translated by John E. Steely (Nashville: Abingdon Press, 1974).

Appendix I

Baptism—A Theological Question

The meaning of baptism is thought by many to be found in what the Bible teaches about the rite. But baptism's meaning is essentially one of theology rather than of biblical exegesis. The primary documents are ambiguous about the full import of John's baptism, especially in light of the fact that Jesus submitted himself to it. There is uncertainty about the baptism of the disciples who at Ephesus were baptized in the name of Jesus even though they had already received John's baptism. There are accounts of household baptism and, on the other hand, texts calling persons to believe first and then be baptized. There is reference to the baptism of the Spirit but confusion as to the sequence and relationship between baptism and the coming of the Spirit. Thus, exegesis will not provide a definitive doctrine of baptism.

Biblical exegesis, however, must precede any theological development, as also must the examination of postbiblical practice and interpretation. But at this moment in history it is difficult for exegesis to effect much change in the theology of baptism, for even our analysis of the material is often biased. How is it that the Lutheran finds infant baptism in the New Testament while the Baptist insists that only believers were baptized in those days? The answer is, of course, that both groups have developed theologies of baptism and more than likely do not intend to change them radically.

The futility yet necessity of sound exegesis is demonstrated in the debates on baptism in the New Testament. Besides the host of little argumentative people who, with special interests to foster or protect, have engaged the question, the greats of biblical and theological studies have also been at work and have come out in disagreement. Probably the most notable of these disagreements are in Karl Barth's (*The Teaching of the Church Regarding Baptism*) and Oscar Cullmann's (*Baptism in the New Testament*) debates in the late forties and the running conversations between Joachim Jeremias (*Infant Baptism in the First Four Centuries*) and Kurt Aland (*Did the Early Church Baptize Infants?*). Jeremias actually set forth his comprehensive view in 1938. The English version (1960) is a translation from a revised German edition (1958). Aland's challenge came in 1962. The next year, Jeremias answered Aland in *The Origins of Infant Baptism*. The Jeremias-Aland argument is more detailed, thus it represents more precisely the difficulty of finding the correct exegesis of the texts bearing on baptism. This difficulty is compounded by the fact that Jeremias, in *The Origins,* admitted to a change of mind on whether the children referred to in 1 Corinthians 7:14 had been baptized; he now holds that they had been.

Jeremias's arguments for infant baptism are that there is no biblical evidence of two kinds of Christians—the baptized and the unbaptized; there is no indication that the Old Testament custom of family solidarity had been abandoned; there is no special rite for infants as opposed to adults; and there is no evidence that infants were baptized only in a small party or sect. He wrote in conclusion that

> both East and West are at one in tracing infant baptism back to apostolic tradition, and it is highly questionable whether this tradition should be so quickly put on one side as a dogmatic *petitio principii,* as occasionally happens. For the Gospel of John could scarcely have formulated in so unqualified a manner the proposition that only those begotten by water and the spirit can enter the kingdom of God (John 3.5), if in its time baptism had been withheld from children of Christian parents (*Infant Baptism,* pp. 57-58).

Aland counters Jeremias point by point, concluding that the New Testament does not indicate when baptism should be administered and that from the glimpses that we have of how baptism was practiced "we must conclude that infant baptism was not practised at that time . . ." (*Did the Early Church,* p. 113). It was only at the end of the second century that infant baptism came to be practiced, and here it was a theological issue, he asserts. Aland clarifies what he means:

Appendix I

". . . so long as the Church assumed that children born of Christian parents were sinless, it abstained from infant baptism; so soon as it recognized the falsity of this presupposition, it began to ask for and introduce infant baptism" (p. 113).

The arguments in this Jeremias-Aland debate are so detailed that to report them here would be to reproduce the works themselves. However, an example or two will demonstrate the refinement of the discussion. In his discussion of the *oikos* formula, Jeremias acknowledges that the baptism of infants or children is not explicitly singled out, but he holds that everyone was surely included in the baptism of households. The households of Cornelius, the jailor at Philippi, Lydia, Crispus, and Stephanas did not, in Jeremias's reading of sociological data from the period, include a significant contingency of slaves. Rather, the reference is to the children of the house (*Infant Baptism*, p. 20). Aland responds that only in the case of the baptism of Lydia is household baptism explicit; and, in further disagreement with Jeremias, suggests that it is more than likely that Lydia, the jailor, Cornelius, and Crispus had domestic slaves and that they, not the children, are the referents in the *oikos* passages (*Did the Early Church*, pp. 89-90).

Jeremias held that the *oikos* formula was adopted very early by the Christian community from Old Testament cultic practice (*Infant Baptism*, p. 21), whereas Aland holds the connection to be greatly exaggerated both in substance and in the circle of inclusion (*Did the Early Church*, p. 93). The same kind of arguments continue in regard to the New Testament pericope on the blessing of the children and also in regard to evidence beyond the New Testament document.

Aland finally asserts that the question of baptism is not simply a historical one but a theological question. Thus is he able to maintain that, although he finds no evidence for infant baptism in the New Testament and ancient church, he himself holds to the theological necessity of infant baptism. His case is persuasive, but it need not concern us here, for in raising the question of baptism to a theological one he has made more legitimate the existence of divergent views on baptism.

My own four-reality view on the awakening to faith favors the theological validity of believer's baptism. Such a validity is not set exclusively over against infant baptism but is the view most consistent with other theological and psychological considerations in my theory of nurture. Thus, believer's baptism as the rite for Reality 3—affirmation—is not so much proposed as an indispensable view, but as a more proper one, to use Barth's word. Also, it simply has to be admitted that the believer's baptismal mode is so much a part of the author's heritage that to hold to any other would represent too radical a departure, a departure seen as neither desirable nor probable.

The development of biblical theology ought to be left to the scholars; thus I will not attempt to offer original justification for holding to the practice of believer's baptism. Rather, I will depend on Barth's view of baptism in the New Testament laid out in *The Teaching of the Church Regarding Baptism,* a work in which he calls infant baptism a half baptism and suggests that the proper baptism is of the adult.

The first foundation of baptism, for Barth, is that it belongs to, is "part of the errand of the Church," rather than to the individual (pp. 31, 37). In his words: "The Church of Jesus Christ on earth originates, grows and persists through the divine 'adding thereto' (Acts ii, 47) of those who, through their baptism as believers, publicly proclaim themselves as saved and are publicly acknowledged as such" (pp. 31-32). The second principle is that the individual, the one to whom the baptism is given, must be willing and ready "to receive the promise of the grace directed towards him and to be party to the pledge of allegiance concerning the grateful service demanded of him" (p. 40).

Since Barth is here referring to the ordering of baptism, it has to be noted that he is not suggesting that other baptism is without validity and effectiveness, but any other is a "clouded baptism" and a "wound in the body of the Church," for it is not "correct" or "done in obedience" (p. 40). The person is not brought, but comes, for baptism (p. 42), and the one who comes must be an "active partner" (p. 41). This rules out the baptism of infants. Not even the texts on the blessing of the children or 1 Corinthians 7:14 can be interpreted to condone such baptism. Further, the arguments from the *oikos* passages are mere "thin threads." In pondering these texts with their emphasis on preaching, faith, and baptism, one "wonders whether one really wants to hold to this thread" (p. 45). Cullman demurs, holding that "infant Baptism is in every detail congruous with the *doctrine* of baptism" (p. 70) when baptism is viewed as general (defined on page 20, *Baptism in the New Testament)* and as incorporation into the church.

For Barth the meaning of baptism is "participation in the death and resurrection of Jesus Christ"; "it implies a threat of death and a deliverance to life"; thus it deals with the estrangement problem, for the baptized "is now dead to sin [and] has become alive unto God for an existence in His service" (p. 11). Baptism does not redeem (p. 28), for it cannot produce effects but rather is dependent on God (pp. 21, 23). As holy and hallowing, baptism is a representation, a seal, a sign (pp. 13-14). As an eschatological sign, says Barth, "it [baptism] points also into the heart of the life which the baptized is living here and now; to his past, and to his future at the time of that Aeon, which is present with us and hastening towards its goal and end" (pp. 62-63).

The so-called main-line churches are proponents of infant baptism. Baptists are among the champions of believer's baptism. W. T. Conner, Baptist theologian, held "that the only person properly qualified for baptism is one who has heard the gospel, accepted its message, and believed in Christ as his Savior" (*Christian Doctrine*, p. 282). Another, Augustus Hopkins Strong, wrote that baptism is for the regenerated, those who "have entered by faith into the communion of Christ's death and resurrection" (*Systematic Theology,* p. 945). Dale Moody, while assuming "the priority of grace to faith," believes in the "primacy of faith in baptismal theology" (*The Word of Truth*, p. 460). However, Southern Baptists have, in practice, compromised these convictions and the Barthian defense of believer's baptism by turning to child baptism. This shift in practice has come predominantly without any knowledge of its implications for the doctrine of baptism. We thus have gotten ourselves in the uncomfortable position of preaching one doctrine, but practicing an altogether different one. Most of us simply accept the child for baptism and utter the same formulas as for the baptism of a believer. For integrity's sake, our duty is either to hold to the doctrine and change the practice or hold to the practice and change the theology.

A Baptist pastor, Warren Carr, refutes the claim that we must make a choice between the actual practice and the stated theology. In his 1964 work *Baptism: Conscience and Clue for the Church,* Carr says such a state "may be providential" (p. 183). He suggests that Baptists should come into the open with the practice of child baptism because "baptizing a child old enough to make a personal response militates against the magic elements of infant baptism and the harsh legalism of the rite when administered to believers" (p. 184).

Carr does not see himself as simply lowering the age for believer's baptism. His work is an apology for the baptism of children on the theological ground that baptism is essentially initiation into Christ and the church. Infant baptism, while objective and a sign of God's grace, is defective in its isolation from the profession of faith; if confirmation is sacramental, then it is an "affront" to infant baptism (pp. 88-94). Believer's baptism is too subjective and ignores the initiatory nature of baptism (pp. 81-84) and obscures God's grace "by an inordinate accent upon man's act of faith" (p. 176).

Baptism, according to Carr,

> . . . spells out personal faith and confession; the work of God in the giving of the Spirit and salvation; the glorifying of God in the atoning death and triumphant resurrection of Christ the Lord; death to sin and the newness of life to come; cleansing for ethical and moral life; identification with the death, burial, and resurrection of Christ; and a community of faith as the arena of the Spirit's visitation upon the one whose faith has brought him to the water (p. 165).

Another Baptist, William E. Hull, in a summer, 1980, sermon, "When Should a Child Join the Church?", compliments Carr's view but believes that it is based too much in reaction to the weaknesses of infant and adult baptism. Hull would rather draw from the strengths of both. He believes that child baptism can uniquely symbolize the initiation by circumcision into the covenant community as in the Old Testament and adult initiation in the New Testament, because the baptism of children who have grown up in the church comes at a time in their development when these meanings "overlap." For Hull "baptism may be understood as the mid-point of a 'salvation history' that spans all of childhood, gathering up the prevenient grace operative even before birth and anticipating the autonomous faith achieved only in adulthood" (p. 10). Moody, though titling a section in his systematics "Initiation into the Church: Baptism," doubts that child baptism "can pass for a repentance baptism that involves guilt and forgiveness" (*The Word of*

Truth, p. 463). The difference in infant and child baptism is "the transfer of belief from the parents to the child" (p. 463).

Persons attracted to Carr's and Hull's arguments for child baptism on the basis of covenant theology and the competence for personal choice should weigh this position against that of Thomas Droege, a Lutheran theologian. In *Self-Realization and Faith,* Droege parallels Carr in holding that infant faith defined in adult terms of acceptance is problematic and that adult faith is based too much in the power of logic. However, rather than attempting to find a middle ground in initiatory baptism in childhood, Droege stays with his Lutheran heritage of baptizing infants but redefines infant faith as self-reception. The infant is receiving, unconsciously of course, "the promise of God, which not only sustains faith but gives it birth" (p. 51). Faith begins here, and its emphasis is on God's action and promise. That promise, made in baptism, is fulfilled in confirmation when the adolescent completes the faith-development cycle from self-reception to self-realization. Droege writes: "The self which was received by grace through the promise of Baptism realizes its potential for fulfillment through the development of faith" (p. 71).

Because Carr, Hull, and Droege base their views partly on psychological assumptions, their work should be evaluated in terms of the developmental stages of Erikson's psychosocial theory, Piaget's cognitive theory, Kohlberg's moral reasoning theory, and James Fowler's faith development theory. Droege did, in fact, do his homework on Erikson's psychology and has been in close contact with Fowler in Candler's Center for Faith Development.

Finally, can anyone doubt the proposition that baptism is a theological problem? Here we have before us two eminent theologians (Barth and Cullmann), schooled in the Scripture, but disagreeing on its interpretation. We have New Testament scholars (Jeremias and Aland) disagreeing over biblical evidence for infant baptism but agreeing that it ought to be practiced. We have two Baptist pastors (Carr and Hull, the latter also a New Testament scholar) calling for child baptism, in one case to offset the abuses of infant and believer's baptism and in the other to draw from their strengths. And we have a Lutheran theologian (Droege) who, in facing the same weaknesses and strengths, holds to his persuasion for infant baptism. Rather than finding all of this confusing, we should find it clarifying: Baptism is a theological question!

Appendix II

Bushnell's Idea of Christian Education

From the time in 1846 when he told the Hartford Association that the child is to grow into adulthood as a Christian and not ever remember not being a Christian, Horace Bushnell, a Congregational pastor, was in trouble. He had set forth his basic idea two years earlier in a journal article, "The Kingdom of Heaven as a Grain of Mustard Seed," which later appeared in his book *Views of Christian Nurture and Subjects Adjacent Thereto*. Bushnell wrote:

> In place of a doctrine so false and pernicious, we hold that children are, in a sense, included in the faith of their parents, partakers with them in their covenant, and brought into a peculiar relation to God, in virtue of it. On this ground, they receive a common seal of faith with them, in their baptism; and God, on his part, contemplates, in the rite, the fact that they are to grow up as Christians, or spiritually renewed persons. As to the precise time or manner in which they are to receive the germ of holy principle, nothing is affirmed. Only it is understood, that God includes their infant age in the womb of parental culture, and pledges himself to them and their parents, in such a way, as to offer the presumption, that they may grow up in love with all goodness, and remember no definite time when they became subjects of Christian principle. Christian education is, then, to conform to this view, and nothing is to be called Christian education which does not (p. 165).

Bushnell was charged with being a naturalist and of denying the fact and power of sin. If one reads all of Bushnell, but especially *Christian Nurture* and *Nature and the Supernatural*, one will find a more balanced view of what is meant. For Bushnell,

> Nature . . . is that created realm of being or substance which has an acting,

a going on or process from within itself, under and by its own laws. . . . It is still to our scientific, separated from our religious contemplation a chain of causes and effects, or a scheme of orderly succession, determined from within the scheme itself (*Nature and the Supernatural,* pp. 36-37).

On the other hand, the supernatural is that which "is either not in the chain of natural cause and effect, or which acts on the chain of natural cause and effect, in nature, from without the chain" (p. 37). The supernatural is superior to the natural which exists for the former. It is a "system not under the law of cause and effect, but ruled and marshaled under other kinds of laws and able continually to act upon, or vary the action of the processes of nature"; he spoke of nature and supernature as the one true system of God (p. 38).

What Bushnell was teaching is that God can work in a supernatural way through the organic unity of the family so that the child will grow up knowing the Christian way and choosing it over the sinful way. There is no conceivable way that education can be termed Christian education unless it is ordered along this central process; it is, otherwise, to be termed un-Christian education, for it educates the child to the belief that one must grow up in sin and then turn from that sin at a mature age, then, but not before, to be called a Christian.

This organic unity is the supernatural work of God through the family; yet the parents are not mere passive conduits of God's power, just as the child is not a mere vessel of parental piety. Parents make decisions and act certain ways toward their infants, and in this action and decision making they are impressing the child with what it means to be a Christian. This nurture is more than influence, although that is a part of it, especially after about age three. Prior to this age it is rather an impression made in the life of the infant when the infant is yet unable to understand. The child receives these impressions imperceptibly, just as parents often transmit them without being conscious of what they are doing. Once the age of impressions is passed, the child becomes capable of conscious reception of parental influence and of making decisions. These receptions and decisions may, but do not necessarily, involve struggle, fall, and rescue.

Bushnell's central thesis is strengthened by his belief that one can know God intuitively and is, therefore, not confined to rational processes. This intuitive knowledge, this mystical experience is not anti-

Appendix II

rational, but neither is it limited by logical reasoning. It is possible, then, for a person to experience God directly. Taken together, the organic unity of the family, the belief that nature and the supernatural form the one true system of God, and the conviction that knowledge of God can come intuitively—all of these—comprise the true idea of Christian education.

Bushnell struck another blow to a rationalistic approach to the essence of being Christian with his view on language, set forth as an introductory essay in *God in Christ*. Language, in terms of its use in shaping religious concepts, is not exact, Bushnell held, and therefore cannot be literal in its expression. Rather, language must approach truth as paradox, as enigma, and be expressed primarily in images, as in poetry. This does not invalidate argument, inference, clarification, and other logical action by which a teacher or writer communicates, but it does emphasize that religion is so far above logical reasoning that language simply cannot express it adequately. Understanding this about Bushnell, one is in a better position to begin to understand what he meant by what he wrote. To fail to appreciate his imagery, his respect for language, and his understanding of its limitations is to consign oneself to the great company who are bewildered by this man whose thought came as a fresh spring rain over the Connecticut valley nurturing a budding view of humanity which the winters of stern Calvinism had stunted.

Appendix III

Coe's Theory—Salvation by Education

George Albert Coe was a remarkable person whose thought dominated religious education theory in the first quarter, if not the first third, of this century. Although Bushnell antedates Coe and is most often the beginning point in any consideration of religious education theory, Coe formulated the first comprehensive theory. One may wonder whether, in fact, Coe had three theories, one in *The Spiritual Life,* another in *A Social Theory of Religious Education,* and a third in *What Is Christian Education?* Regardless, on analysis these three works taken together, plus others, firmly establish Coe's place as a pioneer in religious education theory.

Coe's *The Spiritual Life* was written a year before William James's Gifford lectures on "The Varieties of Religious Experience." His *A Social Theory* appeared the same year as Walter Rauschenbusch's theological rationale for the social gospel. In *What Is Christian Education?* he set forth a creative principle which was an early blend of romanticism (not idealism) with empiricism.

One of the threads throughout Coe's thought is the idea of salvation by education. If he did not create the phrase, he at least gave it status when he asked, "Is it not strange that salvation by education has never received doctrinal recognition?" (*The Religion of a Mature Mind,* pp. 294-295). It is, of course, a question to which he already had an answer, as the form of the question betrayed. He believed the notion should have the same validity as does the belief that God works in the conversion of an adult. ". . . children may be reared under Christian presuppositions," he held with Bushnell, "so as never to know themselves as being anything but Christian" (p. 325). Education that does not recognize that it is itself a saving work leads children to equate salvation with forgiveness of sin and deliverance from guilt and thereby encourages "them to count themselves as outside the fold until they are rescued from a life of sin" (p. 368).

Coe makes frequent reference to the belief that children are to be reared from within rather than without the kingdom. The adult who willingly sins is required to "repent and be converted, but children, already possessing the life-principle of the kingdom, require spiritual development" (*Education in Religion and Morals,* p. 46). If the developing child is within the kingdom, "the adolescent transition, when it comes, [will be] a step, not into the Christian life, but within the Christian life" (p. 48).

Education which is based on the assumption that children are within the kingdom also assumes "that the child has a positive religious nature" (p. 61). This does not mean that everything is all right with them, that they naturally grow properly, that they need no help in their growth, or that they are necessarily conscious of God. Positively, what it means, Coe wrote, is:

> (a) That the child has more than a passive capacity for spiritual things. . . . (b) That nothing short of union with God can really bring a human being to himself. . . . (c) That the successive phases in the growth of the child personality may be, and normally are, so many phases of a growing consciousness of the divine meaning of life (p. 62).

A major source of misunderstanding the true nature of education as a saving reality is in the concept of the new birth. Coe challenged the term "new birth," suggesting that the Bible really says and teaches that man is "born from above." Whereas "new birth" means a sudden change, "born from above" implies a kind of life, as Coe put it, "The life from above is a *kind* of life, and its source is God. There is here no antithesis to education or development" (p. 65).

Holding to salvation by education eliminates the necessity of asking when religious education should begin, Coe said, "for it really begins with the beginning of experience, and it goes forward with experience." The question becomes one of a kind, he continued: "Shall it be positive or negative, symmetrical or distorted, repressive or emancipating?" (p. 207).

This call for a doctrine of salvation by education is consistent with Coe's view of God as educator and as immanent, as he wrote:

> Salvation by education is a possibility and a fact because education is not merely something that we do to and for the child, and not merely this united with the child's own efforts for himself. God is the central reality of the whole. He is the moving force, the giver of the inner law, and the goal of all human development. Through education he extends his saving grace to the child (*Mature Mind,* pp. 319-320).

It follows then, that far from making God unnecessary to salvation, education construed as being the means of salvation "becomes a means of making him [man] conscious of the God in whom he lives and moves and has his being" (p. 320).

Salvation by education is set over against total depravity. Depravity holds "that there is nothing in the child that is worth bringing out, that development can do nothing for him, that he must wait for something to happen to him before he can so much as begin to be religious" (*Religion and Morals,* p. 50). Thus to hold to total depravity is to nullify the idea and role of religious education (p. 49). On the other hand, although total depravity contradicts the possibility of education, salvation by education does not deny that evil tendencies are present or that decisions do not need to be made. Coe held that evil tendencies "find a continuous corrective in divine help" and decisions remain important because "normal growth takes place only through co-operation of the individual will with the inner divine impulsion" (p. 56).

In his later writings, Coe argued that the education that is effectual is social education. "Society," he said, "is not merely one educator among many; it is the prime educator within all educational enterprises" (*Social Theory,* p. 14). Coe, by this time, had come to assess as inadequate the conception of education as helping the child actualize his potential by simply aiding his unfolding powers. The social view of education required that the child be helped "to discriminate between them [powers], and while promoting the growth of some, to prevent the growth of others" (p. 15). This view requires social interaction and precludes a highly individualistic education.

Coe, however, did not envision the total absorption of the individual in the group. Either extreme—the individual turned completely on himself, or given blindly to the mass—is unacceptable. The ideal end is "regard of individual for individual, reciprocal regard of the individual for his group, and of his group for him, and regard of one group for another" (p. 38). This can happen only in a social setting, as Coe said, ". . . in the last analysis, social experience is the only thing that can thus socialize any one" (p. 19). In more specific reference to religious education Coe made it clear that social experience provides children with "conditions in which love is experienced, practised, wrought into steady and deliberate living by the help of both intellectual analysis and habit formation, and developed into a faith that illumines the crises and the mysteries of life" (p. 80).

Appendix IV

Educational Theory Since 1940

Kendig Cully, Wayne Rood, and Harold William Burgess have provided helpful attempts at reviewing and grouping religious education theories. Cully's *The Search for a Christian Education—Since 1940* (1965) organizes the theorists under categories, such as liberalist, psychologically oriented, relational, biblically based, fundamentalist and neo-evangelical, and church-focused. Within each of these categories, Cully further divides the theorists. For example, in the category "Biblical Bases of Nurture," he includes James D. Smart, Iris Cully, and D. Campbell Wyckoff.

Cully makes a good case for his classification and includes most of the "names" in the wide field of theories of religious education. A conspicuous exception is Findley Edge, a Southern Baptist who at the time of Cully's writing had produced *A Quest for Vitality in Religion*, an experiential philosophy of religious education based in a neoorthodox theology.

Cully calls on religious education theory to learn the importance of historical perspectives from the revival of biblical theology and the ecumenical movement. By discovering its roots, religious education theory, in Cully's opinion, will have more appeal to the theological student, will engage in dialogue with other disciples, and will provide the church a more solid basis for the practice of education. His is a worthy summons. However, more than fifteen years after the summons most theorists have been more influenced by the psychologists than by these other movements.

Five years after Cully's work, Wayne R. Rood, in *Understanding Christian Education*, attempted to provide religious education theory with categories parallel to what others had done for general education. He suggested three: experimentalism, personalism, and essentialism. He roots experimentalism in John Dewey, personalism in George Albert Coe, and essentialism in Maria Montessori. In terms of theorists after 1940, Rood's and Cully's lists are almost parallel. A major name, Randolph Miller, is missing; Ernest Ligon is added.

Experimental (or pragmatic) Christian education has Christian character as its purpose, the reconstruction of life as its goal, and moral and spiritual values as its content. For personalism, the purpose is Christian maturity, the goal is creative love, and the content is interpersonal relations, a category similar to Cully's understanding of psychologically oriented nurture. The purpose of essentialist education is confrontation with the Word, with the Bible and the creed as the content. The goal of this category is acceptance of a restored relationship with God.

Rood experienced the same problem Cully had already admitted to and which all who attempt to "classify" also know, namely, the fact that a single theorist cannot usually be put exclusively under one category. For example, Cully had to choose whether to put Reuel Howe with psychologically oriented nurture or with relational education. On analysis, Rood has the same problem, most notably with Coe who might be an experimentalist as well as a personalist.

Five years after Rood's work, Harold Burgess, in *An Invitation to Religious Education*, names four theoretical approaches to religious education theory: the traditional approach, the social-cultural approach, the contemporary theological approach, and the social-science approach. The traditional theological approach parallel's Cully's fundamentalist and neo-evangelical category and Rood's essentialism. The social-cultural approach is most closely identified with Coe's thought, with what Rood termed personalism. The contemporary theological approach in Burgess is different from the traditional approach in that the former is concerned more with the place of the Christian community and a small group methodology, whereas the traditional approach emphasizes the communication of a divine word by an authority figure. This category crosses many of Cully's classifications. The social-science approach is based in the teaching-learning process and is neutral as concerns theology. Burgess finds only James Michael Lee as a proponent for the social-science approach and makes enthusiastic claims for its originality as a comprehensive theory. However, some Protestant education, at least in practice, has operated along this line, especially in superimposing the methods of progressive education onto a conservative authoritarian theology.

In addition to these reviews and evaluations of theories and theorists, there are the compilation-staples which provide overviews of the field: *Introduction to Christian Education* and its sequel, both edited by Marvin Taylor; *An Introduction to Evangelical Christian Education*, edited by J. Edward Hakes, *Exploring Christian Education*, edited by A. Elwood Sanner and A. F. Harper; and *A Survey of Religious Education*, edited by J. M. Price *et al*. Similarly there are single-author works, such as Peter P. Person's *An Introduction to Christian Education* and J. Donald Butler's *Religious Education*.

These attempts have served useful purposes, but current interest in this kind of work is not high among theory makers. Rather, the intrigue is in at least four areas: religious education and theology, psychology and religious development, phenomenal guiding ideas, and how to talk about the field.

One strand in religious education theory is the continuing discussion of the relation between theology and education. In spite of Harrison Elliott's suggestion that there is no one faith which religious education is responsible to communicate, and Lee's suggestion of a theologically neutral social-science approach, Miller's concern for theological concern continues to attract theorists. The question is not a simple one of finding a theology to fit Christian education, but of understanding the relationship between the two and of how to work responsibly in that relationship in light of other dynamics. Sara Little is correct that we will not likely find a suitable theology; however, she does not suggest that the quest be abandoned *(Foundations for Christian Education in an Era of Change)*.

Among contemporary dialogues on theology and education, process theology is receiving the major attention, although Nels F. S. Ferré was discussing it in relation to education over fifteen years ago *(A Theology for Christian Education),* and God in Coe's social theory was certainly in process. (See *Process and Relationship,* edited by Iris and Kendig Cully; Randolph Miller's *The Theory of Christian Education Practice;* and the symposium in *Religious Education,* May-June, 1973.)

The discussion concerning theology and education has been carried on mostly by educators; the major theologians have pretty much ignored educational theory. The luminaries in religious education theory have dealt materially with theology, but the major theologians have not written on religious education. Occasionally theological types will come over to our journals and tell us how Teilhard's or Whitehead's thought might affect religious education (albeit an instructive contribution), but theological journals and books rarely take note of educational theorists. Some theologians, to the benefit of all, have written books on faith and education, e.g., Thomas De Wolfe's *Teaching Our Faith in God,* but from the relationship of theology the giver, education the receiver. The Presbyterians and Lutherans, a few years ago, demonstrated the essential interplay between education and theology when in response to the affiliative needs of their children and the ritual concerns of the church they reapplied their doctrines of baptism and Communion.

A second strand is the interest in shaping or at least explaining religious education in terms of the major psychologies. The influence of the cognitivists, the psychoanalysts, the phenomenologists, and the behaviorists is immense. Jean Piaget, Carl Jung, and Erik Erikson receive much of the attention in theory making. However, Abraham Maslow, Carl Rogers, Gordon Allport, Erich Fromm, and B. F. Skinner have high respect in the more particular concern of learning and teaching. Theorists who attempt to build educational theories around these psychologies will meet only futility; if it is difficult to build on a theology, how much more on a psychology. However, theorists who find in these psychologies the personal dynamics behind what we do in religious education will help clarify religious education. In addition, one of the valuable contributions of this turn to the psychologists is that we have seemingly lost interest in building religious theory from general educational theory.

Some notable work has come out of this interest in the major psychologies. Ronald Goldman (especially in *Religious Thinking from*

Appendix IV

Childhood to Adolescence) and John Peatling (in *Character Potential: A Record of Research,* vol. 7, October, 1974, and *Knowing and Helping Youth)* have concentrated on researching the development of religious thinking along Piagetian lines. James Fowler (especially in *Stages of Faith*), in dialogue with Piaget, Erikson, and Kohlberg, has conducted original research and set forth a comprehensive faith development scheme. David Elkind (especially in *The Child and Society)* has conducted more limited research, but from his work and postulations from Piaget's work he has made stimulating proposals concerning the cognitive nature of unfolding faith. Mary Wilcox *(Developmental Journey)* has conducted original research and, drawing from Piaget, Kohlberg, and Fowler, has suggested the shape of a faith journey. Theologian Thomas Droege *(Self-Realization and Faith)* has laid down directions for nurture, utilizing the personality dynamics of Erikson's affective psychology. John Gleason, a chaplain *(Growing Up to God),* has sketched a suggestive relationship between Erikson's ages and religious development. Christian educator John Westerhoff III *(Will Our Children Have Faith?)* has proposed a thoughtful four-style, faith-enculturation theory which, though not research-based, is in accord with significant research and philosophical dialogue.

This affinity between psychology and religious education theory shows in *Modern Catechetics,* edited by Gerald Sloyan, and *Contemporary Approaches to Christian Education* by Jack L. Seymore et al. The connection is also in works concerned with a particular age group, e.g., Lucy Barber's *The Religious Education of Preschool Children,* Iris Cully's *Christian Child Development,* Charles Stewart's *Adolescent Religion,* and *Knowing and Helping Youth,* edited by G. Temp Sparkman. The relationship itself is explored in many places, as in two more recent books: John Peatling's *Education in the Psychological Key* and John Elias's *Psychology and Religious Education.*

The third strand is perhaps more simply a factor in religious education theory, namely, the student of theory is interested more in a phenomenon, a whole, than in categories and classifications. Thus is the theorist concerned with guiding ideas for religious education that will endure beyond the pursuit of theoretical categories. Interest in Thomas Groome's "shared praxis" and Westerhoff's "enculturation" demonstrates this concern. Idea seedlings appear regularly in anthologies, such as Gloria Durka and Joanmarie Smith's *Emerging Issues in Religious Education,* and in fresh journal articles. These have a way of defining cutting edges which eventually become full-blown guiding ideas.

Of course, these already useful and used guiding ideas will endure: Horace Bushnell's "true idea of education" *(Christian Nurture),* George Albert Coe's "creative principle" *(What Is Christian Education?),* Harrison Elliott's "question" *(Can Religious Education Be Christian?),* Randolph Miller's "clue" *(The Clue to Christian Education),* Lewis Sherrill's "struggle" *(Struggle of the Soul),* Howard Grimes's "redemptive community" *(The Church Redemptive),* Wesner Fallaw's "church education" *(Church Education for Tomorrow),* David Hunter's "engagement" *(Christian Education As Engagement),* Joseph Ban's "crossing point" *(Education for Change),* Roger Shinn's "incorporation" *(The Educational Mission of Our Church),* and Findley Edge's "quest" *(A Quest for Vitality in Religion).* Though not educational theories, James Loder's *Transforming Moment* and Fowler's work in faith development are sure to plant a seed in the mind of some budding theorist and to enrich the thinking of some theoretician whose theory making is in progress.

Westerhoff's enculturation idea has caused theorists to reevaluate the psychic and physical energy invested in the church school. Earlier, James Smart in *The Teaching Ministry of the Church* and Roger Shinn in *The Educational Mission of Our Church* exhorted educators to see that in the end it is the whole church which teaches and incorporates. We may not have taken these voices as seriously as we should, but Westerhoff has so stated the case that he is not being ignored. His argument has already produced fruitful dialogue within the family of theory makers.

The fourth strand is the renewed interest in what to call the field. Westerhoff, perhaps in dialogue with Catholic educators, appears to be the agent of the revival. He is preaching a return to an old word, *catechesis,* to name what has been most commonly termed religious or Christian education. Catechesis has been the property of the Catholic tradition; some among that group have therefore come forward with pointed critiques of catechesis as the umbrella term, e.g., Thomas

Appendix IV

Groome in *Christian Religious Education*. Groome prefers to call the field by the title of his book, which turns out to be the same as one from the 1930s by Austen DeBlois and Donald Gorham. They employed the term to set Christian religious education off from general and character education and from Moslem religious education, Jewish religious education, etc.

Some have supposed that the term "Christian education" is parochial and limited to indoctrination, an altogether defective understanding. The term "Christian education" is too prevalent in reputable circles to be accused of such myopic concentration. However, Peter Person in the 1950s did clarify that he was using the term to mean evangelical Protestant Christian education. Incidentally, he later utilized the term "Christian religious education" *(An Introduction to Christian Education)*.

Another view is that religious and Christian is the difference between liberal and conservative education. However, the "liberal" movement in education is identified closely with associations which have religious in their corporate titles while at the same time Southern Baptists use the term "religious education." Numerous evangelical groups designate the enterprise as Christian education, also a favored term of that liberal, George Albert Coe, who was active in the founding of the "Religious" Education Association.

About two decades ago Wesner Fallaw, in *Church Education for Tomorrow,* proferred the term "church education." He defined it in marked contrast to the Sunday school, which he considered inept and which he identified with pragmatism and character education. In its genesis it sounds much like what some mean by Christian education, that is, something the church does over against general education. Although one sees this term around, it apparently did not catch on as an umbrella term.

It is evident in this whole discussion that we are up against the inherent problem of definition, namely, that any term has a history and has to be defined and that, even when carefully delineated, any term raises additional and diverse images in the mind of others. Thus, the argument goes on *ad infinitum* within the unlikelihood that any sweeping changes in terminology will be made. *Ad interim,* it makes good copy for journals, gives convention planners an interesting topic for conference time, and requires all of us to rethink what we are doing, even if we are unwilling to rename it.

Appendix V

The Celebrative Rites

One of the great questions of theological and ecclesiological history is how the worshiping congregation might concretely ritualize, recognize, and celebrate its moments of faith awakenings, of heightened religious awareness, of commitments. There is wide divergence in practice, and even where the practice is similar, the underlying theology is distinct. That is why I offer alternative rites for each of the four realities in the awakening to faith. In addition, I propose numerous "passage recognitions," which will complement the celebrative rites, and commissioning litanies for persons taking on special assignments. There is a concluding word on death, the final passage.

The Infancy Rites

Let us look at two rituals for this moment of faith awakening: the rite of presentation and the rite of infant baptism.

The Rite of Presentation

The rite of presentation is focused in the touch. Because this rite has no certain theological history or consistent practice, I am suggesting in some detail how it might proceed and have created materials for its doing. It consists of a litany of presentation, participated in by the parents and the minister, and the singing of a hymn. There is nothing magical in this uncomplicated rite, nothing transferred from minister to child. No one should suppose the rite confers regeneration. The rite is a simple, yet arresting, symbol that the child is a child of God and that this status is a gift of God, not of parent, minister, or church.

A Covenant of Presentation

Minister: We are here today to present Emma to the church and to consecrate her to God. Who brings the child for this holy purpose?

Parents: We, her parents, bring Emma to be dedicated to God.

Minister: What can we affirm about Emma?

Congregation: That she is made in the image of God and is a child of God by creation.

Minister: As Emma grows in our congregation, how will we show her that she is a child of God?

Congregation: We will give her our love and will include her in the experience of the congregation.

Minister: As Emma grows into childhood, what will we tell her about her history?

Congregation: We will tell her about Abraham, the father of our faith; about Sarah, the mother of Isaac; about Moses, who led our ancestors out of bondage; about Ruth's example of faithfulness; about the Jewish hope for a Messiah; about Jesus Christ the Savior; and about the history of the church as the people of God.

Minister: What will we expect of Emma?

Congregation: We look to the day when she will sit with us at the Lord's Table, declare faith in Jesus Christ, confirm the heritage which we will pass along to her, and come as an adult to full commitment to God's will and work.

Minister: Do you, Emma's parents, assume your primary responsibility for keeping Emma in touch with such expectations?

Parents: Yes, we happily and genuinely accept this serious duty.

Minister:	And do you, the congregation, pledge to work toward creating a nurturing environment for Emma?
Congregation:	Yes, we do, for she belongs to us as well.
Minister:	Then may God be with us.
Congregation:	God help us. Amen.
Minister:	Amen.

The Touch

One way to administer the touch is for the parents to hold Emma, facing the congregation, then have the minister lay hands lovingly on Emma's head, saying: "Emma, your parents have given you birth; you are made in God's image and you are a daughter of God. All of us promise to nurture you in faith. Amen."

A Hymn

In God's Image

All are made in God's own image,
In God's likeness, made we all.
From the hand of the Creator
Free gift not lost in the Fall.

In our birth, the gift is given
Work cannot its beauty earn.
Yet, it carries high intention:
Trusteeship, its grand concern.

Though comes sin the gift obscuring,
Still it stands as God-imbued.
Comes the Christ the gift unveiling,
In his life it is renewed.

O what joy such news resounding,
O what tidings on the wing:
Liberated from sin's binding,
We are free to work and sing.

Words copyright © by G. Temp Sparkman, 1980
To be sung to Stuttgart hymn tune, 8.7.8.7., by Christian F. Witt

The Rite of Infant Baptism

The baptism of infants is an ancient rite, and each church practicing it has its own meaning and method. To the Episcopalian, baptism is a "sign of Regeneration or New Birth," a grafting into the Church, a sealing of the forgiveness of sin and "adoption to be the sons of God," a confirmation of faith (*The Book of Common Prayer*, p. 608). The Lutheran believes that "In Holy Baptism God adopts us into the household of faith and establishes a covenant that he does not break" (*Affirmation of the Baptismal Covenant*, p. 7). To the Presbyterian, baptism has more of a covenantal character, signifying that the child is "enrolled, entered, and received into the covenant and family, and so into the inheritance of the sons of God" (*Power to Permit Children at the Lord's Table*, p. 5).

It would be presumptuous of me, out of a believer's baptismal theology, to attempt a reinterpretation of infant baptism or to suggest how it is to be celebrated. However, I can hope that the practice would give more place to sonship–daughtership as gift of creation, a gesture which would not be in violation of covenant theology, as the Presbyterian statement demonstrates. While the rite may carry the promise of regeneration, if it actually offers infant regeneration, then the rite cannot symbolize the import of the religious reality of sonship–daughtership.

The Middle Child Rites

We examine now the rite of child baptism and the rite of the Lord's Supper as each relates to the heightened religious awareness of the middle child.

The Rite of Child Baptism

Child baptism may find its meaning in three sources. First, it may favor the language of infant baptism, signifying that the child is being brought under the covenant of grace. This position would borrow from the covenant idea in the Old Testament, involved integrally with the solidarity of child and father and the religious function of the family.

Second, child baptism may borrow its language from believer's baptism, signifying repentance from sin and symbolizing death to sin and resurrection to new life. Because this is the predominant meaning of child baptism, formulas abound for the practice. Third, the baptism of the child may be viewed as Christian initiation into the household of faith, into membership in the congregation.

Of the three, only initiatory baptism, though it goes further in its meaning than my concept of belonging, can convey the belongingness which is the religious reality of middle childhood. Currently, no formula exists for this particular meaning of child baptism. (See Appendix I, "Baptism: A Theological Question.")

The Rite of the Lord's Supper

The participation of the middle child in the Lord's Supper proceeds from two directions. It continues that which was symbolized in the infant rite and anticipates the declaration of faith which is yet to come. It reminds children that they are children of God, a status given by God. It tells them that they also are children of the congregation where their parents are participating members. At the same time, it identifies them as children of promise who will, in appropriate seasons, declare faith and make more lasting commitments.

To the Presbyterians, "The Holy Table is none other than Christ's Table. He invites those who put their trust in him to share in the feast which he has prepared" (*Power to Permit*, p. 34). The Lutheran statement on Communion holds that it is a baptized child's birthright. It says of the children who come for the first time, "They have learned how in sharing the bread and wine of Holy Communion we remember Jesus' death and his rising to life again on that first Easter day, and how eating the bread and drinking the wine makes us one with him and brings us closer to each other" (*Affirmation of the Baptismal Covenant*, p. 13). Baptist confessions of faith include the Lord's Supper as a memorial to Christ's death and as a sign of fellowship with one another and communion with Christ.

Any of these views of the meaning of the Lord's Supper are compatible with the rich meaning of belonging as the religious reality for the middle child. The child, in participating, remembers Christ's death, celebrates Christ's resurrection, fellowships with the community of faith, and anticipates God's completion of salvation. (See Appendix VIII, "The Lord's Table.")

A Celebration of Belonging

(For use with baptism and/or first Communion)

Minister: Today we celebrate a grand moment in Emma's faith journey.

Congregation: Emma has grown among us as a child of God. We have lovingly nurtured her in the faith we all share in common. In many ways we have shown Emma that she is part of us.

Minister: What more shall we say to her?

Congregation: We now say to her more dramatically that she belongs. We welcome her to the Lord's Table, a sign of God's continuing grace in her life and of this congregation.

Minister: Emma, we have come often to the Lord's Supper to remember the life of Jesus Christ and to find strength in each other's faith. Today, by having you participate with us, we add new joy. You belong to us. But this moment holds additional celebration.

Congregation: As Emma takes first Communion we sense a promise that in a few years she will come to affirm her heritage of faith and decide for herself her relationship to Jesus Christ and the church.

Minister: We have talked of belonging and promise. What else can we affirm?

Congregation: In receiving Emma as Jesus accepted the children, we commit ourselves again to our own responsibilities as followers of Jesus Christ, on mission through the church.

Minister: So let it be! So let it be! Amen.

Appendix V

(Note: In cases when more than one child is involved, substitute "children" and/or "our children" for "Emma"; change verbs and singular nouns and pronouns to the plural.)

A Hymn

(For use with baptism and/or first Communion)

Let the Children Come

Children belong where parents' faith
In rich devotion lives;
Where congregation worships God
And Christian nurture gives.

Salvation planted by God's grace
Now comes to bud and grows
By secret power small seeds hold,
Till the full flower shows.

Jesus said, "Let the children come,
Forbid them not their place,
For in their simple faith reside
The kingdom's joy and grace."

(A stanza for first Communion for children who were baptized in infancy)

Welcome, dear children, to the Lord's
Table spread out for you,
The bread and cup now gladly take
And to Christ e'er be true.

Words copyright © by G. Temp Sparkman, 1982
Hymn tune, St. Agnes, CM, by John B. Dykes

The Rites of Affirmation

There are two rites presented here to mark the faith awakening of adolescents.

The Rite of Believer's Baptism

Believer's baptism is of a person who has declared faith in Jesus Christ, a declaration coming from an understanding of sin, its meaning and consequence, and of faith, its origin and blessing. It signifies a self-assumed faith at a time in one's life when choice between sin and faith is most critical. It symbolizes one's continuing death to sin and resurrection to walk in a new life. In this, it is confirming a process that has been at work in the life of the child from birth, but only now self-consciously acted on. Thus, it qualifies supremely as a fitting rite for the religious reality of affirmation.

Affirmation of Faith and Baptism

Minister: The Scripture reads: "Then they that gladly received his word were baptized." Today, Emma comes to be baptized. Many years ago, as an infant made in the image of God, she was presented by her parents to the congregation and consecrated to God. In childhood she was assured that she belonged to the life of the community of faith. Emma has appraised that heritage and confirmed it; she has faced her life situation and affirmed faith in Jesus Christ.

Choir: Alleluia.

Minister: Behold, the baptismal water; behold the believer. Is there anything to hinder Emma from being baptized?

Congregation: No; as Emma has grown among us, we have seen God's grace at work in her, and now that she has come to this moment to assume heritage and faith, we joyfully welcome her baptism.

Choir: Alleluia.

Minister: Emma, repeat after me:
I understand that in this baptism
I am willingly and openly
Confirming my heritage in faith

Appendix V 213

|Minister:| and declaring faith in Jesus Christ.
Emma, upon your confession of faith I joyfully baptize you.
Choir: Alleluia.
All Sing: "We This Declaration Speak"

A *Hymn*

For use with baptism or affirmation of baptismal vows.)

We This Declaration Speak

We this heritage appraise, Faith's own history we raise;
Child of God in infant birth, Told and shown our given worth.
To the congregation made   To belong without our aid,
As the Christ who in the way   Blessed the children of his day.

We this heritage confirm; Our baptismal vows affirm;
Grateful for God's keeping grace; Taking consciously our place.
We believe; declare Christ Lord; Heeding both his life and word.
Vowing God's own will to seek, We this declaration speak.

Words copyright © by G. Temp Sparkman, 1982
Hymn tune, St. George's Windsor, 7.7.7.7.D. by George J. Elvey

The Rite of Light

Many adolescents come to the time for a declaration of faith from a long background of membership in the church. They were baptized as infants and admitted to participation in Communion in middle childhood. Traditionally, these children have been given the rite of confirmation. However, because of the wide understandings and uses of the term "confirmation," some churches have looked for new ways of ritualizing the adolescent experience of faith. The Lutherans, for example, call such experience "an affirmation of the baptismal covenant" and end the service with the exchanging of the sign of the peace of Christ. An appropriate symbol, light, deserves consideration as the rite of affirmation in instances where persons have already been baptized. Already a familiar feature in worship, especially at Christmas and Easter, the lighted candle comes to symbolize the affirmed believer's coming out of darkness into light. The light has been present since birth and has been overcoming the darkness as God's grace has worked in the child. But now, in adolescence, the person understands more clearly the struggle between the light and the darkness and is able to bear more responsibly the meaning of being light in the world.

Affirmation of Baptismal Vows

The affirmants process with unlighted candles or, if seated already, are called to stand at the front of the sanctuary, facing the congregation.

Minister:	People of God, see before you the children of God, children of this congregation.
Congregation:	We see and we rejoice.
Choir:	Alleluia.
Minister:	Children of God, children of this congregation, see before you those who brought you for baptism and nurtured you in faith.
Affirmants:	We see and we give thanks.
Choir:	Alleluia.
Minister:	Besides your gratitude to these people, what do you bring today?

Appendix V

Affirmants:	We bring ourselves. We come to affirm the baptismal vows made in our behalf before we were old enough to know and respond to God's grace. We come confirming the heritage of faith in which we have been reared. We come confessing Jesus Christ as Lord.
Choir:	Alleluia.
Minister:	It is a day of fulfillment. Those whom we consecrated to God do this day come to give themselves to God, to confess for themselves faith in the Christ.
Congregation:	It is a day of joy. Those whom we loved and whom we taught the faith do this day respond personally to God's love and take on for themselves the faith of the church.
Choir:	Alleluia.
Minister:	See before us the shining light, the Christmas candle, the Easter candle, the symbol of Christ's presence among us.
Congregation:	We behold his glory, the only begotten of God.
Minister:	See around us the spreading light, giving light to the world.
Congregation:	The light shines in the darkness and the darkness does not overcome it.
Minister:	See within us the warming light, lighting our lives.
Congregation:	Jesus is the true Light, lighting all persons who come into the world.
Choir:	Alleluia.
Minister:	Now to symbolize the meaning of this holy moment of affirmation, put your candle to that light as an act of faith; pull your candle away and see that you, too, are light, as Jesus said.

The Affirmants light their candles.

216 THE SALVATION AND NURTURE OF THE CHILD OF GOD

Minister: Child of God. Child of promise. Child of faith. Light in the world. Rejoice in your salvation. Go as light into the world.

Choir: Alleluia.

All sing, "We This Declaration Speak." (See p. 213.)

Affirmants recess to the vestibule.

The Rite of Creative Trusteeship: Laying On of Hands

Except for ordination to the career ministry and, in some churches, ordination to the lay ministry of the deacon, there is little attention given to heightened adult religious experience and decision. Of course, the continuous participation of the adult in the celebration of the Lord's Supper is a concrete expression of the possibility for the renewal of one's religious experience. However, something more is needed. The congregation needs a way to establish the expectation that adults of some Christian maturity will face their responsibility to join the generational stream as the bearers of nurture and the missioners for the gospel in the world. Adults who come to this point are ready to make public demonstration of their commitment to creative trusteeship.

Upon the occasion of such commitment, the congregation will applaud the decision and commission the person as a creative trustee. The blessing will be communicated through the rite of the laying on of hands. This rite completes the cycle. At the beginning of life, the minister, either by the touch or by baptism, led the congregation in worship as parents presented the infant for consecration. In middle childhood the child was, by admission to the Lord's Table or by baptism,

Appendix V

shown to belong to the community of faith. Later, either by water or by light, the minister and the congregation celebrated the youth's declaration of faith. Now the congregation touches the adult, giving its blessing, as the adult becomes a creative trustee for God in the world.

Celebrating Creative Trusteeship

Minister: In creating humanity, God said, "Let us make man in our image, after our likeness; and let them have dominion over all the earth." And God blessed them and said to them, "Be fruitful and multiply, and replenish the earth, and subdue it."

Congregation: We are made in God's image and are to exercise dominion over the earth.

Minister: The psalmist said, "Thou madest him to have dominion over the works of thy hands; thou hast put all things under his feet."

Congregation: We are made in God's image and are to exercise dominion over the earth.

Minister: Our ancestors in the faith taught, "You shall love the Lord your God with all your heart, and with all your soul, and with all your might. You shall love your neighbor as yourself."

Congregation: Jesus Christ affirmed and fulfilled these great commandments.

Minister: As the People of God we are to follow the example of Jesus and thus complete the command to have dominion in the earth. We are to exercise creative trusteeship in our world.

Emma has understood this example, this command, and has committed herself to be a creative trustee for God. She will now come to tell us how God brought her to this fulfilling decision.

Emma recounts her awakening to faith.

Minister: Emma has shared her faith journey with us and has responded to the call of God to be a creative trustee. What is your response?

Congregation: We affirm Emma in her decision and pledge to pray for her as she lives out her commitment.

The minister asks Emma to kneel facing the congregation, then invites anyone who wishes to come by, lay hands on Emma, and give her a blessing.

At the end, Emma faces the congregation and all sing, "We Are God's People."

A Hymn

We Are God's People

This is God's world, all things belong
To some design, some good intent.
Nothing is earned, it all is giv'n;
It all is lent.

This is Christ's church; he gives it life.
He is its founder, is its Lord.
The church begins and ends in him;
Lives by his word.

We are God's people, God's trustees.
We live God's purpose to unfurl.
We are Christ's servants, his own priests
In church and world.

Words copyright © by G. Temp Sparkman, 1982
Hymn tune, Oldbridge, by Robert N. Quaile, 8.8.8.4.

Commissionings for Particular Functions

Special tasks vital to the church's mission require the commissioning of persons who take on particular tasks for the whole congregation, such as committee assignments, deacon, elder, or presbyter service, and mission trips. Salt, oil, spices, and water can be used appropriately

Appendix V

and meaningfully to symbolize the import of these commissionings. Consult regular worship books for materials for such occasions or see *Writing Your Own Worship Materials* (G. Temp Sparkman, published by Judson Press), chapter 5, on readings and litanies. Toward the end of these readings, alter them so as to make transition to the use of the following symbols.

Salt Commissioning

The participants, facing the congregation, ask: "By what concrete sign may we symbolize our commissioning?" The minister, lifting a bowl of salt with both hands, says: "Jesus taught that Christians are the salt of the earth. You who today commit yourselves to this significant task are being salt in the world." The minister then turns to the first person in the group and, holding the bowl with both hands, looks into the person's eyes, calls the person by name, and says: "You are the salt of the earth." That person then takes the bowl and does the same thing. And so it goes around the group. (Eye contact, calling by name, and holding the bowl in a serving fashion are important to the meaning of the celebration.) After all have been served, the minister again lifts the bowl and says: "Let us go from this place to be the salt of the earth."

Oil or Spice Commissioning

The minister, with back to the congregation, lifts a bowl containing the oil or spice and says: "This oil (or spice) is the sign of God's energy within you and the seal of God's support as you undertake your work." The minister then hands the bowl to a helper who stands next to the minister. Beginning with the first participant, with all participants facing the congregation, the minister dips into the bowl and touches the person's forehead, rubbing it three times, then, calling the person's name, says: "As a sign of your commitment, verbalized in the company of this congregation and before God, I do now anoint you for your work." After all have been anointed, the minister says: "Let us go into the world as those anointed for special work for God."

Water Commissioning

The participants face the congregation around a table on which is placed a bowl of water and a towel. The minister, with back to the congregation, extends both hands toward the bowl and says: "Jesus washed the feet of his disciples and in so doing showed himself to be servant, an acted parable of his teaching that those who would be greatest must be servant of all. In that same spirit, you have today taken vows of service. Thus will I now wash your hands as a sign of servanthood and as a reminder that as you serve others you are serving God." Each participant will individually approach the bowl, putting both hands into the water. The minister will lift the participant's hands from the water, raising them to chest level, then will take the towel and dry the hands, and will say: "Go and do the same."

Passage Recognitions

Besides celebrating intensified religious experiences through the four celebrative rites, a congregation should recognize other significant passages in the life cycle. Gifts, litanies, citations, and symbolic acts may accompany the acknowledgement of these passages.

Age-Related Passages

Entrance to first grade
Entrance to middle or junior high school
The obtaining of one's driver's license
Graduation from high school
Graduation from college or other kind of school
Marriage
Twenty-fifth and fiftieth wedding anniversaries
Career changes
Retirement

Wound-Embracing Rite

In addition to these age-related passages, the congregation needs a "wound-embracing rite" by which it acknowledges the reality of divorce, death, and other separations and embraces in love the persons who are caught in the throes of such crises. We do this quite easily when a person grieves over the death of a close one, but we have difficulty admitting to the reality that there are, as Robert Frost wrote

Appendix V

in the poem "The Hill Wife," ". . . finalities besides the grave."*
Take divorce as an example. A wayward brother or sister who comes for confession and rededication is heartily received; divorced brothers and sisters slip back into worship as into glass houses, without an including embrace. Obviously, this is a very sensitive issue, but if we are a true community of faith, we will find ways to embrace the wounded, and as the wounded, to be embraced.

Death: The Final Passage

Death is the final passage, and the funeral is the last rite. The grave mysteriously draws us into a three-dimensional experience in which we look backward, we look within, and we look beyond. We look back in time to acknowledge a human life which, to paraphrase Rupert Brooke, "saw dawn and sunset and the colors of the earth." We look within to acknowledge the grief which such loss brings and, perhaps in some measure, to grieve over our own mortality. We look beyond the existential moment in hope. The funeral, or grave rite—if one wants to term it a rite—should then include both the recognition of loss in the experience of the living and the inheritance of the resurrected life by the dead. Without this dialectic, the funeral will become either an orgy of weeping as of people who have no hope, or a platitudinous exercise in unreality, denying the seriousness of earth's part in eternity and the intense pain of separation.

*From "The Hill Wife" from *The Poetry of Robert Frost*, edited by Edward Connery Lathem. Copyright 1916, © 1969 by Holt, Rinehart and Winston. Copyright 1944 by Robert Frost. Reprinted by permission of Holt, Rinehart and Winston, Publishers.

Appendix VI

Image and Fall

Person is made in the image of God. ("Person" is a substitute for "man".) This is a clear teaching of the Old Testament even though the fall of person outweighs the image of God in contemporary views of human nature. Therefore, the two notions, person in God's image and fallen humanity, go together as classical doctrines of the church.

The Image of God

The three uses of the phrase "image of God" in the Old Testament are in Genesis and from the Priestly strand of biblical tradition (Genesis 1:26-27; 5:1-3; 9:5-6). The older Jahwist account of creation does not include the phrase. The Old Testament writer simply announces that person is made in the image of God, but does not interpret the assertion. Some interpretation is in Psalm 8 and in two Apocryphal works: Ecclesiasticus 17:3ff. and the Wisdom of Solomon 2:23. To our dismay, the New Testament writers do not bother to exegete the Genesis passages. However, beyond the Bible there is a wide body of speculation and a plethora of notions as to the meaning and implications of the *Imago Dei*. The most comprehensive review of these interpretations from the Fathers to contemporary theologians is in David Cairns's *The Image of God in Man*, written in 1953, but since revised.

The Meaning of the Image

The major Old Testament theologians—Edmond Jacob, Gerhard Von Rad, Walther Eichrodt, and Theodorus Vriezen—consider the image of God to be a central reality in the Old Testament. For example, Jacob, while acknowledging surprise that the notion is in a document so strong on God's transcendence, insists that "it is not a truth mentioned in passing but a quite fundamental reality" (*Theology of the Old Testament*, p. 168). That it is central seems established; it is its meaning that is so controversial.

Theodorus Vriezen believes that "image of God" indicates a special relationship to God. Out of this relationship God gives person dominion over the animal world. So "image" does not mean "dominion." Person is "God's vice-regent on earth," but more importantly reflects "in his nature the nature of God." Although in Genesis 2, person is shown as being in harmony with God, as being in innocence, being in the image does not mean a state of rightness (*An Outline of Old Testament Theology*, pp. 413-414).

Gerhard von Rad, finding no explicit explanation for the meaning of the image of God, focuses on the reason for person being made in that image. That reason is that "man should uphold and enforce his—God's—claims as lord." This signature, "lord in the world," is not solely spiritual or intellectual but is also physical. But rather than making God anthropomorphic, it makes "man as theomorphic" (*Old Testament Theology*, vol. 1, pp. 145-146).

Walther Eichrodt studies the Hebrew words for "image" and "likeness" and holds that the writer's use of "likeness" clearly refutes that physical correspondence between God and person is adequate to describe the meaning of being in the image of God. He points out that the word "likeness" only is used in Genesis 5:1 and argues that this means that the writer did not want the reader to establish too close an identity of the human form with God. Rather, held Eichrodt, the writer wanted to set forth the thought of "the absolute otherness and transcendence of the divine nature," "a correspondence between God and Man which could only figuratively be characterized as the endowment of Man with God's 'image'" (*Theology of the Old Testament*, vol. 2, pp. 122-126).

Edmond Jacob considers the image to mean that person is representative of God and exists in "relationship with and dependence upon" God. He joins the other theologians in interpreting the image of God to mean a peculiar kind of relationship between God and person, but

Appendix VI 225

not a state of goodness in the sense of moral perfection (*Theology of the Old Testament,* pp. 166-171).

The systematic theologians carry the argument forward. For example, Karl Barth holds that the image of God "is not a quality of man. Hence there is no point in asking in which of man's peculiar attributes and attitudes it consists. It does not consist in anything that man is or does" (*Church Dogmatics, III*-1, p. 184). Person is "partner . . . capable of action and responsibility . . . a counterpart . . . [a] copy and reflection" of God's own being (pp. 184-185). But Barth moves on to the New Testament to affirm what Paul believed, namely, that Jesus Christ is in fact the express image of God. As partakers with Christ, we then can be said to possess the image, for it becomes a human reality (pp. 190, 202-203).

Emil Brunner postulates two aspects of the image of God. They are the formal and the material. The formal is the Old Testament image and it "consitutes his [man's] specifically *human* quality" (*Dogmatics, II, The Christian Doctrine of Creation and Redemption,* p. 57). It is not one's rational beingness, but one's "relation to God as responsibility, as responsible personal being" (pp. 77-78). The material image, on the other hand, is the predominant doctrine of the image in the New Testament. Here person has the image of God through Jesus Christ who is the true image of God. It is a restored image, "the new creation of the original image of God in man" (p. 58). In these opinions, Brunner is going against Luther's belief that Adam existed in a state of original righteousness, and against Luther and Calvin who held that a relic of the image was still present (David Cairns, *The Image of God in Man,* pp, 152-169).

In Paul Tillich's thought the image of God means that person has an "essential center" from which to view both self and world (*Systematic Theology,* vol. 2, p. 49). The image is good in that in it one "is given the possibility and necessity of actualizing himself and of becoming independent by his self-actualization, in spite of the estrangement unavoidably connected with it" (*Systematic Theology,* vol. 1, p. 259).

The systematic thinkers have taken us beyond the Old Testament and into the New, where we find no attempt by any writers to analyze the Old Testament texts. However, the image is there, and it is shown in three different ways: First, the Old Testament sense; second, the presentation of Jesus Christ as the image of God; and third, person as being in the image through faith in Jesus Christ (*The Image of God in Man*, chapter 2).

The first, or Old Testament sense, is that in which the image refers to one's humanity and is inclusive of all people. That the New Testament writers do not study these Old Testament texts does not mean that this sense is not present. Some passages believed to carry this "assumed" sense are:

James 3:9, "With it [the tongue] we bless the Lord and Father, and with it we curse men, who are made in the likeness of God."

1 Corinthians 11:7, "For a man ought not to cover his head, since he is the image and glory of God."

Acts 17:28 (by inference), "For 'in him we live and move and have our being'; as even some of your poets have said, 'For we are indeed his offspring.'"

Luke 20:22-26, "'Is it lawful for us to give tribute to Caesar, or not?' But he [Jesus] perceived their craftiness, and said to them, 'Show me a coin. Whose likeness and inscription has it?' They said, 'Caesar's.' He said to them, 'Then render to Caesar the things that are Caesar's, and to God the things that are God's.'"

The meaning of image in these New Testament texts is to show one's humanity. The chief difficulty with this use of image is when the presence of the image is thought to be soteriological, thus relieving person of responsibility for sin. Still it stands as a simple acknowledgment that all persons are created in the likeness of God and that their defection from the Maker's purpose does not alter such a primary truth.

Texts supporting the second meaning are:

Colossians 1:15, "He [the Son] is the image of the invisible God, the first-born of all creation."

Hebrews 1:3, "He reflects the glory of God and bears the very stamp of his nature, upholding the universe by his word of power."

In these texts Cairns believes that image of God means "Christ's singular dignity and divine Sonship" (*The Image of God in Man*, p. 40). Jesus is spoken of as the image of the invisible God, and the Hebrews passage in the King James Version of the Bible uses the phrase "the express image of God's glory." A check in a concordance will also show that in the majority of cases the references to God's Fatherhood are to God as the "Father of our Lord Jesus Christ." This use, however, is not the central one.

The central sense of image in the New Testament is, according to Cairns, the third one, wherein the word is used to "describe Christ's perfect humanity, in which by faith men can share, and in which they hope to be perfected" (*The Image of God in Man*, p. 43).

Romans 8 (see entire chapter), verse 29, "For those whom he foreknew he also predestined to be conformed to the image of his Son, in order that he might be the first-born among many brethren."

This third sense is by far the most commonly held one, for it shows us to be children of God through Jesus Christ. Those who accept the work of Jesus and declare personal faith in him become the children of God. It is in this use of the image of God (that is, that we are conformed to the image through the Son) that the questions of sin and salvation, of responsibility and decision are pertinent.

A quiet reflection on this brief examination of the meaning of the image of God produces two dominating thoughts. One, while image has a substantive meaning for the Old Testament theologians, it is closely connected with God's intention that person have dominion in the world. Second, it is clear that in one case we all share in being made in God's image, but that in another, we share in it only through faith in Jesus Christ who is depicted as being the express image. Thus it is appropriate to talk, with Brunner, of a formal image, which is our humanity, and of a material image, which is a new humanity. It is not only appropriate, but it is also inescapable, for while we are children of God in the most basic sense of origin, we do not relate to God as faithful children.

The Effect of the Fall

It has been impossible to discuss the doctrine of the image of God without also touching on another central doctrine—that of the Fall. And to talk of the Fall is at the same time to enter the old and involved discussion of evil and of individual sinfulness, of which the Fall is one explanation. Although the word "fall" does not appear in the Bible, it has become an official and permanent word in the theological vocabulary.

There are two stories of the Fall in the Old Testament, the well-known Adam story in Genesis 3 and the less-known angel story in Genesis 6. But the New Testament gives its attention to the Adam story. There are references to fallen angels in Jude, verse 6, and 2 Peter 2:4, but the dominant theology of sin in the New Testament is that of Paul in which Adam's fall is of primary importance. As to Jesus' theology on the Fall, N. P. Williams found none of the Gospels as revealing that Jesus taught anything about it (Norman Powell Williams, *The Ideas of the Fall and of Original Sin*).

Although there are few direct biblical texts dealing with the Fall, there are many that present the reality of sin and person's involvement in sin. The Synoptics do not define sin, and Jesus, while certainly acknowledging it, did not attempt to explain it. Paul gives it many meanings, including the idea that sin is a missing of the mark and an external power that controls unredeemed person. In the rest of the New Testament sin is presented essentially as acts of wrongdoing and lack of faith in Jesus Christ (Alan Richardson, *A Theological Word Book of the Bible*).

Our central concern, however, is not with definition but effect. It may seem like an inverted sequence since the Garden story of the Yahwist is older than the image texts, but the question is whether, in being driven from Eden, Adam and Eve lost the image and likeness of their Creator.

The Old Testament theologians cannot find evidence that the image is lost. Jacob states that "neither the fall nor the flood destroyed the image of God" (*Theology of the Old Testament,* p. 166). Vriezen holds that "The *image of God"* in man was not lost, nor yet mutilated . . . . not even by sin, because it rests upon God's will and is, therefore, founded upon the Creation" (*An Outline of Old Testament Theology,* p. 413). Von Rad agrees: "So it cannot be said that the image of God is lost . . .," then renders a qualifying word: "But as to the way in which these (grave disturbances in the Fall) affected the image of God in man, the Old Testament has nothing explicit to say" (*Old Testament Theology,* vol. 1, p. 147).

Appendix VI

The systematic theologians are concerned with the question of the Fall and, as one would expect, are attempting to reconcile what they understand the Old and New Testaments to be saying.

Brunner held that "in the thought of the Old Testament the fact that man has been 'made in the Image of God' means something which man can never lose; even when he sins he cannot lose it" (*Dogmatics, II*, p. 57). However, in the New Testament the image "is spoken of as having been lost and indeed as wholly, and not partially lost" (p. 58). "Even the sinner is a personal being, and in this fact, even as sinner, he resembles the personal God; but this similarity does not alter the fact that through sin, in another sense, he has *completely* lost his 'likeness' to God" (p. 123).

Barth said that the "likeness" is not lost. "We certainly cannot deduce from this (the Old Testament Scriptures) that man has lost it (the likeness) through the fall, either partially or completely, formally or materially" (*Dogmatics, III*-1, p. 200). Since one does not possess (as a quality) or accomplish this creation, person "is in no position to endure, let alone to reverse it" (*III-1*, p. 190). Since this position puts Barth squarely over against Brunner, it is noteworthy that Brunner said of Barth's view: "He (Barth) now admits this 'structural' concept of the *Imago*, which is found only in the Old Testament . . . as the element in the Image of God which cannot be lost, as opposed to that which can be, and has been, lost" (Brunner, *Dogmatics, II*, pp. 44-45).

Alan Richardson, a New Testament theologian, picks up on Calvin's thought in this quote: "Man's capacity for truth, beauty and goodness is thus seriously impaired, and God's image in man is defaced. But it is not destroyed." Person is depraved in the sense that "there is no part of him which remains unaffected by the 'Fall'" (*A Theological Word Book of the Bible*, p. 14). Calvin's own term for the fallen remains was "frightful deformity" (*Institutes, I*, p. 189).

What, then, up to this point, are we left with? The experts in Old Testament Scripture find no belief that the image of God is lost; in fact, the evidence is that it is very much intact after the Fall, and this is in spite of the wide-ranging view of person's potential and sinfulness in the events recorded in the old documents. On the other hand, the average reader of the New Testament finds a compelling call to a fallen humanity to partake of God's image through belief in Jesus Christ, himself the image.

It is clear that we are left with this: Person indeed was created in the image, after the likeness of God. This is not nullified by the events told in the account of Adam and Eve leaving the Garden of Eden. But by the time of the New Testament such a likeness is so obscure as to be thought virtually nonexistent. Thus the strongest strain of New Testament thought talks about being conformed to the image of Jesus Christ as the way to be in the image of God, since he (Jesus Christ) "bears the very stamp of [God's] nature" (Hebrews 1:3).

And if we follow the lead of this language of "obscurity," that is, that the image is not lost but neither very evident in sinful person, then we can speak of the image as being forever present but renewed in the person of Jesus Christ. The Old Testament writers had enough empirical evidence to conclude that person was more like the beast over whom one was to have dominion than like God the Maker. Yet the chroniclers refused to say that the image had vanished. That the weight of New Testament writing assumes that the likeness was lost merely reinforces the extent to which the obscurity had developed. (And it must be remembered that some believe that the Old Testament sense of the image of God was simply assumed by some New Testament writers.)

Thus we return to Brunner, for what happens in Jesus Christ materially restores what the original intention was with the formal image. Also, Calvin's thought is on target in one respect, for in Jesus Christ we are indeed reformed as creatures in the image and likeness of God. Then, Barth's position also holds in that just as we have no control over the image, either to create or reverse it, neither can we initiate its renewal in Jesus Christ.

So person is created in the image of God still. But that image is pitifully obscured, sadly inoperative in the work of humanity. Yet such obscurity must not lead to despair, for in hope we believe in the redeeming work of the Author and Finisher of our faith.

The Relationship of Image to Sonship/Daughtership

We come now to the most difficult theological task of Reality 1, namely, showing a tie between the image of God and sonship/daugh-

Appendix VI

tership without suggesting a universal salvation. Does being created in the image mean that we are thereby children of God? That question has already been answered in the affirmative. But the affirmation is not universally held. Tillich claimed that "man in his essential nature . . . has such a relation [sonship] to God," but that "this relation has been lost by man's estrangement from God. . . . Sonship to God has ceased to be a universal fact" (*Systematic Theology, vol. 2*, pp. 109, 110). Calvin believed that only "those who are directed to the good by his Spirit" may be recognized as children of God (*Institutes, II*, p. 809).

Archibald Hunter, New Testament theologian, does not find a universal sonship/daughtership in Jesus' teachings. "He spoke of God as his own Father, and taught that others might become his sons. . . . Not sons of God by nature, they might become sons by grace" (*Introducing New Testament Theology*, p. 32). Joachim Jeremias makes the same point in this passage: ". . . according to the earliest tradition, Jesus addressed the designation of God as 'your Father' *only to his disciples*, and never to outsiders. That indicates that Jesus did not see the Fatherhood of God as something to be taken for granted, a common possession of all men, but as a privilege enjoyed by his disciples . . ." (*New Testament Theology*, p. 180).

However, Jeremias, in discussing the parable of the prodigal son uses the term "lost children." Of course the main point of the parable is clearly the father's love, and there is no attempt to show proof of or to discuss sonship apart from the primary focus. Still there comes to the mind of any sensitive reader the thought that the parable simply assumes that all are sons of God, though some are faithful, some wayward.

David Cairns is not so cautious about such an interpretation of this parable. He utilizes it as the primary argument for such a sonship. Cairns makes it clear, however, that he is not talking about a universal salvation which denies man's sinful situation or the necessity of a new birth (*The Image of God in Man*, pp. 49-50). Under such an argument, the question of sonship/daughtership is an anthropological question, not a soteriological one. (See Jacob, *Theology of the Old Testament*.)

Augustus Hopkins Strong, Baptist theologian at the turn of the century, is emphatic that being created in the image of God means that all are children of God. He extends this status even to sinners. "God is Father of all men, in that he originates and sustains them as personal beings like in nature to himself" (*Systematic Theology,* vol. 2, p. 474). This is, however, a natural fatherhood; special fatherhood is reserved for "those who have been regenerated by his Spirit and who have believed on his Son" (p. 474). God is Father of all persons in the sense of origination, impartation of life, sustentation, likeness in faculties and powers, government, care, and love. "In all these respects God is the Father of all men, and his fatherly love is both preserving and atoning," said Strong (p. 474).

Two lesser-known writers make strong argument for all persons being children of God. That they are not so well known or widely quoted does not diminish the wisdom in what they have to say. One of them, W. B. Selbie, contends that Jesus "envisaged God as the Father of all men whether they acknowledged the relationship or not" (*The Fatherhood of God,* p. 83). One of Selbie's most pertinent and interesting sections is his argument that Jesus' attitude toward children shows his belief in God's Fatherhood for all (p. 84). He then writes, "Children are children of God not merely because He has created them in His image, but because He loves them and claims them for His own" (p. 85). In another place he holds:

> The issue here is quite a simple one and needs to be sharply stated and pressed home. Children are either born children of perdition and of the devil, or they are children of God, made in His image and made for Him. No middle way seems to be possible. The idea that children can be made children of God by baptism savours too much of pagan magic ever to be acceptable to thinking minds. The baptism of infants can never be anything but a symbolical acceptance or declaration of the fact that they are children of God (p. 86).

John MacKintosh Shaw introduces an interesting distinction between childship and sonship. All persons have "childship" since they are born as children of God. "But childship is not in itself sonship. It is only the potentiality of sonship" (*The Christian Gospel of the Fatherhood of God,* p. 169). ". . . sonship means more than mere natural relationship or descent, it means spiritual likeness or affinity, the sharing of a common spirit" (pp. 169-170). Shaw goes on to say that only Jesus

Appendix VI

has developed fully from childship to sonship (p. 171). It is an interesting, but weak distinction, since by analogy to be a child is to be either a son or daughter, and to be either is to possess a sonship/daughtership relation. From this point on, adjectives such as faithful can only be used to indicate the quality of relationship.

Where are we, then, with this question of the tie between being made in God's image and being thereby God's sons and daughters? We are left with a self-evident truth which has not been given the attention it deserves, except by those who wish to argue for a universal salvation. Thus, since, as someone has said, where the experts disagree we common folk can take a little liberty, we will hold with full assurance that we are sons and daughters of God by creation and that a Christian nurture which recognizes our true humanity must begin with such a truth. It is a universal status but not a universal salvation.

If it does seem, and it must to many, that such an assertion is unscriptural, does it not merely again reinforce the extent to which the relation of person to God was viewed in New Testament times as so discontinuous as to be nonexistent? It is a pity the New Testament authors did not make a thorough interpretation of this point of sonship/daughtership and image of God and, that because they did not make it, we feel bound to ignore so arresting a truth—all are children of God by God's own making. Without our merit, we are God's children. By God's grace in Jesus Christ we may also become God's redeemed children.

Appendix VII

Tillich's Doctrine of Estrangement and Salvation

Paul Tillich, German theologian until 1933 when he had to give up his post at the University of Frankfort, taught in the United States at Union and Harvard. His doctrine of sin and salvation is included in his *Systematic Theology, vol. 2* (1957).

Tillich believed that person (my word for man) exists in a state of estrangement, cut off from God, self, and others and, thus, is no longer of one's true essence. The biblical depiction of humanity from Eden and Babel to Paul's theology is one of estrangement. Tillich does not wish to replace the word "sin" with "estrangement," for the latter is one's state, and in that state there is sin. Sin is an expression of that estrangement.

Sin, as an expression of estrangement, shows up in the forms of unbelief, hubris, and concupiscence. Unbelief is more serious than failure to believe the creeds and dogmas; it is rather "the disruption of man's cognitive participation in God" (p. 47). It is more serious than denial of God or disobedience or self-love. "Man's unbelief is his estrangement from God in the center of his being," said Tillich (p. 48). Hubris is when person "elevates himself beyond the limits of his finite being and provokes the divine wrath which destroys him" (p. 50). Person, as a fully centered being, is off center from God's will and is estranged. Hubris is better compared with self-evaluation than with pride. In unbelief person turns from one's ground of being; in hubris one turns toward oneself and refuses to "acknowledge his finitude."

Driven by hubris, person mistakes "partial truth with ultimate truth" and "limited goodness with absolute goodness" (p. 51).

Concupiscence is "the unlimited desire to draw the whole of reality into one's self" (p. 52), whether it be hunger, sex, power, or wealth. "It is the unlimited character of the strivings for knowledge, sex, and power which makes them symptoms of concupiscence" (p. 53). In themselves, these are not sinful, but in their distortion they express one's estrangement from God. Concupiscence in knowledge is "the desire . . . to draw the universe into one's self and one's finite particularity"; concupiscence in sex is "unlimited sexual striving which prevents a creative union of love with the sexual partner"; concupiscence in power is the attempt to draw "the universe into himself in terms of the power to use for himself whatever he wants to use" (p. 53).

Sin is both a universal fact and an individual act. The two aspects are inseparable (pp. 55-58). Similarly, estrangement is both individual and collective. The individual creates the collective estrangement, thus cannot be separated from it. The two become intricately intertwined (pp. 58-59).

Person, as estranged from the Ground of Being, has being in the form of existence, not as essence. The estrangement means that person is not in the condition of essential essence but is under the terms of existence. The Christ, as the New Being, conquers "the gap between essence and existence" (p. 119). "The estrangement of his existential from his essential being is conquered in principle, i.e., in power and as a beginning" (p. 119). In Christ the new arrives, and the old is overcome; essential being is manifest, not just possible, but actual. He is "the presence of the New Being . . . under the conditions of existence" (p. 124).

Thus, salvation (healing) is come. "In this sense," held Tillich, "healing means reuniting that which is estranged, giving a center to what is split, overcoming the split between God and man, man and his world, man and himself" (p. 166). It has a universal significance; and all before Jesus, during and after his life, participate to a degree in it, for in this event he became the symbol of salvation for all time, past, his present, and the future. As persons participate in the New Being, they participate in "faith instead of unbelief, surrender instead of *hubris*, love instead of concupiscence" (p. 177). This dimension of salvation is not to be thought of as a mere subjective decision, but as the "state of having been drawn into the new reality manifest in Jesus as the Christ" (p. 177).

For the above, Tillich reserves the word "regeneration," the first character of salvation. The second he names justification. This character of salvation is acceptance. First there is an objective dimension in which God accepts us, though we are in our estrangement unacceptable. Then there is a subjective, namely, our own acceptance of God's acceptance of us, knowing that there is nothing in us which enables God to accept us (p. 179). "The cause is God alone (by grace), but the faith that one is accepted is the channel through which grace is mediated to man (through faith)" (p. 179). While God's acceptance of us is a given from which justification springs, it is our role to receive such good news, that though divided and alienated, we are accepted by the Ground of Being.

Salvation, then, is regeneration and justification, but it also is sanctification. Tillich calls this the transformational character of salvation. It is the "process in which the power of the New Being transforms personality and community, inside and outside the church" (pp. 179-180). It means that we are being changed, that our acceptance by God and our acceptance of that acceptance can take hold in our lives and make a difference.

Appendix VIII

The Lord's Table

The Lord's Table in contemporary Christianity is a table in a place of worship, a table from which priest or minister serves the Lord's Supper or Communion or leads the Eucharistic celebration, uttering formulas of varying interpretations. Neither of these, the isolated table nor the formula, is of the oldest tradition. Rather, the table was one around which Jesus and others were eating, and his words were more communal than theological. These meals which Jesus attended were not always with disciples; and when he was host, anyone was allowed to come and eat. Remember his inclusive activity and teaching—how he ate freely with sinners and how in his parable of the great supper he has the host calling anyone to the feast.

One such meal which Jesus hosted for his disciples, commonly known as the Lord's Supper, has evolved into a central event in the history of defining or identifying the Lord's Table. In this development, the Table has become a subject around which differing views have gathered. These divergent positions relate to which of the written traditions is oldest, to the character of the Supper, and to the most responsible interpretation of the biblical material. These differences are not simply the uninformed opinion of novices. Competent scholars have approached the questions of text, setting, and meaning and have come away in disagreement.

Take, for example, the problem of text and setting. On the one hand, Karl Ludwig Schmidt holds that Luke 22:15, 16, and 18 is the oldest extant tradition (*Twentieth-Century Theology in the Making*, Vol. 1, ed. Jaroslav Pelikan, pp. 343-352). On the other, Willi Marxsen argues that Luke has formulated his text from 1 Corinthians 11:23-25 and Mark 14:22-24 (*The Beginnings of Christology*, trans. Paul J. Achtemeier and Lorenz Nieting, p. 92). Both investigators, however, agree that the event from which the tradition (oral and written) has evolved cannot be absolutely identified as one in which Jesus was instituting what has become the Lord's Supper (Marxsen, p. 104; Pelikan, p. 348).

The interpretations given to the event are too numerous to reference or review. From the biblical accounts, the early Fathers, and other material from the early church, the meaning of the Lord's Supper (Eucharist, the most common term after A.D. 100) diverges so much that Friedrich Wiegand could surmise: "The material from the first thousand years is so slight, and so indefinite in its terms, that every side in the disputes of the present day can find its own view reflected there" (Pelikan, p. 358). As with baptism, the doctrine of the Lord's Supper has gone through much theological transformation and there is no single view which can rightly claim to be "the biblical view." From this point, neither can history give us an authoritative word.

The creeds and confessions of the church provide sources for demonstrating diversity of views on the Lord's Supper. One major disagreement is whether Christ's body and blood are actually present in the Supper (Philip Schaff, *The Creeds of Christendom*). The Roman and Eastern creeds teach the real presence of Christ in the elements: The Canons and Decrees of the Council of Trent (1563), The Profession of the Tridentine Faith (1564), The Longer Catechism of the Eastern Church (1839), and The Old Catholic Agreement (1875). The Tridentine states that Christ is present "truly, really, and substantially" (vol. 2, p. 208). Among the evangelical Protestant confessions, Luther's Small Catechism (1529), The Augsburg Confession (1530), The Belgic Confession (1561), The Formula of Concord (1576), and the Saxon Visitation Articles (1592) uphold, though in a different manner, the real presence, as Augsburg reads: ". . . the body and blood of Christ are truly present and are communicated to those that eat in the Lord's Supper" (vol. 3, p. 13). The Saxon Articles speak of "the true and natural body of Christ which hung on the cross, and the true and natural blood, which flowed from the side of Christ . . ." (vol. 3, p. 182).

Appendix VIII

Refuting the literal presence of the body and blood of Christ are Zwingli's Ten Berne Theses (1525), the Scotch Confession of Faith (1560), the Heidelberg Catechism (1563), The Thirty-Nine Articles of the Church of England (1571), The Irish Articles of Religion (1615), the Westminster Confession of Faith (1647), Methodist Articles of Religion (1784), and Articles of Religion of the Reformed Episcopal Church in America (1875). The Church of England statement, repeated in later creeds, adds to Zwingli and is representative: The body and blood of Christ being literally present "can not be proued by holye writ, but is repugnaunt to the playne wordes of scripture, ouerthroweth the nature of a Sacrament, and hath geuen occasion to many superstitions" (vol. 3, pp. 505-506).

As to the effect of participation, there are several themes in those confessions. The notion of nourishment is predominant, as in Trent where the sacrament is "spiritual food of souls" (vol. 2, p. 128), and in the Irish Articles, a seal "unto our spiritual nourishment and continual growth in Christ" (vol. 3, p. 542). In partaking, Christians are, in the Second Helvetic Confession (1566), "more kindled, more strengthened and refreshed" (p. 894). Westminster adds to this theme, "a bond and pledge of their communion with him, and with each other" (p. 664). Old Catholic also includes "communion with one another" (vol. 2, p. 551). The Moravian Church (1749) calls it a "pledge of grace" (vol. 3, p. 804). Several documents continue these views, adding that of "memorial of our Redemption," as in the Reformed Episcopal creed (1875) (p. 823), and in the statement of the National Council of Congregational Churches of the U.S. (1833), "a symbol of His atoning death, a seal of its efficacy, and a means whereby He confirms and strengthens the spiritual union and communion of believers with Himself" (p. 915). The Supper is a "token of faith in the Saviour, and of brotherly love" (p. 733) in the Congregational Union of England and Wales statement (1833). Luther's Small Catechism uses the stronger language: ". . . the remission of sins, life and salvation are given us in the Sacrament" (p. 91), as do Trent, "preserved from mortal sins" (vol. 2, p. 128), and Tridentine, "Christ is received" (p. 208).

Baptists, though having no official theology and holding creeds in suspicion, have a long history of producing confessions. These statements typically were written by one or more prominent persons and were not submitted to critical, group discussion.

Such ambiguity, that is, holding to a document which is representative but not officially binding, presents a difficult methodological problem, therefore, there can be no attempt to analyze these documents as if they were dogma. However, one can find in them certain threads of thought which have persisted, in spite of the nonconformist streak in our history.

A reading of the more notable Baptist confessions and some of their forerunners reveals the following understandings of the Lord's Supper. The Eighteen Dissertations of Balthasar Friedberger (really, Balthasar Hubmaier) in 1524 do not mention Lord's Supper or Eucharist but do assert that "The Mass is not a sacrifice but a memorial of the death of Christ" (William L. Lumpkin, *Baptist Confessions of Faith,* p. 20). This motif of memorial to Christ's death continues in the other Anabaptist confessions, with the addition in the Hutterite confession of the Supper as "a sign of the community of Christ's body" (p. 40).

The confessions of English General Baptists emphasize the Supper as communion with Christ and other Christians, e.g., John Smyth's confession: "That the Lord's Supper is the external sign of the communion with Christ, and of the faithful amongst themselves by faith and love" (p. 101). All three themes—memorial, fellowship, and communion with Christ are included in the local confessions of early English Baptists. Similarly, the general confessions, when they interpret the Supper, include these motifs, e.g., the 1677 Second London Confession: "The Supper of the Lord Jesus, was instituted by him . . . for the perpetual remembrance . . . [of] his death . . . and to be a bond and pledge of their communion with him, and with each other" (p. 291).

As to American Baptist confessions, the earliest, the 1742 Philadelphia Confession, left unchanged the article on the Supper found in the Second London Confession. Some of the other early documents do not interpret the meaning of the Supper. The 1833 New Hampshire Confession holds that in the Supper members of the church "commemorate together the dying love of Christ" (p. 366). The Free Will Baptists' treatise and the Baptist Bible Union articles include the same meaning for the Supper. Some other pivotal confessions do not interpret the

Supper, but simply set forth its necessity and prescribe who may participate.

After 1853 the American Baptists circulated the New Hampshire Confession, with some additions, and in 1925 the Southern Baptist Convention adopted a revised version of the New Hampshire document. The 1925 articles were adopted in revised form by the Southern Baptist Convention in 1963. The article on the Lord's Supper was not changed from its form in the New Hampshire Confession. It is most significant to the nonconformist spirit of Baptists that the conventions of 1925 and 1963 asserted in the preamble to the articles of faith that the articles are not "complete statements of our faith, having any quality of finality on infallibility. . . . only guides in interpretation, having no authority over the conscience . . ." (p. 392). The Baptist faith and message is depicted as "a consensus of opinion of some Baptist body, large or small, for the general instruction and guidance of our own people and others concerning those articles of the Christian faith which are most surely held among us" (p. 392). However, as in 1833, 1853, 1925, and 1963, the articles were not submitted to scholarly analysis or to substantial public debate. This phenomenal achievement is due in part to our historic view that the articles are not binding on any person or group of Baptists, and, therefore, for the sake of unity we have trusted our leaders to draw up statements for us.

So the common thread of thought among the lineage of Baptist confessions includes the Supper as a memorial to Christ's death and as a sign of fellowship with one another and communion with Christ. Not all confessions include all three themes, and some do not interpret the Supper at all.

Once one comes to a position on the meaning of the Lord's Supper, a second question follows: Who may sit at the Lord's Table? Some uninformed, some quite responsible, and some surprising answers have been given this question.

Who is worthy to come to the Lord's Table? The problem of worthiness is dealt with in two passages from 1 Corinthians—10:14-33; 11:17-35. In the earlier text, Paul, in addressing the worship of idols, considers it unworthy for Christians to come to the Lord's Table while at the same time deliberately identifying with other competing philosophies or styles of faith. M. H. Shepherd, Jr., writes: "It [Communion with Christ] is of such holiness and power that profanation of it by association with the communions of either Jewish or pagan sacrifices provokes the Lord to 'jealousy'" *(Interpreter's Dictionary of the Bible,* p. 161). Leitzmann holds that Paul meant to warn Christians against participating in the Lord's Supper and in heathen sacrificial meals *(Twentieth-Century Theology,* p. 389). Werner Georg Kümmel believes that "Paul intends to emphasize that the participants in the Lord's Supper enter into personal communion and sit at the same table with the risen Lord, and from this he draws the inference that the Christians cannot also sit with demons at their table *(The Theology of the New Testament,* p. 221). Raymond B. Brown agrees: "A Christian cannot participate in both the Lord's Supper and suppers held in honor of pagan gods" *(Broadman Bible Commentary,* vol. 10, p. 348)."

If indeed the above context speaks to the unworthiness question, then clearly the contemporary application is that one must not come to the Lord's Table with competing loyalties. Such an application stirs the imagination when one considers the contending allegiances held by modern Christians who regularly take the Lord's Supper.

In the second text, Paul is speaking to a factious situation in the church, in this case, how Christians came to and participated in the Lord's Supper. As the entire text demonstrates, the meal in question is the fellowship meal before the agape and the Eucharist were separated; thus it cannot be understood as referring exclusively to the "bread and the cup." In Paul's mind, the Lord's Supper *(kuriakon deipnon)* is patterned after the Last Supper. Unworthiness and profanation apply to sharing the food with others and discerning the body. Some were satiated, others hungry—such behavior clearly was unworthy of the Lord's Supper; it was not in discernment of the body of Christ.

If the phrase "discerning the body" is made into a violation of Christ's actual body, then one holds a magical view of the Supper, as if in taking it we are taking Christ's flesh and blood. If "body" should, in this text, mean Christ's body, then John sets the record straight that it is participation in Christ's spirit that gives life, not the actual eating of his flesh. (See John 6:25-65.) Kümmel believes that "the point is not the inadequate regard for the 'elements' of the Lord's Supper by the community—Paul knows nothing at all of such—but rather the neglect of a sharing in the food and consequently a 'not discerning the body [of Christ]'" (11:29) *(The Theology of the New Testament,* p. 221). Neither is the point that worthiness is "a state in which I must find myself *before* reception," in Ernst Käsemann's view, but rather "it means the attitude toward the sacrament itself" (footnote in *First Corinthians* by Hans Conzelmann, p. 202). In Conzelmann's words: "It is eating unfittingly when the Supper of *the Lord* is treated as one's 'own supper'" (p. 202). However, Brown includes in his commentary on the text the possible interpretation that the "'not discerning the body' means not recognizing that the bread represents the body of Christ," an interpretation similar to his own view that one may profane the body of Christ by coming to the table without having examined "oneself in the light of the meaning of Christian faith and Christian love" (*Broadman Bible Commentary,* p. 359).

Does worthiness, either in Scripture or contemporary practice, assume a profession of faith on the part of the participant? The Presbyterians and Lutherans have addressed such a question. The General Assembly of the United Presbyterian Church in the U.S.A., amended, in 1971, *The Book of Order,* 41.06, to read as follows:

> The session is charged with maintaining the spiritual government of the congregation, for which purpose it has power . . .; to permit baptized children of the church, when their families deem it appropriate, to receive the Lord's Supper with the congregation before such children shall have made formal profession of faith.

The above is from a letter sent to all pastors of the church and is contained in a document entitled *Power to Permit Children at the Lord's Supper,* published in 1971 by the church's Board of Christian Education. In addition to the pastoral letter, the document contains the argument for permitting children to the Table, some continuing questions, and supporting studies.

The argument in the document proceeds along three lines. First, the document establishes from *The Book of Confessions* that baptized children are members of the church. Second, *The Book of Order* contains two views of admission to the Supper, one a strict view that only the examined may be admitted; two, a more inclusive view that does not require examination. The document then asks by what logic strangers visiting in the worship service may participate in the Lord's Supper but baptized children may not. Third, psychology and pedagogy are appealed to:

> It is of the greatest importance that his [the middle child's] aspiration and volitions be stimulated not only by instruction and command, but also by participation and involvement. It is at an early age that participation with the worshiping community in the Lord's Supper can have a formative influence on his attitudes and on his identification of himself as a member of the Christian community and as a sharer in its faith and ideals. He now realizes that he is accepted as a participating member and is not limited to being a spectator or outsider. The child's participation in the Lord's Supper is based on his baptism which is a sign and seal of God's grace offered to him before he possessed the capacity for a fully cognitive response (*Power to Permit,* pp. 6-7).

Next the document turns to the matter of confirmation, which up to the time had been required before the child could participate in the Supper. The document sets forth the hope that in separating confirmation and first Communion confirmation "may become less a graduation from classes into a technical membership and more an event in an unconcluded series of events confirming one's Christian faith in life" (p. 8).

At the same time the Presbyterians were studying the problem of children and worship, so were the Lutheran churches. In a booklet, *Affirmation of the Baptismal Covenant,* published in 1975, the Lutherans set forth a revised way of looking at how the child comes to faith. It recommended a three-stage approach, beginning with baptism in infancy. First Communion, the next stage, is to be offered in middle childhood, a sign of belonging and a reminder of the meaning of baptism. The third stage is the affirmation of the baptismal covenant, most likely at age fifteen or sixteen years, a time when the children own the faith for themselves. This rite replaces confirmation. Operating throughout all three stages is the "catechetical ministry."

Communion is recognized as "the birthright of the baptized" (p. 12), and it should be recognized naturally and not burdened down with too many dramatics lest the children get the impression that they are entering a new status in the congregation. The hope is that this will reinforce the real meaning of baptism as the admission to the church.

While both the Presbyterian and Lutheran studies have emphasized that the subject of their work is the already baptized child and that the allowance of First Communion in middle childhood is meant to continue the meaning of that baptism, both churches were led into the problem by considering the meaning of worship and the place of children in worship. The Presbyterian study made special note of this origin both in the argument and in the supporting studies. The Presbyterian supporting documents also consider but do not resolve the problem of unbaptized children. However, the documents suggest that in some instances even the unbaptized should be included because of their connection with parents who are believing members but who, for some reason, have chosen to delay the baptism of their children.

The Baptist Confessions are clear on this point: Only the baptized may participate in the Lord's Supper. (See Hugh Wamble's survey "The Lord's Supper," November 21, 1961.) Baptist theologians A. H. Strong and W. T. Conner uphold the tradition of the confessions of faith. Conner, in a defense of closed Communion, wrote: "Baptism certainly does precede the Lord's Supper, and we believe the argument that Baptists should not invite to the Supper those whom they do not regard as baptized is a valid argument" (*Christian Doctrine,* p. 290). Nonetheless, some churches currently allow unbaptized children to participate, especially at family Communion services during Thanksgiving and other special times of the year. Where it has been allowed, the practice has been primarily a recognition of family solidarity. If the practice is to continue, it should be from a theological base which is compatible with believer's baptism, and which begins with the laborious exegesis of the bibical material. Further, if children are to sit at the Lord's Table, the rationale must issue from a salvation perspective which recognizes two facts: (1) that faith in its incipient forms is imperceptive to the subject of faith as well as to observers, and (2) that through God's mercy and the church's faithfulness, grace and faith operate before as well as after our individual decisions of faith and commitment.

Appendix IX

Dominion, Priesthood, Trusteeship

In the image text of the Priestly creation, Elohim commissions humanity to have dominion (*radah*) "over all the earth" (Genesis 1:26) and "over every living thing" (v. 28); to subdue (*kabash*) the earth (v. 28). In the Yahwist text, Yahweh-Elohim puts "the man" (no reference to image of God) in the garden "to dress it and keep (*shamar*) it" (2:15). For *radah*, "have dominion, rule," the Arabic cognate is "tread, trample" (William Gesenius, *A Hebrew and English Lexicon of the Old Testament*, pp. 921-922). For *kabash*, "subdue, dominate," the Arabic is "press, squeeze, knead, attack, assault"; the Aramaic is "tread down, beat or make a path, subdue" (p. 461). *Shamar*, "to have charge of," refers in Canaanite terms to an overseer (pp. 1036-1037). In Psalm 8:6 the Lord (Yahweh) makes man to "have dominion" (*mashal*), and, in allusion to the imagery of the cognate words, the Lord "has put all things under his feet." Here the form is "cause to rule" (p. 605).

The Old Testament theologians interpret the Priestly texts to mean that dominion is the vocation which God has given to humanity. It was a work of stewardship, as Vriezen suggests: "Because man stands in a special relationship to God he is entrusted by God with dominion over the world," is "God's vice-regent on earth" (*An Outline of Old Testament Theology*, p. 413). Von Rad interprets the image texts to mean that God has put "man in the world as the sign of his own sovereign authority, in order that man should uphold and enforce his—God's—claims as lord" (*Old Testament Theology*, vol. 1, p. 146).

The Old Testament exegetes will not allow this truth to be reduced to an individualistic corruption. Humanity is the trustee. "The stewardship over the world," writes Hans Wolff, "is therefore entrusted to the great company of mankind . . . they all partake in the dominion over creation" (*Anthropology of the Old Testament,* trans. Margaret Kohl, p. 162). Eichrodt, while not connecting image and dominion, finds in the Genesis text that dominion is given "by a special creative act of blessing" on the whole human race as a "common universal task" in which "he (man) is made the responsible representative of the divine cosmic Lord" (*Theology of the Old Testament,* vol. 2, p. 127).

In Israel this general charge to humanity was caught up in "covenant." God made an everlasting covenant with Abraham and his seed (Genesis 17), a covenant renewed in the call to Moses (Exodus 3 and 6), at Sinai (Exodus 34), and after Sinai (Deuteronomy 5). The covenants at and after Sinai emphasize law and ordinance more than generational fruitfulness and redemption. This law comes often in particular form, such as in the Ten Commandments and the codes in Deuteronomy, but it also has a larger form as in Jeremiah who speaks of a covenant renewal involving a law written within (Jeremiah 31:31-34), and in the familiar commands to love God with heart, soul, and mind (Deuteronomy 6:4), and to do justice, love kindness, walk humbly (Micah 6:8), and to love your neighbor as yourself (Leviticus 19:18).

The words "dominion," "rule," and "subdue" do not, in the New Testament, refer to humanity's stewardship of the world. One hopes the notion is simply assumed as a part of the church's Hebrew heritage. Hebrews 2 refers back to Psalm 8 as if to say that humankind who has not been faithful to the task of trusteeship must look to Jesus, as Hans Wolff suggested: "through the mode of sovereignty of the One who was crucified, mankind's stewardship over the world is snatched back from self-destruction, and the image of God once more emerges in all its freedom" (*Anthropology,* p. 165).

The emphasis in the New Testament is on love, service, and priesthood. Jesus sees himself as fulfilling the law. Although Matthew and Mark offer two forms of the Great Commandment, and both are different from the Deuteronomy text, Jesus recalls the Shema and another commandment: that you love your neighbor as yourself (Leviticus 19:18;

Appendix IX

Matthew 22:39; Mark 12:33. Also, see the Gospel of John and First and Second John).

Service texts in the New Testament are too numerous to cite. It is best seen in the concrete actions of Jesus serving his disciples and washing their feet. Jesus extends the term beyond the table to service to the sick, imprisoned, the hungry, etc. And, of course, there is the grand thought and act of the Son of man coming, not to be served, but to serve. By this "every *charisma* is a gift entrusted to man with the condition that the man who has been blessed by it should serve as a good steward of the manifold gifts of God" (*Theological Dictionary of the New Testament,* vol. 2, ed. Gerhard Kittel, p. 86).

To serve (*diakoneo*) was, in the Greek mentality, an unfulfilled life for persons; to be a ruler was the desired status. In secular Greek the most comprehensive meaning was "to serve." To a lesser extent it meant "provide or care for" and more infrequently, "to wait at table" (*Theological Dictionary,* p. 83). In Judaism, the status of servant was elevated in importance, especially in relation to serving God, so that only the most worthy could be the waiters at the table. The Greek meanings were present in Judaism, but Israel added "to obey" and "to render priestly service."

Priesthood (*hierateuma*) is another New Testament emphasis. In 1 Peter 2:1-10 "the predicates of salvation and dignity, namely, possession, temple and priesthood . . . are consistently transferred from Israel to the Gentile Christian community" *(Theological Dictionary,* vol. 3, p. 250). This priesthood belongs to the new people of God and "is a ministry of witness to all humanity" (pp. 250-251).

Catholic theologian Hans Küng, in *The Church,* has formulated an exceptional treatment of the doctrine of the priesthood of the believer or, as he puts it, the royal priesthood of all believers. His discussion of this reality is a part of a larger doctrine which holds to the high priesthood of Jesus Christ and to the necessity of an ecclesiastical ministry. In between these two dimensions of the doctrine, Küng proposes five aspects of this royal priesthood of all believers: direct access to God; spiritual sacrifices; the preaching of the word; the administering of baptism, the Lord's Supper, and forgiveness of sins; and mediating functions.

On the question of direct access to God, Küng adds nothing to the common understanding of liberty of conscience and free moral agency before God. As to spiritual sacrifices, he adds much, referring not to ceremonial ritual in the sanctuary but to the Christian offering oneself as a sacrifice in the world. "This," he holds, "is the true sacrifice of the New Testament priesthood" (p. 374) and breaks down the artificial distinctions between sacred and profane. On the ministry of the word, Küng extends the word "preaching" to include "proclaim, announce, preach, teach, explain, speak, say, testify, persuade, confess, charge, admonish, etc." (p. 375), and he means also that in many instances these functions will be performed by the believer-priest in the worship service. He has high regard for the place of the lay preacher and lay theologian.

In regard to the administering of baptism, the Lord's Supper, and forgiveness of sins, Küng understands that every Christian is to participate. He asserts:

Every Christian has the power to baptize (and to teach) . . . . *every* Christian is fundamentally empowered to take an active part in the forgiving of sins. . . . *every* Christian is fundamentally empowered to take an active part in this eschatalogical meal of commemoration, thanksgiving and covenantal fellowship (p. 380).

Küng does hold that persons may be authorized to lead in these Christian privileges and duties, but as servants, not as lords, masters, or superpriests. The priesthood belongs to all Christians, and each Christian is thereby a priest. Leaders are appointed by and for the church, but these persons are not to be elevated to a position between God and persons, for such is "contrary to the New Testament message: both the message of the *one* mediator and the high priest Jesus Christ and that of the priesthood of *all* Christians" (p. 383). Minister, bishop, elder, rector, priest, pastor, pope, and archbishop are not privileged positions for vainglory or private gain but have honor as offices of service, as Küng writes of the pope: "The Petrine ministry can be correctly and biblically described as a primacy of service, a pastoral primacy: *primatus servitii, primatus ministerialis, primatus pastoralis*" (p. 477).

Along with this understanding of the activity of a spiritual sacrifice, Küng considers the mediating function of the Christian to represent the central work of the priest. This mediating act means taking the faith into the world. It is the duty of the priest, writes Küng, "to mediate between God and the world, by revealing the hidden works of God and making effective his acts of power" (p. 381). Thus the mediator is not one who stands as a go-between in a situation of required intercession but is one who assists in bringing together. It is an unselfish, but self-fulfilling ministry: "The priesthood of all believers is a fellowship in which each Christian, instead of living for himself, lives before God for others and is in turn supported by others" (p. 381).

With this background, my phrase "be a creative trustee" appears to be an appropriate representation of dominion in the Old Testament and service and priesthood in the New Testament. Steward, partner, disciple, priest, minister, or servant, joined with "creative," would be appropriate terms. Stewardship is perhaps too identified with the giving of money; discipleship, with learning, narrowly, or broadly with evangelism; priest and minister, with an official priesthood or ministry. Servanthood is neither overused nor overpracticed, and "creative servant" would be a worthy term for the Christian vocation. Partnership suffers somewhat from the implication that we might be equal partners with God, but it is clear that dominion meant that we were to work with God. The term "creative," however, includes this notion that we are active in the process of being steward, servant, etc.; thus creative partnership appears a little redundant. At first, creativity as a single word had a certain appeal; however, this term has been much too overworked in the literature. Finally, then, "let them have dominion," "subdue the earth," "dress it and keep it," "when you did it to the least of these," "you are a royal priesthood," are caught up appropriately in "be a creative trustee for God in the world." That is our calling.

Appendix X

Erikson's Wisdom

American psychologist Erik Erikson, postulating from years of clinical experience, has given the world a wise view of how the personality develops from infancy into old age. Though Erikson knew Freud, and his work is out of the psychoanalytic wing of psychology, his is a psychosocial model rather than a psychosexual one. Erikson does not ignore the significance of the sexual modalities of each developing age (e.g., anal modality in early childhood) but views these in larger social terms and sees their purpose as contributing to a vital personality. This anal modality "is not restricted to the sphincters. A general ability . . . develops to alternate withholding and expelling at will and, in general, to keep tightly and to throw away willfully whatever is held" (*Identity: Youth and Crisis,* p. 107). Society becomes a partner in one's development, challenging and supporting the growing individual.

For Erikson, vitality comes as the developing person realizes a new sense, with each ascending age. In infancy the child is vital who emerges from the first two years with a basic sense of trust, i.e., a confidence in one's significant others and in oneself. In middle age, vitality is in generativity, in assuming responsibility for preserving creatively the culture for the sake of the present and the next generation. Not to realize this vitality is to become stuck at an age.

In each age a crisis develops, a crisis out of which either vitality or failure is possible. The crisis is a critical period in which one either goes forward or retards, either builds or rests. These crises are epigenetic; they have a more pregnant moment of appearance, coincident with age and socially related factors, when they can best be realized. In Erikson's own words, epigenetic is the principle "that anything that grows has a *ground plan,* and that out of this ground plan the *parts* arise, each part having its *time* of special ascendancy, until all parts have arisen to form a *functioning whole*" (*Identity and the Life Cycle,* p. 53).

Erikson warns that such a plan does not mean that development is an achievement scale so that, when a task is mastered, one is done with it. Rather, both positive and negative aspects of each crisis appear throughout life. However, if there is any wisdom to Erikson's scheme, then it must be clear that if a crisis is mastered appropriately at its time of epigenetic ascendancy, and vitality results, then a degree of positive residue is taken over into the next crisis. Erikson expresses it briefly in his description of the autonomy stage: "For the growth of autonomy a firmly developed early trust is necessary" (*Identity: Youth,* p. 110).

Epigenetic also involves the truth that dynamics of future developmental crises appear in earlier crises, and the dynamics of earlier crises reappear later. The most evident example is seen in the identity crisis of adolescence: the residue from the earlier stages contributes to vitality in adolescence, and dynamics appear that will only later come to full flower, as, for example, intimacy, a young-adult crisis. This perception is seen when Erikson characterizes the identity crisis as a time when the youth attempts to find unity "out of the effective remnants of his childhood and the hopes of his anticipated adulthood . . ." (*Young Man Luther,* p. 14).

If the identity crisis of adolescence is the one which draws from and anticipates other crises, the generativity crisis of middle adulthood is the most pregnant with the possibility of giving birth to full humanity or settling for something less. In this critical time, the adult either finds an existential *kairos,* the sense of this being one's time, or falls victim of *chronos* and lives in the tedium of passing time. But for Erikson the social import of this development is enormous. The generative adult takes on responsibility for generational perpetuity, not in a static preservation of the past but in a creative conservation of the continuity and identity resident in the traditions and institutions of society.

Erikson's well-known and oft-cited "ages of man" are laid down in Erikson's *Identity and the Life Cycle, Childhood and Society,* and *Identity: Youth and Crisis.*

Appendix XI

Piaget's Discovery

The Swiss psychologist Jean Piaget, who died in 1980 at the age of eighty-four, discovered, from extensive clinical interviews over decades with his own and others' children, that children's thinking follows an accommodation-assimilation process with potentialities and limitations at each stage of development. The Genevan was not so much concerned with mental ability as with ways of thinking; thus, he often would tell his protegés to be alert to children's mistakes in reasoning inasmuch as the mistakes often hold more secrets to the kind of thinking that is going on than do "correct" answers.

As with Erikson, Piaget saw development in holistic terms, and he spoke often of affective development (e.g., in his and Bärbel Inhelder's *The Growth of Logical Thinking*), but he was most attracted to cognitive aspects of development and he devoted his long life to discovering their dynamics. This emphasis on the cognitive or the way of knowing led some to label him a genetic epistemologist, a label which may well be the one which endures as Piaget, now that he is gone, will come under the scrutiny of historical perspective.

Only perilously does one attempt to characterize Piaget's thought. It may perhaps be done best according to the accommodation-assimilation-equilibrium model in which Piaget concludes that the child mind has within it a propensity toward equilibrium. This energy sets in motion activity which both contributes to the fulfillment of mental structures and suffers from the limitations of existing structures. "In short," Piaget wrote, "thought in all realms starts from a surface contact with the external realities, that is, a simple accommodation to immediate experience" (*The Construction of Reality in the Child,* p. 383). The child's limited experience, lack of "schemas," hinders the process of true assimilation of the external reality, although the young child assimilates in a highly egocentric fashion. In turn, this egocentrism impedes accommodation. The two, assimilation and accommodation, work against each other and together throughout life with "the filtering or modification of the input" being assimiliation, and "the modification of internal schemes to fit reality" being accommodation (*The Psychology of the Child,* p. 6). (Also see *Biology and Knowledge.*)

A child, for example, seeking equilibrium as regards the change in form of a ball of clay, runs up against certain limitations during the preschool years that prevent a full assimilation of whatever transformations are taking place, but early in the school years this same movement toward equilibrium succeeds, for the structures are, at that period of development, ready for the challenges. "We shall say," wrote Piaget, "that there is equilibrium when this external intrusion is compensated by the actions of the subject" (*Six Psychological Studies,* p. 151).

This makes experience and education vital to development, for they aid in the actualization of potential, but neither of these can cause the child to perform prematurely at levels for which the structures do not exist. Thus, the school child—regardless of the amount of hard work, memorization, reward, and punishment—cannot throw off the limitations of concrete thinking in order to solve problems which only formal operational thought permits.

Piaget admitted to the possibility of the existence of innate structures, spatial perception for example, and that Kant was possibly correct in positing innate or a priori categories (*Biology and Knowledge,* pp. 53, 268-269). However, Piaget clearly preferred what he termed "operative" thinking as he wrote, "To know is to assimilate reality into systems of transformations. To know is to transform reality in order to understand how a certain state is brought about" (*Genetic Epistemology,* p. 15). Knowledge is not static as in purely empirical or a priori knowledge but is a product of the action, of continuous construction in which something new is formed "which did not exist before, either in the external world or in the subject's mind" (p. 77). The subject

Appendix XI

assimilates something of the object to oneself and at the same time accommodates something of self to the object. This is learning (*Psychology and Epistemology*, p. 108).

Another way of characterizing Piaget's work is by direct examination of the periods of development which he postulated from his research. By now, these are also well known and often cited.

A Sensori-Motor Period, roughly the first two years, in which the child masters the notion of the permanent object, space and time, and causality.

A Pre-Operational Period, a preschool, transitional period in which the child matures in the ability to develop mental symbols of the external world, but still cannot free the mind from perceptions which prevent one from performing operations, as in the case of the conservation experiments where the child believes that water poured from one glass to another increases in volume.

A Concrete Operational Period, the school years, in which the concrete operations of conservation, for example, are mastered but which is imprisoned by the concrete, unable to perform mentally when the material is abstract.

A Formal Operational Period, adolescence, in which the child is freed from the limitations of concrete thought and enjoys the wide range of deductive and inductive reasoning.

These periods are set forth in brief form in Piaget and Inhelder's *The Psychology of the Child*. In *The Child and Reality* Piaget gives these stages of cognitive development the age identifications often missing in other works. The Sensori-Motor Period is given full treatment in Piaget's *The Construction of Reality in the Child*. The movement through the Pre-Operational Period is traced in *The Language and Thought of the Child*. His best discussion of adolescent development is in his and Inhelder's *The Growth of Logical Thinking: Childhood to Adolescence*. In *Six Psychological Studies,* a group of essays with a valuable introduction by an American interpreter of Piaget, David Elkind, Piaget discusses significant themes.

Piaget was not an educator; thus we have no Piagetian book setting forth an educational scheme according to his findings. Any attempt to formulate such a scheme is bound to futility, or at least incompleteness, for Piaget's overriding concern was with genetic epistemology, not language, pedagogy, sociality, or affectivity. However, his discovery can certainly be recommended as the ruling base for what happens cognitively in any school, so that curriculum makers will not attempt to make of children what they are not yet ready to become while at the same time help them to mature at just the points where they are structurally ready. It is the way children are made; it should be the way we aid their making. Piaget put it this way: "While the adult educates the child . . . every adult, even if he is a creative genius, nevertheless began as a child, in prehistoric times as well as today" (*The Psychology of the Child*, p. ix).

References for Appendixes

Affirmation of the Baptismal Covenant. Prepared by Lutheran Church in America, The American Lutheran Church, The Evangelical Lutheran Church of Canada, The Lutheran Church—Missouri Synod.
Aland, Kurt, *Did the Early Church Baptize Infants?* Translated by G. R. Beasley-Murray. Philadelphia: The Westminster Press, 1963.
Ban, Joseph D., *Education for Change.* Valley Forge: Judson Press, 1968.
Barber, Lucie W., *The Religious Education of Preschool Children.* Birmingham, Ala.: Religious Education Press, Inc., 1981.
Barth, Karl, *The Teaching of the Church Regarding Baptism.* Translated by Ernest A. Payne. London: SCM Press, Ltd., 1956.
——————, *Church Dogmatics, The Doctrine of Creation,* III, 2. Translated by Harold Knight et al. Edinburgh: T. & T. Clark, 1958.
The Book of Common Prayer. New York: The Church Pension Fund, 1945.
The Broadman Bible Commentary. Edited by Clifton J. Allen et al., vol. 10. Nashville: Broadman Press, 1969.
Brunner, Emil, *Dogmatics: Vol. II, The Christian Doctrine of Creation and Redemption.* Philadelphia: The Westminster Press, 1979.
Burgess, Harold W., *An Invitation to Religious Education.* Birmingham, Ala.: Religious Education Press, Inc., 1975.
Bushnell, Horace, *God in Christ.* New York: Charles Scribner's Sons, 1876.
——————, "The Kingdom of Heaven as a Grain of Mustard Seed,"

in *Views of Christian Nurture and of Subjects Adjacent Thereto.* Hartford: Edwin Hunt, 1847.

———, *Nature and the Supernatural, As Together Constituting the One System of God.* New York: Charles Scribner's Sons, 1887.

Butler, J. Donald, *Religious Education: The Foundations and Practice of Nurture.* New York: Harper & Row, Publishers, Inc., 1962.

Buttrick, George A., ed., *Interpreter's Dictionary of the Bible,* vol. 3. Nashville: Abingdon Press, 1962.

Cairns, David, *The Image of God in Man.* London and Glasgow: Collins Press, 1973.

Calvin, John, *Institutes of the Christian Religion,* vols. 1 and 2. Translated by Ford Lewis Battles. Philadelphia: The Westminster Press, 1960.

Carr, Warren, *Baptism: Conscience and Clue for the Church.* New York: Holt, Rinehart and Winston, 1964. Copyright © 1964 by Warren Carr. Reprinted by permission of Holt, Rinehart and Winston, Publishers.

Coe, George Albert, *Education in Religion and Morals.* Old Tappan, N. J.: Fleming H. Revell Company, 1911. Used by permission of Fleming H. Revell Company.

———, *The Religion of a Mature Mind.* Old Tappan, N. J.: Fleming H. Revell Company, 1902.

———, *A Social Theory of Religious Education.* New York: Charles Scribner's Sons, 1927; reprinted ed., New York: Arno Press and the New York Times, 1969. Reprinted with permission of Charles Scribner's Sons.

———, *The Spiritual Life.* New York: Eaton and Mains, 1900.

———, *What Is Christian Education?* New York: Charles Scribner's Sons, 1929.

Conner, W. T., *Christian Doctrine.* Nashville: Broadman Press, 1962.

Conzelmann, Hans, *First Corinthians.* Philadelphia: Fortress Press, 1975.

Cullmann, Oscar, *Baptism in the New Testament.* Translated by J. K. S. Reid. Philadelphia: The Westminster Press, 1950.

Cully, Iris V. and Kendig B., eds., *Process and Relationship.* Birmingham, Ala.: Religious Education Press, Inc., 1978.

References for Appendixes

Cully, Kendig Brubaker, *The Search for a Christian Education—Since 1940*. Philadelphia: The Westminster Press, 1965.

Droege, Thomas A., *Self-Realization and Faith*. Chicago: Lutheran Education Association, 1978.

Durka, Gloria, and Smith, Joanmarie, *Emerging Issues in Religious Education*. Ramsey, N. J.: Paulist Press, 1976.

Edge, Findley B., *A Quest for Vitality in Religion*. Nashville: Broadman Press, 1975.

Eichrodt, Walther, *Theology of the Old Testament*, vol. 2. Translated by J. A. Baker. London: SCM Press Ltd., 1967.

Elliott, Harrison, *Can Religious Education Be Christian?* New York: Macmillan, Inc., 1941.

Erikson, Erik, *Identity and the Life Cycle*. New York: W. W. Norton & Company, Inc., 1980.

——————, *Identity: Youth and Crisis*. New York: W. W. Norton & Company, Inc., 1968.

——————, *Young Man Luther*. New York: W. W. Norton & Company, Inc., 1958.

Fallaw, Wesner, *Church Education for Tomorrow*. Philadelphia: The Westminster Press, 1950.

Ferré, Nels F. S., *A Theology for Christian Education*. Philadelphia: The Westminster Press, 1967.

Gesenius, William, *A Hebrew and English Lexicon of the Old Testament*. New York: Houghton Mifflin Company, 1907.

Gleason, John, *Growing Up to God: Eight Steps in Religious Development*. Nashville: Abingdon Press, 1975.

Grimes, Howard, *The Church Redemptive*. Nashville: Abingdon Press, 1958.

Groome, Thomas H., *Christian Religious Education*. New York: Harper & Row, Publishers, Inc., 1980.

Hakes, Edward, ed., *An Introduction to Evangelical Christian Education*. Chicago, Ill.: Moody Press, 1964.

Hunter, Archibald, *Introducing New Testament Theology*. Philadelphia: The Westminster Press, 1958.

Hunter, David, *Christian Education As Engagement*. New York: The Seabury Press, Inc., 1963.

Jacob, Edmond, *Theology of the Old Testament.* New York: Harper & Row, Publishers, Inc., 1958.

Jeremias, Joachim, *Infant Baptism in the First Four Centuries.* Translated by David Cairns. Philadelphia: The Westminster Press, 1960.

_____, *The Origins of Infant Baptism.* Translated by Dorothea M. Barton. Naperville, Ill.: Alec R. Allenson, Inc., 1963.

_____, *New Testament Theology.* New York: Charles Scribner's Sons, 1971.

Kittel, Gerhard, *Theological Dictionary of the New Testament,* vol. 2. Translated by Geoffrey W. Bromiley. Grand Rapids, Mich.: Wm. B. Eerdmans Publishing Company, 1964. Vol. 3 published in 1965.

Kümmel, Werner Georg, *The Theology of the New Testament.* Nashville: Abingdon Press, 1973.

Küng, Hans, *The Church.* Translated by Ray and Rosaleen Ockenden. New York: Sheed and Ward, 1967.

Loder, James, *The Transforming Moment.* New York: Harper & Row, Publishers, Inc., 1981.

Lumpkin, William L., *Baptist Confessions of Faith.* Valley Forge: Judson Press, 1959.

Marxsen, Willi, *The Beginnings of Christology.* Translated by Paul J. Achtemeier and Lorenz Nieting. Philadelphia: Fortress Press, 1979.

Miller, Randolph C., *The Theory of Christian Education Practice.* Birmingham, Ala.: Religious Education Press, Inc., 1980.

_____, *The Clue to Christian Education.* New York: Charles Scribner's Sons, 1950.

Moody, Dale, *The Word of Truth.* Grand Rapids, Mich.: Wm. B. Eerdmans Publishing Co., 1981.

Pelikan, Jaroslav, ed., *Twentieth-Century Theology in the Making,* vol. 1, *Themes of Biblical Theology.* Translated by R. A. Wilson. London: Collins Press, 1969.

Person, Peter P., *An Introduction to Christian Education.* Grand Rapids, Mich.: Baker Book House, 1958.

Piaget, Jean, *Biology and Knowledge.* Translated by Beatrix Walsh. Chicago: The University of Chicago Press, 1971.

_____, *The Construction of Reality in the Child.* Translated by Margaret Cook. New York: Basic Books, Inc., 1964.

————, *Genetic Epistemology*. Translated by Eleanor Duckworth. New York: W. W. Norton & Company, Inc., 1971.

————, *Psychology and Epistemology*. Translated by Arnold Rosin, New York: Viking Press, 1975.

————, *Six Psychological Studies*. Edited by David Elkind; translated by Anita Tenzer. New York: Vintage Books, 1968.

Piaget, Jean, and Inhelder, Bärbel, *The Psychology of the Child*. Translated by Helen Weaver. New York: Basic Books, Inc., 1969.

Price, J. M., et al., eds., *A Survey of Religious Education*. Nashville: Thomas Nelson, Inc., 1940.

Richardson, Alan, *A Theological Word Book of the Bible*. New York: Macmillan Publishing Co., Inc., 1951.

Rood, Wayne R., *Understanding Christian Education*. Nashville: Abingdon Press, 1970.

Sanner, A. Elwood, and Harper, A. F., eds., *Exploring Christian Education*. Kansas City, Mo.: Beacon Hill Press, 1978.

Schaff, Philip, *The Creeds of Christendom*, vols. 2 and 3. Grand Rapids, Mich.: Baker Book House, 1919. Reprinted by Baker Book House and used by permission.

Selbie, W. B., *The Fatherhood of God*. London: Duckworth, 1936.

Shaw, John MacKintosh, *The Christian Gospel of the Fatherhood of God*. New York: George H. Doran Co., 1924.

Sherrill, Lewis J., *Struggle of the Soul*. New York: Macmillan Publishing Co., Inc., 1963.

Shinn, Roger, *The Educational Mission of Our Church*. New York: United Church Press, 1962.

Sloyan, Gerard S., ed., *Modern Catechetics*. New York: Macmillan Publishing Co., Inc., 1963.

Smart, James D., *The Teaching Ministry of the Church*. Philadelphia: The Westminster Press, 1971.

Stewart, Charles W., *Adolescent Religion*. Nashville: Abingdon Press, 1967.

Strong, Augustus Hopkins, *Systematic Theology*, vols. 1 and 2. Valley Forge: Judson Press, 1979.

Taylor, Marvin J., *Introduction to Christian Education*. Nashville: Abingdon Press, 1976.

Tillich, Paul, *Systematic Theology,* vol. 1. Chicago: The University of Chicago Press, 1951.

———, *Systematic Theology,* vol. 2. Chicago: The University of Chicago Press, 1957. Reprinted by permission of The University of Chicago Press. Copyright 1957 by The University of Chicago Press.

Von Rad, Gerhard, *Old Testament Theology,* vol. 1. Translated by D. M. G. Stalker. London: Oliver and Boyd, 1962.

Vriezen, Theodorus, *An Outline of Old Testament Theology.* Oxford: Blackwell, 1970.

Westerhoff, John H., III, *Will Our Children Have Faith?* New York: The Seabury Press, Inc., 1976.

Williams, Norman Powell, *The Ideas of the Fall and of Original Sin.* New York: Longmans, Green & Co., Ltd., 1927.

Wolff, Hans, *Anthropology of the Old Testament.* Translated by Margaret Kohl. Philadelphia: Fortress Press, 1974.

Subject Index

Accommodation, 88, 89, 98, 99, 106, 175, 257-259
Affective development (affect, emotion, feeling), 47-56, 61, 62, 70, 78-82, 86, 89, 90, 93, 113, 176, 177
Affirmation: summarized, 34; characterized, 109, 110; and estrangement, 110; and heritage, 111; and faith, 111, 112
After-Easter dialogue, 165
Age of accountability, 24
Assimilation, 88, 89, 94, 96, 98, 99, 106, 175, 257-259
Authority, 124, 125, 131, 146
Autonomy, 50-52, 55, 56, 114, 151, 256

Baptism: stances toward, 19-21, 27, 181-187; infant, 21-22, 182-184; child, 25, 185-187; believer's, 184-185; Aland-Jeremias debate, 182-183; Barth's view, 184-185 (See celebrative rites.)
Baptist confessions, 241-243
Belonging: summarized, 33, 34; and conversion, 41; characterized, 75-77; referred to, 109, 112, 119, 127, 128, 144, 169, 170
Bible, teaching about, 65, 85, 88, 89, 102-106, 131, 134, 153, 160

Celebrative rites: 35, 205-221; presentation, 205-208; infant baptism, 208; child baptism, 208-209; Lord's Supper, 209-211; belonging, 210; believer's baptism, 212-213, light, 213-216;
laying on of hands, 216-218; commissionings (salt, oil, spice, water), 218-220; passages, 220; wound-embracing, 220-221; death, 221
Child dedication, 20
Child evangelism, 26
Child of God: summarized, 33, 34; and conversion, 40-42; characterized, 43-46; affect in, 51; and initiative-taking 55, 56; and faith, 111, 112; and self-certainty, 119; and heritage, 127, 128; and creative trusteeship, 144, 145, 149, 150, 152
Child of devil, 45
Children's church, 90
Choirs, 138, 139, 167
Christian year, 93, 166
Christmas, 66-69, 100-102
Church (community of faith), bearer of salvation, 31, 43; congregation, 32; confers belonging, 75-77; middle child, 77, 85, 91; adult, 145, 151
Church school: for young child, 69-71; middle child, 93-95; adolescent, 133-135; adult, 158-160
Concrete thinking, 29, 82-86, 96, 98, 105, 258
Confirmation, 20, 22, 23, 35
Conscience, 53, 54
Conventional mentality, 129, 155
Converted (conversion), 22, 23, 35, 40-42, 76, 78, 85, 110
Cooperative curriculum project, 134

267

Creation, 29, 30, 39, 43, 134, 157, 223
Creative trustee: and creation, 29; summarized, 34, 35; and conversion, 41; described, 143-145; relation to generativity and estrangement, 148-156; and worship, 166; relation to dominion, priesthood, 249-253
Curriculum for crisis, 135

Death, 151, 168, 221
Declaration of faith, 22, 23, 24, 34, 41, 82, 85, 109-112, 134, 144, 167
Definition, its limitation, 28, 203, 204
Devotional, 144, 155, 156
Devotion and witness, 163-165
Discipline, 50, 52
Divorced persons, 161, 162
Dominion, 143, 152, 249, 250, 253
Dynamic theology, 153, 154

Easter, 42, and the young child, 66-67; middle child, 101, 102
Ecumenism (ecumenical), 83, 91, 150, 153
Egocentricism, 59, 87, 88, 148, 258
Egostrength, 13, 109, 114, 123
Emma's friends, 71, 106, 140, 167
Epigenetic, 256
Equilibrium, 175, 257, 258

Faith: birth, growth of, 19-28; in theology, 19-32, 129, 133, 145, 154; and belonging, 75-77, 82, 85, 88, 102; and identity crisis, 116-123; and trusteeship, 143, 153, 154, 157, 165
Family, 69-72, 89, 92, 93, 136-137
Female identity, 122, 170
Fidelity, 114, 117
Form and content, 97, 98
Formal operational thinking, 37, 83, 96, 98, 105, 115-119, 126, 148
Freedom of choice, 78, 144

Generativity, 146-149, 255-256
Genetic epistemology, 259, 260
Genetic transmission, 75
Genital maturation, 123, 147
God, teaching: to young child, 62, 63, 70; to middle child, 96-99
Grace, 20, 21, 23, 24, 26, 29, 40, 41, 76, 118, 165

Groups: youth, 137, 138; study and care, 158, 159; study, 159, 160; mission, 160, 161; wound-embracing, 161, 162; support, 161, 162; geographic family, 162; sharing, 164; discipline, 164; choir, 138, 139, 167

Heritage, 75, 90, 91, 117, 132, 144
Historical perspective, 100, 118
Hymns, 207, 211, 213, 218

Identity, 112-114, 120, 124, 256; negative, 114; crisis and faith, 114, 116-126, 146, 177
Ideology testing, 125-126, 146
Image of God, 29, 30, 33, 35, 44-46, 49, 55, 85, 111, 112, 127-129, 143-145, 149, 151, 152, 155, 157, 223-233
Inferiority, 79, 80-82, 86, 114
Initiative, 53-55
Integration learning, 88, 89, 94
Intergenerational experience, 90, 94, 136-137, 162, 167
Intellectual development (cognitive development, mental development): in the young child, 56-61, 68; middle child, 82-86; adolescent, 113, 115, 116
Intellectual problems, 131
Intimacy, 146
Intuitive thought, 60, 82, 116, 190-191
Inventive years, 79
Isolation, 146, 147
I-Thou, 150

Jesus Christ: and the children, 26, 27, 33; centerpiece, agent of salvation, 29, 31, 129, 157; God's Son, Savior, 30, 31, 46, 102, 129; historical Jesus, 40; teaching about, 63-65; faith in, 111, 120, 129, 130, 150; image of God, 46, 145, 226, 229, 230, 250; new being, 236; author and finisher, 230

Knowledge problem, 37-40

Learning environments: young child, 69-71; middle child, 89-93; adolescent, 132-140; adult, 158-163
Life commitment, 78

Index

Life plan, 115, 122, 125
Literalism, 131, 191
Lord's Supper, 20, 24, 35, 88, 130, 132, 144, 145, 166, 209, 239ff

Marginal person, 113, 115, 122, 124, 126
Mental image, 56, 58, 60
Mental symbol, 60
Mission, 111, 129, 137, 144, 145, 151, 152
Mission action, 137, 138, 160
Miracles, teaching about, 94, 100
Moral development, 81, 86-88, 124, 125, 154, 155

Natural order, 152
New birth, 194, 236

Object permanence, 56, 57
Oikos, 183
Operation, mental, 82, 86, 258
Order and status quo, 152
Overlapping region, 112, 113

Parable, 86, 89, 94, 103, 105
Paradox, 128, 129, 151, 166
Parental connection, 75, 76, 77, 109
Passage recognitions, 205, 220, 221
Piety, 145, 155
Play, 58, 70
Prayer, 80, 82, 90
Pre-Easter devotion, 163, 164
Preschool humanism, 62
Productivity, 79, 113
Proverbs, 84
Psychological foundations, 36, 37, 255-256, 257-260
Puberty, 112
Public school, 95, 96, 139, 140
Purpose, 55, 56, 78, 79, 113, 114, 122, 149, 151, 152

Rational, danger of the, 23, 85; limits of the, 151, 190, 191
Readings, responsive, 69, 206, 207, 210, 212, 213, 214-216, 217-218
Rededication (renewal), 20, 144
Reflective thinking, 119, 144
Regeneration, 21, 25, 111, 237
Revelation, 38-40

Religious education terms, 28, 202-204
Repentance, 22, 41, 77, 129
Reversibility, 82
Role experimentation, 121, 177

Salvation: origin, 21, 22, 30, 46; scope, 29, 31; within creation, 29; Jesus, the centerpiece, 29, 30, 31, 129, 130; church, the bearer, 31; realities in, 32-35; child of God, 33; psychology, 36, 37; knowledge, 39; image of God, 45; middle child, 76; adolescence, 110-112; adult, 144, 145, 149; end in creation, 157; by education, 193-195; Tillich's view, 235-237
Santa Claus, 100
Schema, 258
Sectarian education, 91
Self: certainty, 119-121, 144; doubt, 52
Sexuality, 54, 55, 79, 123, 124, 147, 177, 178
Stage transit, 71, 108, 141, 168
Shema, 250
Sin (estrangement), 24, 25, 29, 30, 34-36, 39, 45-47, 50, 81, 85, 87, 88, 102, 110, 111, 120, 123, 127, 129, 143, 149-152, 154, 155, 166, 176, 189, 195, 227-230, 235-237
Socialization, 110, 175, 195, 196
Social development, 86-88, 110, 114, 115
Social order, 152, 170
Social position, 112, 113, 126, 146
Space, concept of, 83
Speed, concept of, 83
Status quo and order, 152
Subculture, 132, 137
Substitution learning, 88, 89, 94
Superego, 47
Symbolic function, 57-59
Syncretism, 84, 85, 106

Technology, 152
Television, 86, 93, 136
Theological thinker, 145, 153, 154, 157, 165
Time, 83, 117-119, 150
Toilet training, 52
Transcendence, 118, 129, 151, 156, 166
Trinity, teaching to young child, 62ff; middle child, 96ff
Trust, 48, 49, 50, 55, 114

Verbalism, 96, 98, 126
Vital personality, 49, 54, 255, 256
Vocational choice, 122
Vocational support group, 162
Volition, 22, 109

Willfulness, 50, 51, 113
Witness, 153, 163, 165
Womanhood, 169-171

Working theology, 145, 153, 154, 157, 165
Work, 29, 30, 76; dignity of, 152
World view, 120, 126
Worship: energizing center, 32; early child, 66; middle child, 76, 90, 95, 101, 102; adolescent, 127, 132, 133; adult, 144, 166-167

Youth church, 132, 133

Studies Index
(By Author)

Educational
Joseph Ban, 202
Lucy Barber, 201
Dan Boling, 179
Harold Burgess, 197, 198, 199
Horace Bushnell, 81, 189-191, 202
J. Donald Butler, 199
George A. Coe, 193-196, 198, 200, 202, 203
Iris Cully, 104, 197, 200, 201
Kendig Cully, 197, 198, 200, 215
Austen DeBlois, 203
John Dewey, 198
Gloria Durka, 202
Findley B. Edge, 197, 202
John Elias, 201
Harrison Elliott, 199, 202
Wesner Fallaw, 202, 203
Dorothy Jean Furnish, 105
Donald Gorham, 203
Howard Grimes, 202
Thomas Groome, 201, 203
J. Edward Hakes, 199
A. F. Harper, 199
Lela Hendrix, 178
David Hunter, 202
James Michael Lee, 199
Ernest Ligon, 198
Sara Little, 199
Randolph C. Miller, 198, 199, 200, 202
Maria Montessori, 198
Walter Neidhart, 173
Peter Person, 199, 203
J. M. Price, 199
Wayne Rood, 197, 198
A. Elwood Sanner, 199
Margaret Sawin, 178
Jack L. Seymore, 201
Lewis Sherrill, 202
Roger Shinn, 202
Gerald Sloyan, 201
James Smart, 197, 202
Joanmarie Smith, 202
G. Temp Sparkman, 201
Marvin Taylor, 199
John Westerhoff III, 201, 202
Mary Wilcox, 87, 178, 201
D. Campbell Wyckoff, 197
Gideon Yoder, 173

Psychological
Gordon Allport, 200
Don Browning, 179
John S. Dacey, 177
David Elkind, 88, 91, 96, 201, 259
Erik Erikson, 36, 48, 49, 51, 52, 54, 55, 79, 80, 81, 86, 112, 113, 116, 146, 179, 200, 255-256
James Fowler (See Theological)
Erich Fromm, 200
John Gleason, 201
André Godin, 98
Ronald Goldman, 63, 65, 70, 91, 92, 98-100, 105, 131, 200
Ernest Harms, 63, 174
Reuel Howe, 198

Bärbel Inhelder, 257
Karl Jung, 200
Lawrence Kohlberg, 81, 86, 178, 180, 201
Kurt Lewin, 112, 113, 115, 116
James Loder, 202
Abraham Maslow, 200
Paul Mussen, John Conger, Jerome Kagan, 174, 177, 178
Diana Papalia, Sally Olds, 178, 179
John Peatling, 201
Jean Piaget, 37, 57, 59, 60, 82, 83, 84, 112, 114, 115, 116, 148, 175, 176, 200, 257-260
Carl Rogers, 200
Britton K. Ruebush, 174
B. F. Skinner, 200
G. Temp Sparkman, 201
Charles Stewart, 127, 201
John F. Travers, 174
Mary Wilcox, 87, 178, 201

Theological

Paul J. Achtemeier, 240
Kurt Aland, 182-184
Karl Barth, 182, 184, 185, 225, 229, 230
Raymond Brown, 244, 245
Emil Brunner, 225, 227, 229, 230
David Cairns, 45, 223, 226, 227, 231
John Calvin, 225, 229, 231
Warren Carr, 185-187
W. T. Conner, 185, 247
Hans Conzelmann, 245
Oscar Cullmann, 182, 184, 185
Harold DeWolfe, 200
Thomas Droege, 187, 201
Walther Eichrodt, 223, 224, 250
Nels F. S. Ferré, 199

James Fowler, 97, 98, 129, 130, 175, 178, 179, 180, 201
Balthasar Friedberger, 242
William Gesenius, 249
William E. Hull, 186, 187
Archibald Hunter, 231
Edmond Jacob, 223, 224, 228
Joachim Jeremias, 182, 183, 231
Ernst Käsemann, 245
Gerhard Kittel, 251
Margaret Kohl, 250
Werner Georg Kümmel, 244, 245
Hans Küng, 36, 251-253
Kans Lietzmann, 244
William L. Lumpkin, 242
Martin Luther, 225, 256
Willi Marxsen, 240
Dale Moody, 185, 186
Lorenz Nieting, 240
Paul, 228
Jaroslav Pelikan, 240
Alan Richardson, 228, 229
Philip Schaff, 240, 241
Karl Ludwig Schmidt, 239
W. B. Selbie, 232
John M. Shaw, 232
M. H. Shepherd, 244
John Smyth, 242
John E. Steely, 180
A. H. Strong, 185, 231, 232, 247
Paul Tillich, 36, 225, 231, 235-237
Gerhard Von Rad, 223, 224, 228, 249
Theodore Vriezen, 223, 224, 228, 249
Hugh Wamble, 247
Friedrich Wiegand, 240
N. P. Williams, 228
Hans Wolff, 250